A Beginner's Guide to Directing Theatre

A Beginner's Guide to Directing Theatre

Robert Marsden

methuen | drama
LONDON • NEW YORK • OXFORD • NEW DELHI • SYDNEY

METHUEN DRAMA
Bloomsbury Publishing Plc, 50 Bedford Square, London, WC1B 3DP, UK
Bloomsbury Publishing Inc, 1385 Broadway, New York, NY 10018, USA
Bloomsbury Publishing Ireland, 29 Earlsfort Terrace, Dublin 2, D02 AY28, Ireland

BLOOMSBURY, METHUEN DRAMA and the Methuen Drama logo are trademarks of Bloomsbury Publishing Plc

First published in Great Britain 2025

Copyright © Robert Marsden, 2025

Robert Marsden has asserted his right under the Copyright, Designs and Patents Act, 1988, to be identified as author of this work.

For legal purposes the Acknowledgements on p. ix constitute an extension of this copyright page.

Cover image: Woman director directing theatre play during rehearsal in black box theatre (© Corinna Kern / Getty Images)

All rights reserved. No part of this publication may be: i) reproduced or transmitted in any form, electronic or mechanical, including photocopying, recording or by means of any information storage or retrieval system without prior permission in writing from the publishers; or ii) used or reproduced in any way for the training, development or operation of artificial intelligence (AI) technologies, including generative AI technologies. The rights holders expressly reserve this publication from the text and data mining exception as per Article 4(3) of the Digital Single Market Directive (EU) 2019/790.

Bloomsbury Publishing Plc does not have any control over, or responsibility for, any third-party websites referred to or in this book. All internet addresses given in this book were correct at the time of going to press. The author and publisher regret any inconvenience caused if addresses have changed or sites have ceased to exist, but can accept no responsibility for any such changes.

A catalogue record for this book is available from the British Library.

A catalog record for this book is available from the Library of Congress.

ISBN: HB: 978-1-3503-7052-4
PB: 978-1-3503-7051-7
ePDF: 978-1-3503-7053-1
eBook: 978-1-3503-7054-8

Typeset by RefineCatch Limited, Bungay, Suffolk
Printed and bound in Great Britain

For product safety related questions contact productsafety@bloomsbury.com.

To find out more about our authors and books visit www.bloomsbury.com and sign up for our newsletters.

For Carol, my mum, who supported my love of theatre, and didn't worry when I wanted to go to university to study drama!

Contents

Acknowledgements ix

Part One Introduction to Directing

1   What is Directing? 3

2   How This Book is Set Out 7

3   The Role of the Director: What is Directing? 11

4   The Role of the Director: The 'What' and the 'How' 13

5   The Rise of the Director 19

6   Directing without the Director 25

7   Creativity, Breakthroughs and Building Blocks 31

8   Rehearsal and Production Analyses 35

Part Two Stages of Directing

9   Stage One: Choosing and Establishing 41

10 Stage Two: Creating and Forming 71

11 Stage Three: Building and Encouraging 97

12 Stage Four: Shaping and Layering – the Final Stages 117

13 Stage Five: Delivering and Entrusting 135

Part Three Interviews with Leading Theatre Directors

14 **Tamara Harvey** 155

15 **Holly Race Roughan** 165

16 **Josie Rourke** 175

17 **Roy Alexander Weise** 187

References 197
Index 203

Acknowledgements

Dr Kelly Jones, for keeping me on track and for continual wise counsel.

Practitioners Nick Barclay, David Bowen, Laura-Ann Grecian, Steve Fortune, Daniel Jarvis, Gracie McGonigal, Dominic Meir, Sean O'Callaghan, Emmanuel Olusanya, Christian Patterson, Chrissie Perkins, Neil Roberts, Naomi Symeou and Tamur Tohver for additional quotations throughout.

Alex Scott Fairley for going above and beyond as a proofreader.

Anna Brewer, Aanchal Vij and the wider team at Methuen Drama and Bloomsbury for their continued faith and support.

Executive Dean Dr Julie King, and Associate Deans Professor Tony Dodd and Professor Carlton Reeve for enabling this research during my tenure at the University of Staffordshire.

Part One

Introduction to Directing

1. What is Directing?
2. How This Book is Set Out
3. The Role of the Director: What is Directing?
4. The Role of the Director: The 'What' and the 'How'
5. The Rise of the Director
6. Directing without the Director
7. Creativity, Breakthroughs and Building Blocks
8. Rehearsal and Production Analyses

1

What is Directing?

The directing process varies from director to director and the ways in which we rehearse are continually advancing. Put simply, there is no one way of directing a piece of theatre: it changes as a result of the demands of the text, the genre, the style, the architecture of the theatre space and the dynamics of the acting company. Tamara Harvey, Co-Artistic Director of the Royal Shakespeare Company in the UK and one of the interviewees in Part Three of this book, discusses several possible ways of interpreting a text or a scene and is not someone who subscribes to one way of working.

Kolkata-based director and dramaturg Rustom Bharucha has described his experiences of directing actors who speak a different language; when working with actors, he articulates the importance of being open to working differently, often with a translator, rather than slavishly following any pre-determined approach. For Bharucha, the new layers of meaning that emerge from this openness 'contribute to a radical redefinition of the epistemology of direction in actual practice, whereby the director becomes an engaged listener rather than a disembodied conductor of the rehearsal process' (2000: 353). Listening and responding to what is happening before your eyes is therefore paramount for any director. A major note I often give to emerging directors is to lift their attention from the script to engage with what is happening in front of them, in the dynamic and electric space between the actors and the interactions of the characters. Asking stage management or another actor to be 'on the book' is vital, enabling the director's full attention to be with their company.

Walk into several different rehearsal rooms in a Western environment and there will be some similarities. You will often hear similar language, perhaps based around objectives, tasks, wants, needs, stakes and obstacles which has its roots in Konstantin Stanislavski (more on him later). You may recognize similarities in the methods of discussing, analysing or realising these. Frequently, there are ubiquitous cups of tea and chairs dotted about, actors in discussion with directors (or one another) and people taking notes on paper or – these days – on a panoply of electronic devices. Yet delve deeper and beneath these immediately apparent elements, the rehearsal room is a mercurial delight, ever in motion, with differing techniques at play.

That said, the director will be the one to set the tone at the outset for the exploration ahead, often deciding on the choice of text and rehearsal methodologies. Historically, directing and rehearsal room practices have been fairly secretive, with only a select or privileged few allowed to witness and write about this ecosystem in miniature. In recent years, however, many of the myths that have grown up around rehearsal room processes and the role of the director have been debunked. While directors have, until fairly recently, played into the hierarchical power structures that have formed a part of theatre making – with their powerful position in this structure on occasion being abused – it is now evident that the director plays (and should play) the role of a leader within a group of creative equals. The time of the power grab, where directors would leverage their positions to gain authority, must now come to an end. Elizabeth LeCompte, for example, who has directed experimental ensemble The Wooster Group since it was founded in the late 1970s, sees herself as a '"director in a group" rather than "director of a group"' (Radosavljevic 2013: 19).

Rather more intangibly, the type of rehearsal room and the directorial approaches within it may be dependent on what is driving the project in the background. In rehearsing a commercial, globally familiar megamusical such as *Jersey Boys* or *Les Misérables*, for example, the process may be a recreation of the original director's vision, physical shaping (often still referred to as 'blocking') and style. There will also be financial and time restraints: what can happen within a seven-week rehearsal period will be very different in form from a two-week period, regardless of whether the intent and end goal are the same, and the director must cut their cloth accordingly.

As with a companion text in this volume, Jess Thorpe and Tashi Gore's *A Beginner's Guide to Devising Theatre* (2020), this is not a 'one-size-fits-all' text, nor does it advance a particular system of directing. Rather, this text offers a series of approaches and is designed to be dipped into as required by the reader; that said, it can equally be read progressively. Should you opt for the latter, I would caution against a slavish application of the work and methods. Instead, these should be used as a stimulus for each part of the directing process.

This book is also aimed at staff supporting students who are taking Level 3 BTEC, A Level, UAL (in the UK) or equivalent courses, as well as undergraduate students of directing. It may also appeal to nascent directors and to community or amateur directors, who are looking for an introductory guide to text-based theatre making. Drawing together my practical experience as a director since the 1990s in both commercial and subsidized sectors, with over a decade's worth of formal research in the field of rehearsal studies, this book brings the reader up to date with a variety of directing practices and principles. It also brings to the fore contemporary notions of inclusivity, safe spaces, and ethical practices of creating work. I unashamedly point readers towards my previous text, *Inside the Rehearsal Room* (2022), where many of the contextual and theoretical underpinnings behind the ideas in this text can be found. Where appropriate, I will cross-reference to these in the text.

I firmly believe that a director needs to curate 'how' they work in terms of style, tone and principles, as well as what rehearsal methods they employ.

2

How This Book is Set Out

- **Part One** explores the rise of the role of the director, as well as offering a production analysis exercise, in which an emerging director is invited to see a production and critique it through an analytical framework, aiming to shift away from a journalistic opinion piece and towards an informed review. This exercise relates explicitly to the production logic, whereby the production makes sense through a unified interpretation rooted and grounded in the playtext, as opposed to a literary analysis.
- **Part Two** is the heart of the book, adopting – in the words of cultural anthropologist Jane Goodman – more of a 'megapragmatic or "how to"' (2020: 140) approach. Leading the reader through the five stages of selecting the play and pre-production, creating an ensemble, building the production, developing a structure, and finally meeting an audience, this part offers many directing techniques and concrete practical examples, interspersed with contextual underpinning. Readers can dip into Part Two as necessary, although it has been structured in a deliberately progressive way and can equally be read as such. The exercises in this section contain some of my personal 'go-to' exercises adapted from numerous practitioners: the rehearsal methods I have employed while working on more than one hundred productions with professional or student actors. That said, I do not employ one methodological approach through this book and the reasons for this are twofold.

In the first place, I do not personally subscribe to a concrete methodology. I am something of a magpie, taking the things that resonate with me from various rehearsal and acting methodologies or practitioners, and then selecting and adapting techniques as appropriate. This might be to unlock a moment where we are 'stuck' in the rehearsal room, but equally it may be to strengthen and develop something that is working via impulse within the room, but where impulse has only taken us so far in the creative journey and a form needs to be established. Secondly, many college, conservatoire and university syllabi that this text is designed to support likewise do not adhere to a strict system, so this text offers approaches and ideas within the spirit of this.

For anyone who would like to explore a definite A-to-Z methodology, there are a couple of texts that I would recommend. Katie Mitchell's *The Director's Craft* (2009) guides the reader through Mitchell's rigorous and detailed approach to directing, while James Thomas sets out his approach to active analysis in *A Director's Guide to Stanislavski's Active Analysis* (2016). Active analysis is touched upon throughout this text and so for those with whom this resonates, I would have no hesitation in endorsing Thomas's method. Many of the strategies employed do have their roots in a Stanislavskian[1] approach, aiming to find a believable and relative truth within a production style.

- **Part Three** is a collection of interviews with contemporary theatre directors. **Roy Alexander Weise, MBE**, was, until recently, Co-Artistic Director of the Royal Exchange in Manchester and directs for the National Theatre among others. **Tamara Harvey** is – along with Daniel Evans – the Co-Artistic Director of the Royal Shakespeare Company (RSC). **Josie Rourke** is both a theatre and film director, most notably with the National Theatre and Donmar Warehouse, while **Holly Race Roughan** is Artistic Director of Headlong. These voices offer a contemporary context to directorial questions often posed by emerging theatre directors, as well as responding to certain aspects contained within the further and higher education syllabi. Echoing my point above, none of these directors follow one rehearsal system or rehearsal methodology. When pushed on the subject they do, however,

---

[1] Konstantin Stanislavski (1863–1938) was a seminal Russian theatre practitioner. Recognized in his lifetime as both an outstanding character actor and director, his reputation today rests on his 'system', an approach to training actors that emphasizes what he terms 'the art of experiencing' over the 'art of representation'. The former seeks to activate the actor's conscious thought as a means to mobilizing processes such as emotional experience, which are less easy to consciously control. The actor thus seeks inner motives to justify the action and to define the character's objective, referred to as a 'task'. Stanislavski later refined the system with his 'Method of Physical Action', which emphasized active exploration and improvisation over discussion around the table. Stanislavski's ideas crossed several cultural boundaries, at least in the West, and have arguably become so ingrained there that many actors will use them without necessarily being conscious of doing so.

acknowledge that their approach is often rooted in a Stanislavskian foundation, drawing on techniques such as events, actioning and objectives (tasks) which are outlined in Part Two. What all three have in common is a genuine desire to think about the 'how' of directing, rather than the 'what'. What also unites them is the idea that whatever they do in rehearsals as a director must serve the needs of the story.

3

The Role of the Director: What is Directing?

In his introduction to the series *The Great European Stage Directors*, Simon Shepherd states that 'directors have become some of the celebrities of contemporary theatre. Yet for most of its life [...] theatre has managed perfectly well without directors' (2018: 1). He goes on to ponder whether the role of the director is necessary in theatre at all: after all, it has been in existence for less than two centuries. In contrast, in an interview for *The Stage* trade newspaper, contemporary theatre director Rebecca Frecknall argues that the role of director is necessary even within an ensemble setting. A director can lead the ensemble, with Frecknall stating that 'there's this mistaken idea that there should be no leadership' (2023) and that while she ensures that collaboration is key and that the best idea wins, 'collaboration needs direction [and the director] makes decisions' (ibid.). Peter M. Boenisch highlights the fact that 'the term "director" entered English language theatre comparatively late, in the 1950s ... Before this, the theatre director was referred to as "producer", placing the industrial organization of theatrical entertainment and the pragmatics of cultural production over and above any sense of "art"' (2015: 2–3).

Part One also examines original practices in early modern drama. In Shakespeare's time, there was no director and even within a model of 'director-less' theatre, *directing* is nevertheless constantly in play, albeit without the formal, specialist role of the director. Actors frequently direct themselves, led by the needs of the text and, as Boenisch explores, there is a key difference between directing a play (which is more of an activity) and making a performance with, or without, a director in a creative collaborative interpretation (of a play) through a different philosophical lens. Direction of a production (as opposed to directing a play) then 'marks an artistic and aesthetic approach, different from the mere pragmatic execution of stage business' (ibid.: 3), ensuring the production takes on a quality of its own.

4

The Role of the Director: The 'What' and the 'How'

A director has to balance 'what' they do (i.e. the methodologies employed) with 'how' they do it (i.e. being the tone setter of the rehearsal room). Thai director and academic Arunwadi Leewananthawet argues that 'directing students undoubtably need to form abstract concepts and transform them into [a] concrete live performance through their actors' (2016: 5). It is not for the director to improve or to correct the text, but to work with the text, to believe in it fully and to embrace and unlock its creative opportunities, creating a form in which these can be expressed to an audience. The director realizes the script in collaboration with each creative member of their team, whether actor, designer, technician, or otherwise. It is my firm belief that directors must stand by everything that happens on the stage once the production has opened.

What is without question is that the director must lead a company from the stage of any early abstract ideas to a fully realized production, which should be delivered within budget and on time by the opening night. This should be done in an open, collaborative, co-creative way, where the rehearsal process is frequently decided upon by the director, implicitly and explicitly. Tekena Gasper Mark, in his study of Nigerian theatre directors, sums this up perfectly, by stating that the directorial concept 'harmonizes the approaches employed in the interpretation of a play' (2019: 316). Harmonization resonates strongly with me as a director. Harmony implies that there are individual roles and responsibilities with differing opinions, ideas and ways of working, coalescing around both play and production, that the director must bring together. As director Dominic Dromgoole articulates in relation to the Greek chorus, 'it is hard to find greater joy that the shift put in alongside your fellow worker to make something together. The chorus is still the best of us' (2022: 64). The director has to meld this in a crucible being aware, as

Josie Rourke states in her interview in Part Three, of the different backgrounds, lived experiences and acting methodologies employed by the actors.

I always begin my teaching of directing with a definition of rehearsals offered by director, translator and adapter Mike Alfreds, who says that 'the purpose of [a] rehearsal process is to immerse the actors so thoroughly in the world of the play that they'll have the complete confidence and ability to play freshly, with freedom and spontaneity, at every performance, living in the moment, in a continuous creative flow, able to adapt to – and absorb – change, variation and discovery (2010: 141). For me, if this is the purpose of the rehearsal room, then the director's role is to ensure the building of a coherent world within the frame of the production, ensuring it has its own inner logic and building out from the given circumstances of the play. Alfreds's quotation also encapsulates the need for spontaneity in performance, echoing my desire that the sense of liveness should never be lost.

The director needs to ensure that regardless of the play's style or genre, it has its own coherence and internal logic. Whether representational, naturalistic or realistic, presentational or overtly theatrical, the notion of harmonization as proposed by Tekena Gasper Mark above is key and the director chooses a way forwards in terms of 'how' and what'. For director Sue Dunderdale, the 'choices you make create the style of the piece you are making' (2022: 215). One choice the director must make is how to unify the work of the acting company with the scenographic work and the design world. As Dromgoole puts it, 'being there, and pulling everyone else into the same space, is the primary function [of a director]. When this breaks down, problems multiply' (2022: 250). Thus, unification and ensuring that everyone arrives on time at the same destination is a key function. It is also important to accommodate the different approaches actors take, to create and embody their characters.

The 'how' of this varies wildly. There are productions that start with no prior concept or vision, and this is collectively developed on the rehearsal room floor from day one. Rebecca Frecknall is one example of a director who sometimes adopts this approach, following in the footsteps of others such as Michelle Terry, Artistic Director of Shakespeare's Globe, and Declan Donnellan, who co-founded Cheek by Jowl. This is not to suggest that these directors exclusively use this approach, but it is one for which they are known. Many productions, however, start rehearsals with the director and designer having fully created the world, into which the actors then must find their way and inhabit. Ivo van Hove, previous Artistic Director of Toneelgroep Amsterdam, is one such director, whose approach involves having two groups – scenographic and dramaturgical – that work side by side for approximately two years prior to the start of rehearsals. Often, a director will create a directorial vision or concept, and Part Two offers some ideas about how to formulate this. I have seen *Romeo and Juliet* set in space, a black box *Macbeth*, a hyper-naturalistic *All My Sons* and a modern-dress version of *The Crucible*. All of these are forms that house the content: the playwright's story. Terry McCabe, himself a director, has argued that directors should steer clear of big ideas and auteur-style concepts, stating that the 'director's proper role is that of the interpretive artist who communicates, precisely and vividly, the vision of the theatre's only creative artist – the playwright – to the group of interpreters – the actors – who bear ultimate responsibility for communicating that vision to the audience' (2001: 108). I sit somewhere in the middle of this myself, seeing a director as *creatively* interpreting a play for an audience. I am unsure how to 'precisely' communicate a playwright's vision or intent, as I wish to use their work as the centre point of a circle to build out from, widening the circle to encompass my own vision and intent, but anchored to that of the playwright nonetheless. It is worth adding that, for playwrights long since dead, authorial intention can in any case only be assumed or inferred, since it is impossible to ask them about this and increasingly unlikely, the further back in time one goes, that they will have provided any authorial annotation to that end.

In relation to working with the actors, from the very start of the process, my aim is that the actors, by opening night, are in full ownership of the story they are telling and the characters they are embodying. Regardless of my directorial concept, from casting onwards and through every rehearsal strategy that I employ, I want to ensure that the actors are taking ownership and embodying the text and characters, while I slowly step away. This is 'baked in' to my thinking and I encourage all emerging directors to consider how this seesaw of ownership can be achieved. If the actors are still reliant on the director during the run of the play, then the rehearsal period has not fulfilled its purpose: the director needs to be able to disappear with ease, rather than it feeling like a cliff-edge farewell.

I argue that to direct, a director needs to explore why it is that they make theatre in the first place, as well as what the very purpose of theatre itself is. I set out several exercises in Part Two to encourage directors to begin to think about this, but for me, personally, theatre is about a shared experience and this experience must be live, sharing both time and space. A live stream of a production fulfils half of this remit. Watching a recorded version of a theatre piece is simply an archival viewing, at one remove from that shared space and time. The shared experience for me allows for every individual, whether actor or audience member, to share the same air, experiencing a story through being viscerally connected to it. As Canadian playwright Jordan Tannahill puts it, 'plays sit outside our daily routines. They require more of us. And, in their best moments, they can provide us with even more in return' (2016: 38). As a member of the audience, we may enter the theatre individually, but we exit collectively through the shared experience. Naturally, we cannot pause the experience – neither to attend to other business, nor even to put the kettle on – and this immediacy, this being obliged to focus intently on the story, can have various effects. It may allow us, for example, to consider or respond to the world around us in a different way in the case of a drama or verbatim theatre piece; or it may allow us an escape from the world around us, if caught up in the anarchic abandon of a farce or a pantomime. Tekena Gasper Mark states that 'one thing is certain, theatre originated from the ritualistic practice of humans' (2019: 315) and these rituals, for me, require us to share the same time and space as the actors telling the story, in order to become fully immersed in the world of a play. Kene Igweonu and Osita Okagbue, in their overview of performative interaction in African theatre, articulate how 'theatre and performance have always existed in Africa as part of the cultural process of what it means to be human' (2013: 1), so as well as exploring what it means to be a human being, theatre helps us to navigate and make sense of the world around us, all of which is rooted in the early performance cultures and storytelling rituals of Africa. In Africa, argue Igweonu and Okagbue, theatre 'is not just entertainment but is often geared towards fulfilling particular social or aesthetic functions' (2013: 2), thus filtering the reason for making theatre through this particular lens. For a director to be able to articulate *why* they make theatre, as well as *how*, ensures a deep-rooted connection to the story, as well as the impact it can have on a specific target audience.

In my time, I have heard the director called many things: facilitator, conduit, instigator, party host and guide. One thing that a director should never be, however, is a dictator. Cultural representations of directors (and producers) in film and related media are not always pretty: watch movies such as *Singin' in the Rain* (1952), *The Producers* (1967) or *All That Jazz* (1979), and see the representation of directors through the lens of gender, feminist and queer theories. In the case of *The Producers*, for example, women (in as much as they even appear) are represented as 'other' and the male producer as dominant. Gender studies scholar Judith Butler believes that these binaries are constructed through performance, while feminist philosopher Luce Irigaray argues that women are represented as commodities, excluded from the cultural systems of patriarchal society. Woman, denied means of self-representation, becomes man's 'other', as argued in Irigaray's *This Sex Which Is Not One*, whereby 'woman, in this sexual imaginary, is only a more or less obliging prop for the enactment of men's fantasies' (1985: 25), with a limited number of parts that she can play: 'Mother, virgin, prostitute: these are the social roles imposed on women' (Counsell and Wolf 2003: 63). Less sinister, but equally disconcerting, is the representation of the director or producer as sociopathic or narcissistic. From movies, such as *The Goodbye Girl* (1977), and animation, such as *The Simpsons* episode 'A Streetcar Named Marge' (1992), to TV dramas, such as the *Rosemary and Thyme* series finale 'Enter Two Gardeners' (2007), to storylines broadcast as recently as 2021 on BBC Radio 4's soap opera *The Archers* (1951–) the trope of the powerful, male director abusing power or being demonstrably creatively 'unhinged' has been repeatedly reinforced. Given all of this, not to mention the backdrop of the Harvey Weinstein abuse cases and the #MeToo[1] social movement and awareness campaign (and others related to it), it is incumbent on contemporary directors to ensure that rehearsals are ethical and inclusive.

Directors are also often empowered to choose their creative teams and who they need to be in the room, to make the work. In this regard, there has been a welcome rise in intimacy directors and coordinators, as well as well-being support practitioners in rehearsal rooms over the last five years. This is in response to what director and actor Andrea L. Moor calls the 'demand for equity and safety' (2023: 87) and how both training and the profession must respond to this, against the backdrop of contemporary society. As Moor goes on to write, 'producers and directors must understand the role they play in bringing on an intimacy director, learning how to do an intimacy and content audit of the script' (ibid.: 93).

So, how did we go from a theatre profession that did not need a director, to one that often places the director at the centre of the making process? By understanding the rise of the role of the director, we can begin to understand

---

[1] #MeToo is a global campaign that seeks to increase awareness of sexual abuse, with people publicizing their own person experiences. Although the phrase was used as early as 2006, the movement gained increased prominence and traction in the wake of the exposure of multiple sexual-abuse allegations against Hollywood film producer Harvey Weinstein in 2017, with actress Alyssa Milano being one of the first to encourage all those women who had experienced sexual harassment or assault to make this known by using 'me too' as a status or hashtag on social media platforms.

directorial responsibilities and the ways in which this role can still be of value in the contemporary rehearsal room. We may even be able to begin to reverse the trend of the representation in popular culture of the director as a despot or 'unbalanced'. For a comprehensive look at the role of the director, I recommend that readers turn to Edward Braun's *The Director and the Stage* (1982) and *Theatre Histories* (2016), edited by Carol Fischer Sorgenfrei, Bruce McConachie, Tobin Nellhaus and Tamara Underiner. In my own book, *Inside the Rehearsal Room* (2022), I lay out a historical arc of the rehearsal process, from the campfire to the present day, and attempt to identify the development of the director's role throughout this dynamic. Below, however, I will briefly visit several key times and places that will help to illustrate the arc of the shaping of the role of director over the course of two hundred years.

5

The Rise of the Director

While the term 'director' does not firmly find its way into the theatrical lexicon until the twentieth century, both Ronald Harwood (1984) and Tekena Gasper Mark (2019) argue – albeit from different perspectives – that we need to trace the genesis of the directorial figure through the organization of the performance of ritualistic practices and performances of myths or origin stories. Mark dismantles the long-entrenched notion that theatre began in ancient Greece, suggesting that it had its roots instead in the Festival of Osiris 'of ancient Egypt ... at least twelve hundred years before the Athenian festivals of Dionysus' (2019: 318). Priests oversaw the telling of these myths in ways similar to that of traditional Balinese Barong dance, which is still performed today. This dance – which retells an Indonesian myth of the hosts of good, led by Barong, triumphing over the hosts of evil, led by the demon Rangda – has to be coordinated and rehearsed by the *dhalang*, a performer who is often also a priest.

In the Greek and Roman eras, playwrights often acted as teachers, potentially even acting in their own plays in addition, making them akin to what we today would refer to as a 'theatre maker'. Another figure analogous to our producer began to appear around this time, as the *choregos* was fundamentally a sponsor, who would pay for costumes, props, masks, musicians and the choreographer, as well as financing the chorus for the playwright. The dramatist would then fill the role of director, training performers with the chorus leader up to a year prior to one of the institutionalized competitions or festivals, which formed the theatrical milieu of much of city-state ancient Greece. The city's magistrate would draw lots to choose the playwright and lead actor, with the playwright then personally working to secure the second and third actors. As actors were illiterate, rehearsals would have begun with the playwright in a directorial role reading out their words to the actors to memorize by rote, a trend that would continue in later eras, too.

A baton can be discerned in the hand of the *maître du jeu* (literally, 'master of the game') or 'pageant master' in an illustration by Jean Fouquet in the fifteenth-century French prayer book, *Livre d'Heures pour Maître Étienne Chevalier*. We might surmise that this was an early director, marshalling the actors in performance and bringing the choirs in on cue. This admittedly prosaic way of working demonstrates a nascent director/actor relationship in action. Likewise, in medieval England, as has been well documented, town guilds would organize the retelling of prominent biblical stories, often as part of religious festivals, such as the Feast of Corpus Christi. Large carts supporting scenery known as 'pageant wagons' would house a particular part of the story, with spectators moving between each one, their movements echoing a pilgrimage or the journey of a human being through a lifetime and resembling early promenade theatre. A prominent member of each guild, instructed and given licence by the local councils, may have acted here as pageant master to organize logistics, especially with the rise of theatrical machinery and special effects such as fire. They would also have to employ the (mostly male) actors, who would then have rehearsed in the rooms of private houses. Coventry even employed a professional director on a twelve-year contract. There is also evidence of what John C. Coldewey terms '"property-players" who [were] director, stage manager and producer rolled into one' (Beadle and Fletcher 2008: 226), coordinating with others to realize the logistics of the outdoor performances. I will pass over the subsequent early modern period here, as I examine this in detail in the following section, '**Directing without the director**'.

During the French neoclassical period and the Restoration period of seventeenth-century England, playwrights continued to marshal and direct. The French playwright Molière and his troupe were in the king's favour, directing court entertainments for Louis XIV and Molière's plays formed the cornerstone of the French national theatre. In England, poet and playwright William Davenant bought the tennis courts at Lincoln's Inn Fields, transforming them into a stage, with doors either side of the proscenium arch, trapdoors, flying systems and flats that moved in slots. There was a scenic stage (which comprised the set) and a forestage (an acting space) where the scenes were enacted, there being little interaction between the actors and the scenery. With increasingly elaborate designs, the roles of the scenic artist and the costume designer were introduced, coming to the fore of Restoration period theatre. As a principal shareholder and owner of the theatre, Davenant was more of a managerial figure, but the role of persons in control was being cemented. The playwrights continued to guide the actors, instructing them in the emotional tones required for the playing of the lines, as well as relationships and characterization, effectively directing the plays. It must be noted that Davenant (among others) received the royal patronage of Charles II: in England, as in France, individual figures continued to be endorsed by those in authority as bastions of the craft.

Technological advances in theatre production also cemented the role of the director. Within the emergence of the modern world, technology increased, especially in the wake of the Industrial Revolution and from the 1860s onwards: mass production, the printing press, electricity, the motor car and radio communication took off. By 1880, theatres were beginning to incorporate flying, electric lighting, special effects such as giant waterfalls and tricks, such as the well-known Pepper's Ghost, in order to conjure apparitions. All of these developments meant that somebody had to make creative choices to unify a piece: directors, managers and producers, as we know them in the modern sense, began to emerge.

In 1874, Georg II, Duke of Saxe-Meiningen, toured Europe with his troupe of actors. His support for his court theatre, the Meiningen Ensemble, earned him the sobriquet of *Theaterherzog*, or 'Theatre Duke'. As a painter and art historian himself, Georg placed considerable emphasis on historically accurate, bespoke costumes and scenery. This, along with his predilection for large and precisely choreographed crowd scenes and an increasing desire for a realistic or naturalistic aesthetic all gave rise to the role of the director. Georg himself imposed a strong directorial 'vision', demanding that even chorus members develop fully rounded characters with something akin to what we would now recognize as 'backstory' and with characters inhabiting an onstage world that did not acknowledge the presence of the audience. His introduction of longer rehearsal periods may also have facilitated the development of the director. Ludwig Chronegk, who had been a principal actor of the Meininger Hoftheater until the mid-1860s, retired from his acting work in the late 1870s, to essentially become a full-time director, implementing Georg's vision and establishing the 'Meiningen Principles' of theatre, which not only argued for an integrated, unified theatrical aesthetic, but also emphasized the achievement of this through the firm control of a director. Again, the relationship between Georg and Chronegk (originally from a mercantile family) exemplifies how the rise of the director can be aligned with aristocracy, and the rise of the professional classes. Already here a degree of inherent privilege begins to seep into the hierarchical role of the director with their actors in the rehearsal room. Edward Braun (1982) highlights the fact that Chronegk ruled with an iron fist, often forgetting to wear any form of velvet glove.

In France, Émile Zola's *Naturalism in the Theatre* (1881) set the tone for naturalistic acting, as it identified that the behaviour of the character was motivated partly by their environment. Zola was also an artistic adviser to André Antoine's Théâtre Libre company, founded in Paris in 1887. Antoine had gone to see the work of the Meiningen Ensemble in 1888, and although not all of the work was to his taste, the diligently rehearsed productions and carefully crafted characterizations were of great interest to him. He was impressed by actors not turning their backs on audiences, as well as by the notion that the leading actor did not need to occupy the strongest point onstage, with all the other actors orbiting around them. Inspired by these ideas, Antoine strove both for a form of realism and naturalism. His sophisticated lighting designs removed the footlights, and he frequently began rehearsals by crafting accurate sets and unified costume designs that served as an environment in which his actors could explore their characters and behaviours with a high degree of authenticity. Known for his emphasis on truthful, realistic acting styles and appropriate dialects, Antoine would reputedly go so far as to hire untrained performers, believing that the trained actors of his day were too encumbered by artifice to effectively portray real people.

Parallel with Antoine's work in France was that of Konstantin Stanislavski in Russia. Of his famous 'system' Stanislavski stated that people should not slavishly follow his method, but forge their own paths. Stanislavski was a pioneer and while his early work became cemented (for numerous reasons) as the Stanislavkian system, he also directed productions at the Moscow Art Theatre, where he experimented with different rehearsal room practices and systems for physicalizing the text, and continued to explore different ways of working until his death. The playwright Anton Chekhov held him in the greatest esteem as a director of his naturalistic works and it was the reciprocal exchange between the two practitioners that encouraged Stanislavski's mining beneath the written words to find the subtext of the play. Stanislavski had earlier witnessed Ludwig Chronegk at work with the Meiningen Ensemble and initially (and regrettably) imitated Chronegk's somewhat despotic style; this, however, altered over the years, developing into a much more actor-centric approach, culminating in the development of the 'Method of Physical Action' and active analysis, which allow actors to take ownership of their place within the story using a less dictatorial rehearsal room methodology. Stanislavski's later methodologies will be considered more fully in Part Two. Since Stanislavski also saw André Antoine at work, we can trace a connection between directorial styles and theatrical and rehearsal movements between France, Germany and Russia throughout the late 1800s. This was paralleled by the rise of different writing styles, including the naturalistic, realistic and symbolic dramas of Henrik Ibsen, Anton Chekhov and August Strindberg, among others. These plays moved away from romantic and melodramatic forms, demanding different rehearsal strategies that explored behaviour, psychological motivation and environmental influences on behaviour. Directors also worked to unify both the inner work of the rehearsal room with the external work of the design and scenographic elements. Prior to this, costumes and scenery had come out of stock, using what was available and expedient from the stores, with little regard to the playwright's intentions. With this new bespoke scenic design, coupled with the technological advances and the major shifts in acting techniques outlined above, the role of the director became ever more defined, emerging as the one to steer the production.

6

Directing without the Director

Chapter outline	
i. Verse and prose	26
ii. Cue lines	26
iii. Shared lines	27

The role of the director may well be a fairly recent development across well over two centuries of theatre history. Nevertheless, directing has always taken place. Here I would like to explore 'director-less' theatre, even though – as I hope you will see – directing methodologies are in play. I am going to return to the early modern period, which I glossed over above and to the work of Shakespeare in particular. I have chosen Shakespeare partly because there has been a major exploration of original practices in Shakespearean theatre over the past two decades, with the work of practitioners and academics such as Tiffany Stern, Patrick Tucker and Mark Rylance in the UK, Bill Kincaid in the US, Sarah Roberts in South Africa and Jeremy Lopez in Canada, to name but a few. Shakespeare features on many syllabi, so for this alone his work is well worth exploring.

As Peter M. Boenisch argues, theatre makers should rethink 'what it is that "the director does" or what they should do, to what directing does and may do' (2015: 5). Directing can happen without a director, in the same way that actors embrace dramaturgy, even without the role of the dramaturg. Sarah Roberts describes it as follows: 'This actor-centric strategy redefines the creative authority of the director … in favour of those directly encountering each other via the play. The "directorial task", such as it is, becomes one of facilitation and dramaturgical input, along with ensuring that the entire cast is equally attuned to a collective undertaking' (2022: 5). Here, Roberts goes on to examine how *Macbeth* was performed in South Africa, describing how over the course of several years, the Joburg Theatre Youth Development Programme has been exploring 'spontaneous staging of Shakespeare (and other classics) by a cast [with] diverse linguistic preferences and cultural backgrounds' (ibid.).

Let us return to a few of the original practices and conventions that may allow us to think about how the text contains all the clues needed for an actor to fully embody the character in performance. The playwright was the director in many senses, helping the actors to understand what was required from the character. We know that in Shakespeare's theatre there were a couple of group rehearsals, plus a couple of additional ones specifically for dances and fights, and much private study was needed by individual actors to learn the lines. With up to six plays a week to retain in their memories, the actors needed texts that would essentially direct them and offer all the clues for the taking. Given all of this, here are three quick exercises:

i. Verse and prose

High-status characters frequently speak in prose, and low-status characters in verse, so it is something of a problematic persistent myth that verse is for high-status characters only. My simple rule of thumb is this: where there is a change from verse to prose, or vice versa, there is an acting clue that is being afforded to the actor, not always related to status. This may take some figuring out, but it is often linked to an emotional shift, or a deliberate change in tactic on the part of the speaker.

ii. Cue lines

The actors had only their own parts written out, with the three cue words from the lines of the character who had spoken previously. Thus, the actor playing Solanio in *The Merchant of Venice* would have had the following on his cue sheet:

>   _____ *have my bond.*
>   It is the most impenetrable cur
>   That ever kept with men.

With a scene partner, try out the scene below. Here, Shylock defends his right to recoup the loan he gave to Antonio. The other character in the scene, Solanio, is a friend of Antonio. The actor playing Solanio **must** come in on cue with the above line as soon as they hear the words 'have my bond' spoken by Shylock.

> SHYLOCK
>   I'll have my bond. I will not hear thee speak,
>   I'll have my bond, and therefore speak no more.
>   I'll not be made a soft and dull-ey'd fool,
>   To shake the head, relent, and sigh, and yield
>   To Christian intercessors: follow not, –
>   I'll have no speaking, I will have my bond.
>   *Exit*
>
> SOLANIO   It is the most impenetrable cur
>   That ever kept with men.
>
>   (*MV* 3.3. 4–18)

This is my favourite cue line example of all. When I do this exercise, the actor playing Solanio is always frustrated at being interrupted and not being able to be heard. The playwright is therefore tacitly directing us in terms of mood, emotion and psychology.

iii. Shared lines

In verse, a playwright will often complete the verse line between several characters. Try this example from *The Winter's Tale*. Leontes, King of Sicily, believes that his daughter – the 'brat' mentioned in the text below – is actually the child of Polixenes, a friend whom Leontes (wrongly) accuses of having had an affair with his wife, Hermione. Leontes wants the child banished or killed, and a verse line here is shared between Leontes and Antigonus, a loyal friend of Hermione:

> LEONTES
>   You that have been so tenderly officious
>   With Lady Margery, your midwife there,

> To save this bastard's life – for 'tis a bastard
> So sure as this beard's grey – what will you adventure
> To save this brat's life?
> ANTIGONUS   Anything, my lord …
>
> (*WT* 2.3. 158–60)

Again, try this aloud with a scene partner. What did you instinctively feel here? If Antigonus comes in on cue, he is desperate. There is deliberately no pause here: when Shakespeare offers actors pauses, it is through a lack of verse beats. The actor playing Antigonus must rapidly pick up the response, batting the metaphorical ball straight back at Leontes. *The Winter's Tale* is one of Shakespeare's later plays and he is by this point highly adept at playing with language, creating verbal interplay that is often similar to the musical form of jazz. A plethora of shared lines like these give us a directorial clue as to the pace and potential connections between characters. And in case anyone needs a spoiler alert for a play some four hundred years old, here it is: Antigonus does go on to save the life of the child, Perdita.

There are so many more similar clues offered to actors in the text, including the lengths of lines versus the lengths of thoughts, verbal antithesis, the use of rhyme, the use of rhetorical figures and tropes and the alternation between 'thee', 'thou' and 'you' when one character addresses another. You may pick up any Elizabethan or Jacobean dramatic text and play with these practices. All of these techniques are designed to inform and trigger emotional and psychological currents. See how it can invigorate the performance process and support the actors in what writer and actor-trainer Bella Merlin calls 'dynamic listening'. For Merlin,

> dynamic listening requires a sequence of Action-Reaction-Decision. This sequence dominates all human interaction, and impacts hugely on how we get inside a text and build a character. It goes like this: (1) I do something to you (Action); (2) you instinctively respond to my Action (Reaction); and (3) you then consciously decide how you're going to respond to me (Decision).
>
> (2010: 96)

Having experimented with Jacobean or Elizabethan drama, move on to contemporary texts. How can you work within the spirit of original practices to ensure you are engaging in what Jeremy Lopez calls 'text-based dramaturgy' (2008: 307)? This is essentially exploring the inner dynamics of the text, ensuring that, as a director, you are aware of the acting clues and support your actors in finding and honouring these. Honouring the logic of the text in this way allows the actor and director to get closer to the heart of a moment. Researcher Gay McAuley noticed this in a rehearsal room during her rehearsal observation of a production of Michael Gow's *Toy Symphony* by Company B (now Belvoir) in Sydney, Australia, in relation to the logic text[1] of where a word is placed in the sentence:

> Richard [an actor] picked out the word 'right' in that speech, asking 'Why is it there? What does it mean?' Then he said 'Aha!' That's the moment he realises that it was his self-analysis that has silenced him. So Nina [character] has led him to this insight ... Richard's perception and skill and craft led him to pick up this little word that a reader may have skated over and he then used it to carry a huge weight of important emotional, character and plot meaning.
>
> (2012: 66)

Key takeaways of original practices:

1 The actor becomes the key storyteller. Even if you have a director-led approach, the spirit of original practices can be used to flatten the hierarchy of the rehearsal room, giving actors agency in the creative process.

2 The actors listen dynamically to each other, balancing technique with impulse.

3 The text holds all the acting clues. With any play and with any rehearsal period, return to the text if there's an issue and be nothing less than forensic in searching for your answer. Director Katie Mitchell, in *The Director's Craft*, states that the text should be 'the mediator of any conflict' (2009: 120), should a director and actor disagree on a particular issue.

---

[1] Mike Alfreds refers to all the textual clues as 'logic text', where you can 'make sense of the text at its simplest, logical and grammatically structured level' (2010: 196).

7

Creativity, Breakthroughs and Building Blocks

For me, rehearsals are always about pushing the production forward little by little, adding new layers. Nascent directors that I teach sometimes think that directing is always the pursuit of something revelatory during each and every rehearsal. This may happen occasionally, but not always: telling a good story is what counts. Very early on in my career, I assisted director and writer Sir Alan Ayckbourn, who showed me that directing is as much about knowing when *not* to step in. If a scene is working well, then perhaps saying nothing at all is key. In *Inside the Rehearsal Room*, I developed the notion of 'The Four Lenses of Breakthrough' (2022: 113–14). Most rehearsal breakthroughs are tiny moments of individual revelation and discovery, with a few shared breakthroughs, rather than monumental and epiphanous 'wow' moments. This slowly and carefully allows the actors to embody the text, develop their characters and interact with each other and the world around them in the successful telling of the play's story.

Director Katie Mitchell warns against building a rehearsal process around 'the search for a sudden revelatory discovery or epiphany that will unlock everything' (2009: 115); however, when such discoveries do happen, they are from a position of the practitioner having embodied knowledge that is felt and expressed and they often give confidence to the individuals involved. This has profound implications for the rehearsal room in my belief, as the actor or director may experience a sudden boost of confidence following this moment of insight. However, if this moment is not congruent with the overarching frame of the production, a false confidence may ensue, potentially leading the actor down a path of diminishing returns. 'Creators remodel what they inherit' (Brandt and Eagleman 2017: 45) and a so-called 'lightning moment' has been seen as something of a fallacy: 'Many people have figuratively stood in thunderstorms, waiting for the lightning to strike, but creative ideas evolve from existing memories and impressions ... They arise from the interweaving of billions of microscopic sparks in the vast darkness of the brain' (ibid.: 46).

So, we are therefore building and layering in rehearsals and are either 'bending, breaking [or] blending' (ibid.: 49). Why this is important is that it reduces the pressure a director may put upon themselves to:

i. create a production that is somehow entirely 'original'.
ii. produce a rehearsal schedule that is full of interesting and quirky techniques. This may occupy the time, but it may not be useful to the process. It may feel like you are a director, curating a process, but will there be much actual *directing* happening?
iii. always ensure breakthroughs are happening. My Four Lenses model and the research into this concludes that many of these breakthroughs are small moments of recognition or insight, often in relation to a personal acting journey. It is the director's job to create the conditions for the actors to take ownership and discover meaningfully within the frames of the production. As director Pooja Ghai states, 'actors are magicians, and directing is about helping them find the tools to make magic' (Gardner: 2023).

Returning to this idea of creativity and originality through David Brandt and Anthony Eagleman's prism, when 'bending', we take something already in existence and modify it. As the director of a production at Staffordshire University in 2018, I transposed and bent the Restoration world of William Wycherley's *The Country Wife*, first performed in 1675, to contemporary London. These circles within circles are important for me, locating contemporary London within the circle of understanding Restoration England and city life. When 'breaking', we take something apart and reassemble it differently and when 'blending', two different things are pieced together. 'Blending', as a concept through my work in relation to rehearsal room practice, is a reoccurring theme and one to take time to explore. This links to the notion expressed by Darren Henley, Chief Executive of Arts Council England, that without creativity 'nothing new would happen' (2018: ix). In practice, we often build upon previous ideas and blend thoughts so that I might, say, blend one of Russian practitioner Michael Chekhov's rehearsal techniques with one of Katie Mitchell's. By blending, I am bringing together two or more appropriate strategies that will be useful for a rehearsal room moment. *How to Fly a Horse: The Secret History of Creation, Invention, and Discovery* (2015) was written by technology pioneer Kevin Ashton (who coined the term 'Internet of Things', among others) and debunks the myth that creativity is an elusive activity that only a select few can attain, because 'creating is not magic, but work' (2015: viii), paraphrasing a line from a poem by pioneering German theatre maker Bertolt Brecht, 'The Curtains', written in the mid-1950s: 'That this is not magic, but / Work, my friends' (1976: 425). Frances de la Tour, the actress playing Helena in director Peter Brook's seminal 1970 production of *A Midsummer Night's Dream*, testified to this when Brook suggested that there had been a 'most magical moment' (Selbourne 2010: 99) in the scene in which the four lovers quarrel and are then led astray by Puck. In response to this suggestion, de la Tour, 'taken aback, but easily resisting the emotional pressure … says firmly: "I don't admit it to anyone, when I know something magical has happened. It would destroy it"' (ibid.). This 'magic', for the actor, can become a holy grail of discovery: a seismic 'aha' moment which must not be articulated, for fear it may disappear. This is something that is unhealthy and continues to perpetuate the myth that there is magic at work; a myth that the director must bust.

Kevin Ashton defines these 'aha' moments as a 'sudden revelation … apocryphal and unable to survive scrutiny' (2015: 42), but I would refute this, as I reposition breakthrough moments as naturally occurring instants in the rehearsal process. Ashton's argument that creativity and discovery can only come about via 'ordinary thinking' (ibid.: 37) over a period of time, however, as well as the notion he expresses that hard work creates an 'aha' moment is supported by ongoing research into rehearsal room studies and directing practice.

Finally, I'd like to add that I personally use the term 'useful' a lot in rehearsal as a director: is what we are doing *useful* in moving the process forwards or in layering a moment? I then move on to question whether that useful choice is the most *dynamic* or *interesting* choice, without it being purposely gimmicky. Holly Race Roughan mentions in Part Three of this book that, as a director, she is responsible for not allowing a production choice to be what she calls 'cringy', and I see a gimmick as a potential 'cringeworthy' moment. From there, collectively and collaboratively as a company, we must then decide whether we are telling the story both clearly and in the most engaging, dynamic and interesting way we can.

8

Rehearsal and Production Analyses

One piece of advice I am always giving directors in training is to see as much theatre as possible – and theatre of differing styles and genres. This allows an early career director to critically analyse work using an outside eye. Often the work of the director is invisible, but it is useful to analyse a final production which a director has imbued with their work. Whether or not the director has created an explicit stylistic 'vision' (a phrase that incidentally did not exist until the beginning of the twentieth century) the work of the director will be part of the DNA or fabric of the finished production, ideally collectively owned by the company. Working backwards, it can also be of value to look at and analyse rehearsal notebooks, prompt books and scripts from previous rehearsal periods, in order to ascertain choices made in rehearsal rooms and how these impacted on the finished production. Watching theatre is key to approaching the analysis of a production through the lens of the director. The below exercise, with accompanying questions, triggers and provocations, will allow you to consider the end result of the directing process, choices arrived at, and decisions made.

Analysing a production

How to undertake this exercise:
- Find a live production in which you are interested.
- If a live production isn't accessible, then I recommend the resources available through Drama Online (https://www.dramaonlinelibrary.com), which hosts collections including West End productions of Oscar Wilde's Victorian plays, Renaissance drama from Shakespeare's Globe or the RSC and an extensive

collection of Asian theatre productions, or the resources from the National Theatre At Home (https://www.ntathome.com), which – at the time of writing – features an extensive archive of productions from verbatim play *Grenfell* and complex symbolic piece *Angels in America,* to the Restoration piece *The Beaux' Stratagem*, the musical *The Little Big Things* and realist play *The Cherry Orchard.*

- Do a little research beforehand on the playwright, composer or lyricist on why the piece was written, as well as any reviews of the original production and the creative team's approach.
- Watch the production, keeping the following questions in mind:
  - Did the production feel 'as one' overall; i.e. was the overall 'world' (as described in this section) unified? This is regardless of the playwright's style or the play's genre.
  - Did the production work as a piece of theatre?
  - Did the production speak to our time in any way?
  - Was the production engaging? Did it captivate you?
- To help answer the above, use the following proposed production analysis questions:

1 Are the given circumstances of the play honoured or used to build the world? The givens, naturally, relate to what the playwright says about the characters and time scale, or locational, spatial, religious, spiritual, temporal, economic, generational, political, cultural or political facts. These are the facts required to begin to construct a world that makes logical sense. You can also explore what characters say about each other and why. Does this relate to how the characters are interacting and the subtext being explored?

2 Does the production's world or ethos relate (or not) to the world we as an audience are currently living in? In other words, why should we tell this story now?

3 If you are watching a classical play, do the original practices (playhouse or conventions) support in the (re)telling of the story? If so, how? If not, why not? And if not, does it matter?

4 Does the production honour the historical, cultural, political and social concepts of its original world? These will need researching. If so, why? If not, why not?

5 Do the events of the production 'land'? Events are discussed in Part Two, page 55.

6 Is there a rising and falling of tension? Is the dynamism of the story honoured in the production? Have the actors (with

their director) landed the story beats, i.e. is the storytelling clear?
7 Are the wants and needs of the characters clear? Did actors and directors make interesting choices with character?
8 Do the actors marry their technical abilities (energy, movement, dance, song, voice, embodiment) with the needs of the production and the scale of the theatre? Was the casting appropriate and interesting?
9 Does the design (set, costume, lighting, video, sound, music) and/or scenography aid or detract from the storytelling, or were all the elements unified?
10 Does the design and/or scenography add extra layers of narrative that are congruent to the production? Does the design 'fit' or feel congruent with the playing or auditorium space?
11 How does the groundplan (the arrangement of furniture, scenic elements and entrances and exits) allow for tension-making possibilities for the physical shaping (i.e. the blocking) of the scene? Do the movements of the actors and the proxemics between them feel appropriate for the story beat of that moment? Does the blocking feel forced or naturally earned and owned by the actors? Does the choreography tell a story and enhance the narrative?
12 Is there an ease to the production, i.e. does anything seem to have been unnecessarily interpolated or 'crowbarred in', or is there a seamlessness between all elements that aides the storytelling? These elements may include (but are not limited to) movement, choreography, voice, musical numbers, puppetry and fights.

Key takeaways:
- The production arrived at needs to be unified, ensuring that the inner work of the rehearsal room is married seamlessly to the outer work of the scenographic, design and marketing strategies.
- Regardless of previous productions, or the play's genre, the logic of the production world must be unified: each production is built around its own logic.
- Secondary to the above, ask whether the production world presented is rooted in the text or not. If not, there may be a sound logic that is rooted in the above.

- Remember that the term 'vision' in terms of directing is a phrase from the turn of the twentieth century, and thus a very recent development in several thousand years of theatre and production history. A production does not need an obviously bold or explicit vision in order for it to cohere.

Part Two now takes us stage by stage through a rehearsal process, from early through to late stages. This work is underpinned by all of the concepts and ideas outlined throughout Part One.

Part Two

Stages of Directing

9 Stage One: Choosing and Establishing
10 Stage Two: Creating and Forming
11 Stage Three: Building and Encouraging
12 Stage Four: Shaping and Layering – the Final Stages
13 Stage Five: Delivering and Entrusting

9

Stage One
Choosing and Establishing

Chapter outline

Exercises in how to choose a piece	43
Interwoven or intercultural theatre-making practices	45
Choosing a rehearsal strategy and schedule	47
Genres	50
Textual interpretations and preparing a script	53
Casting processes	57
Inclusive and diverse casting	57
Appropriateness for the character and the production	58
Balance of casting	59
Gathering a creative team for the production	61
Sustainability	64
Configurations and spaces: How these impact early rehearsal decisions	65
Research and development stages	68

Creating the conditions for everyone to enter the rehearsal room begins several months prior to the first day's traditional 'meet and greet'.

This first stage examines how a director chooses a story to tell, and how their collaborators are brought together in order to create a bold frame to hold the play and within which to make rehearsal room decisions. In *Inside the Rehearsal Room* I posit the notion that all productions need to be framed.[1] Each collaborator, from actor to designer, needs to understand where the edges of the frame are, in order to work creatively, boldly, meaningfully and fiercely within.

To work in this way actors, especially, need to feel safe. Psychological safety[2] is something that businesses and public sector organizations now widely use in staff training and there is no reason why theatre making should be any different. In fact, I would go so far as to argue that psychological safety is even more important in theatre making, due to the degree of vulnerability actors need to embrace during the creative process. Actors need to feel safe in order not to be or feel ridiculed, to take risks and to fail. Failure is essential. Holly Race Roughan, Artistic Director of Headlong, states in Part Three that she knows what works in a rehearsal by exploring what *doesn't* work. To be able to undertake that exploration, a company needs to feel safe to explore and create without judgement or ridicule, and for me, this needs to be within the frame of the production concept or world. Otherwise, any discovery made could be meaningless. There must be truth and a belief in the inner logic of any world that the characters inhabit.

The foundations of this are to be laid out early in the rehearsal phase. The rehearsal journey begins as soon as the play is chosen or commissioned, with different passengers boarding and alighting at various stations along the way. For these passengers to join safely at any point, the journey must be planned to make them feel welcome onboard and to allow for their contributions to the quest to be acknowledged and explored. The tone of this is set, therefore, before entering any physical rehearsal space. As the tone setter of the whole process – who is responsible for delivering everyone

---

[1] You can find this in Chapter 3 of *Inside the Rehearsal Room*. Along with the notion of the 'world' of the play: 'The frames are a set of conventions that govern and bound the choices made within a rehearsal process including the acting style required (pantomime, for instance, requires a different style from Pinter), the conventions worked within and rehearsal methodologies employed and are often decided upon prior to the rehearsal period. The world of the play is the environment which the characters perceive and therefore operate and respond to. This can consist of both the world of the playwright's words, as well as the world created by the director and designer through the mise en scène' (2022: 53–4).

[2] Psychological safety exercises aim to emphasize qualities such as empathy, authenticity, participation, vulnerability and feedback, in order to create a safe working environment. The goal is to promote an atmosphere in which no team or company member will feel embarrassed or punished for admitting mistakes, asking questions, or volunteering an idea. Many business arenas already use these in the shape of 'meeting icebreakers' (including such standard games as 'Mad Libs', 'Two Truths and a Lie' and 'First Job/Worst Job') as well as team-building activities (including digital game nights and book clubs). Improvisation games – with their emphasis on collaboration and active listening – have also been successfully used, in and beyond theatre milieus.

safely and on time to their destination – the director is essential in creating the conditions for this to occur. So, without the correct early rehearsal foundations, the part of the journey that takes place in the rehearsal room – the main stage of the journey – could prove bumpy, uneven, and even prone to derailment.

I now refer to the stage outside of the physical rehearsal room as the 'early rehearsal stage', rather than 'pre-rehearsal'. If rehearsal is a place of exploration and making meanings, then this starts with the creative team – the director, designer, choreographer, musical director and dramaturg, among many others – locating the destination early on, planning the journey ahead and choosing the vehicles in which everyone is going to travel, as well as plotting the stops along the way and the landmarks that need to be seen. By undertaking this work, the frame of the production is arrived at: everyone then knows what they are collectively trying to achieve.

Exercises in how to choose a piece

Why, why, why?

How to undertake this exercise:

You've found a play, musical or piece that you really want to direct. Find yourself a spot where you can read the play alone, without interference, either human or digital. Try to read the piece all the way through. This can be in your head, or out loud: whatever works best for you. Include all the stage directions. Give yourself a short break where the writer has marked an interval, so that you honour their structure. Once you have finished, ask yourself the following questions about what you have just experienced:

- **Why have you chosen this piece?** What are your gut responses to the piece and why? These are the visceral responses that stay with you. Does it make you laugh? Does it move you? Does it raise questions or debate? Does it polarize thinking? Is it outrageous? Write yourself a list, draw your thoughts or create voice notes. Capture this first-ever experience before you move on to more intellectual notions of why you have chosen it.
- **Why now?** Why should this story be told now? Why should it be told by *you*? If it's a new piece, why is it needed? How does this

story try to make sense of the world around us? If it's a classical play, what themes and images are present within it that makes it inevitable that this story should be re-told? When I chose to direct Shakespeare's *Measure for Measure* a few years ago, it related to abuses of patriarchal power in society, in the wake of the #MeToo movement. Retelling this story through that lens felt pressing and gave it an immediacy that became a constant rehearsal conversation. Writer and director Tristan Fynn-Aiduenu, interviewed in 2023 in *The Stage* newspaper, talks about giving a play 'a new flavour based on historical context and how it can relate to the present day. This comes from questioning as deeply as possible and seeing what comes through. "What is the connection I have to this [text] truthfully, honestly, soulfully?"' (Benjamin 2023). Greg Doran, now a director emeritus at the RSC, has spoken about his job in relation to the classics being about 'refreshing stories that were told many years ago and making them vivid and bright and immediate, now' (2023: 56). Indhu Rubasingham, Artistic Director of the National Theatre from 2025, states that for her, the choice of piece is predicated on whether it offers 'those watching a different perspective or different world view' (Waugh 2023: 121).

- **Why theatre?** Why this medium? Why put this story onstage? Theatre is about liveness and sharing space and time with actors, as opposed to viewing a recorded archive showing, which is not a shared space or time, or a live stream, where only time is shared. This relates to the energy between storyteller and audience and the holistic experience of the verbal and the visual. Think whether this story may be better as an audio drama. Even if it is extremely text-centric, what visual narrative layers, rooted in that text, will you bring to this piece? All of this moves the text away from being a published piece and towards being a production. The creation of this production world is something I explore below in relation to design and what is sometimes termed the 'concept'. I have occasionally spoken to an emerging playwright and suggested that what they have written might be better served by the medium of film, television drama or audio drama. I am not suggesting here that a story can only be told in one medium, but that the story must earn its place on the stage. Think, too, about demographics: filter some of the above answers through the lens of playing to a specific audience in a particular location, or whether the production would tour, or a mixture of the two. This will enable you to consider whether the play resonates with a specific audience, or whether it can create ripple effects across a touring area. Can the microcosm elements of the story reveal something for the macrocosm? Or does this, conversely, become reductionist and problematic, making it less universal? Only by working through this process explicitly might this become clear.

Why it works:

As a director, I frequently come across plays and musicals that I love. The reality, though, is that that alone is not a reason to produce them. They must be anchored in a real need to tell the story for an audience. A reason to tell a story from an aesthetic point of view must be linked to a strong business case for a producer or artistic director of a venue to commission you to direct it, should the play resonate with them as much as it does with you.

Key takeaway:

You get straight to the heart of the relevance of telling this story in the here and now, today.

Interwoven or intercultural theatre-making practices

Intercultural theatre practices – working together with another culture and producing theatre accordingly – were once heralded as inclusive. However, many of these approaches are now being re-examined through our current societal lenses and being evaluated anew. Peter Brook's *The Mahabharata*, a nine-hour play, performed in French and English, which toured the world after its initial performances in a quarry in Avignon in 1985, received, at the time, almost universal critical acclaim. However, more recently, it has been criticized for imposing a dominant Western aesthetic and understanding of theatre making (and even a patronizing orientalism) upon a Sanskrit epic, central to Hindu belief systems. Academic Rik Knowles has argued that the 'tendency of intercultural theatre and its scholarship [is] to split the world into a "west and the rest" binary' (2010: 21), since it can frequently view 'othered' cultures through a Western lens to create theatre which perpetuates a colonial imposition. As a director, to appropriate (rather than appreciate) other aesthetics and theatre-making styles and cultures can, if done without due care and attention, remove 'elements of performance from the social, cultural, and theatrical or ritual contexts that produced them and where they produce their meanings' (ibid.: 19). As a director's role is about making and shaping meaning through the work they produce, to remove and re-graft performance elements out of context can be seen as cultural appropriation or theatrical vandalism. Even if this is not the intent of the theatre maker, audience reception needs to be considered. In *Theatre and Empire*, Benjamin Poore discusses the contentious performance piece 'Exhibit B', initially staged in Edinburgh in 2014, in which black actors stood on plinths as tableaux vivants, depicting the evils of the colonial era. One part of the performance even labelled contemporary asylum seekers as 'found objects'. Whatever the directorial intentions behind the piece, Poore observes that 'the intentions behind the work [cannot] prevent some members of the audience from reacting to its structural properties' (2016: 10).

Erika Fischer-Lichte, Professor of Theatre Studies at the Freie Universität Berlin, has instead recently invited theatre makers to consider what she terms an 'interwoven' cultural approach, which encourages the practitioner to enter a genuine collaboration when working alongside other theatre-making cultures. For Fischer-Lichte, intercultural theatre is seen as a 'heuristic tool developed mainly in Anglo-American theatre...proclaim[ing] equality' (2014: 9). She argues that bringing together two or more cultures in a theatre piece implicitly presupposes that they are both different. In the case of Brook, it is the dominant, Western, white, male director who used another culture in the making of their work. Interwoven theatre, for Fischer-Lichte, centres around consciously threading strands, with interconnectedness being key to the making of the work, rather than 'homogenising differences' (ibid.: 12). This should be the case where another theatre-making culture or aesthetic is drawn upon within a production, whether that is sensitively handling the bringing in of Japanese butoh or Noh theatre-making techniques, or certain music or costumes from Indonesian wayang puppetry theatre: the starting point should always be a place of cultural sensitivity and appreciation, and not one of cultural appropriation.

Underpinning all these factors in the choice of play is the fact that the director is the storyteller who pulls together all the multifarious elements to create a unified whole. This leads me to ask the following question: If the story that you want to tell is too far removed from yourself, is it morally right to direct that story? I was once approached by a producer who asked me if I would be interested in directing Sue Townsend's 1982 play *Bazaar and Rummage*, which centres around three acutely agoraphobic women who attend a jumble sale organized by their female social workers. During the course of the story, the three central characters reveal many intimate details about their various lives, including the suffering engendered by their shared phobia. This is so far removed from my experience, that I questioned the producer as to why they had approached me; they understood and appreciated my honesty. I bring this up because the play you choose to direct should ultimately be one that speaks to you or reflects in some manner your thinking about the world. This is not to say that you should not tell the story if the narrative of a play is outside of your lived experience. But you do need to make sure that there is a strong connection to the material and that in your bringing together a team of creatives and actors, you ensure that – through them – lived experience can be brought directly into the room. In his book *My Shakespeare: A Director's Journey through the First Folio*, Greg Doran discusses the 2004 production of *Othello* by the RSC. The casting of two South African actors[3] in the production, each of whom had differing but direct lived experience of apartheid, shifted the way the story was told for Doran as a British director.

Choosing a rehearsal strategy and schedule

A director, working with their creative and production team, often leads on both the rehearsal strategy (i.e. how the company will work) and the planning of the rehearsal schedule, in terms of what will be rehearsed when. Here, I would like to posit my approach to the decisions I need to make during the early rehearsal period. This is an approach that I have been developing over several years which helps me consider things in advance, as directors need to discuss some of the production concepts and frameworks with producers, artistic and creative directors, casting directors and actors at auditions, as well as with their wider team.

---

[3]Sello Maake Ka-Ncube played Othello and Antony Sher played Iago; the two discussed the way their experiences influenced their playing of the roles in an article in the *Guardian* newspaper: https://www.theguardian.com/stage/2004/may/25/theatre2.

I start initially with how I want to rehearse in terms of personal values, prior to working out the scheduling. A director should aspire to living and breathing their values through the work that they make. To take one example, Katie Mitchell has spoken widely about how she tries to ensure that sustainability is a quality that is threaded both through her approach to rehearsals and theatre making, and the content produced. I will return to sustainability, particularly in the context of eco-dramaturgy, a little later. To offer a more personal example, I recently undertook an exercise where I asked numerous producers, actors and creatives that I had worked with to describe my rehearsal room and ways of working in terms of values. I then asked several colleagues to narrow this down. The six adjectives they arrived at were:

- Collaborative
- Committed
- Creative
- Authentic
- Inclusive
- Reliable

Taking each of these values in turn, I will demonstrate how these might translate into tangible ways of working:

Collaborative	The director may wish to flatten rehearsal room hierarchies, ensuring that all voices are valued and heard in a compassionate and open manner. This does not mean a free-for-all with no boundaries. Everyone needs to work within the frame of the production style, as well as being aware of the length of the rehearsal period. Even the shortest rehearsal period can result in genuine collaboration through listening to ideas and honouring the contributions of individuals, either from their lived experiences, creative endeavours or the wider research undertaken.
Committed	A director leads by example. A committed director is one who has taken time to prepare properly, undertaken their pre-production preparation and read the script numerous times from several different angles, embracing textual and production analysis exercises such as those above.
Creative	A director's role is also to ensure that everybody else involved in the creative process can undertake their own work and bring their skills and expertise to the table. The director must then curate the conditions for everybody's creativity to come to the fore. An actor's job is to develop a character within the frame of the production and to use their creative thinking and imagination to analyse and respond to the text and the given circumstances.

I used to sit with the lighting designer throughout all the sessions dedicated to plotting the lights. This, however, is completely counter-productive, since it does not allow the lighting designer to create within the brief. Lighting is the lighting designer's art form, and creatives will always surprise you with their artistic and technical skill and interpretations. The National Advisory Committee on Creative and Cultural Education (NACCCE) defined creativity as 'imaginative activity fashioned so as to produce outcomes that are both original and of value' (1999: 30). To me, the important words here are 'fashioned' and 'value'. Creativity's freedom is contained, to create an outcome that is of value: in this case, to the production.

In terms of aesthetics, being creative doesn't mean creating a concept merely for the sake of it and a production world can be original in so many ways. A black-box production of *Macbeth* told simply through light, sound and the bodies of the actors is just as much of a creative response to that story as is a high-concept visual world.

Authentic Being your authentic self is key in the rehearsal period. Pedagogic research over the years has demonstrated that educators need to present themselves authentically and directors should follow suit. To be humble and honest and to state when you don't know the answer to something is essential. Building an ensemble is about taking a collective and collaborative approach to a moment or a scene; it is not about pretending to know all the answers.

Inclusive If one of the director's main tasks is to enable everybody else to do their job effectively, then it must follow that being inclusive is fundamental in achieving this. Inclusivity in terms of casting and production teams means ensuring that diversity is embedded within the recruitment process, through opening up opportunities for access.

This means ensuring that carers are not disadvantaged by scheduling, for example. A move towards fewer evening and weekend rehearsals, as aligned to the 'Reset Better' charter, suggested by the Production Managers' Forum (PMF),[4] may enable a greater degree of inclusivity, in contrast to the increasingly old-fashioned idea of working 'morning, noon and night'.

Inclusivity must also form a part of casting processes: artists whose lived experiences are being presented by characters in the play must be able to audition for these parts. The creative team a director assembles (including intimacy and well-being coordinators) will also be key; even if a particular organization does not have certain roles, there are approaches that can mitigate this, which are discussed below.

---

[4] The Production Managers' Forum is an online resource aimed at all those involved in the management and technical production of theatre. Their 'Reset Better' charter – the product of pooling ideas of how to construct an industry with a better work/life balance in the wake of 'The Great Pause' of 2020–21 – can be viewed here: https://www.productionmanagersforum.org/reset-better/.

	A sensitivity reader may be employed, for example, to support a new writing piece which is at the edge of, or outside of, immediate experiences. They can read the script from the point of view of their lived experience and advise accordingly.
	Access needs must also be considered; for casting to be open and diverse, support workers such as signers may be needed from the audition stages onwards. Reasonable adjustments should also be made for actors with neurodiversity, including dyslexia, dyspraxia and aphantasia.
	While this is a responsibility shared by everyone in the room, the director must set the tone, ensuring that space is available for everyone to do their best work. Time should also be available for debriefing, checking in and coming out of character ('de-roling'). Stage Three draws on recent research and development into performance training and practice to explore this further.
Reliable	Reliability means much more than merely being punctual: it is also about saying that you will do something and delivering it at the agreed time. If a producer needs a props list by a certain date, this needs to be delivered for their workflow to run smoothly. This also allows the production team – in this example – to deliver their best work, which aligns with the spirit of creativity and inclusivity discussed above.
	Consistency is key here, too. For example, if a director purports to work in one way, but in practice then works in another, mistrust can develop within companies. If a director says they are going to do a run-through, or work on a particular scene and (without a valid reason) does not, then the director/actor relationship may begin to break down. This is particularly the case when an actor has prepared for a fight or an intimate scene, or is psychologically and physically prepared for a run-through.
	Finally, reliability means bringing in a production on budget and on time: the opening night date will have been fixed long ago. If nothing else, in practical terms, this will mean that the director stands a good chance of being hired again!

Now, explore your own values and how this might relate to how you work.

Genres

Rehearsal periods never look the same. Throughout *Inside the Rehearsal Room*, I suggested different ways of working, depending on whether it is a contemporary play, classical play, musical, pantomime or comedy that is being undertaken. I refer to this as 'genre-thinking'. Directors must consider the genre or style within which they are working, to figure out what rehearsal strategies they may need to fashion a production that is teeming with life, crackles with energy and story, bursts with events and essentially honours the creative possibilities that the text presents. I offer some suggestions for idiosyncratic approaches to a handful of genres below, which may importantly affect scheduling when working.

Comedy and farce	• Move onto the rehearsal room floor as soon as possible. I once assisted on a farcical comedy; by the beginning of week two, we were still sat around the table, actioning and breaking down the text. At the end of the day, after rehearsal, the actors were in a state of anxiety and dismay, as they were desperate to begin to physicalize the text and encode the material into their bodies, timing jokes and shaping the physical business.
Pre-1800 classics	• Factor in early work on unfamiliar language, word meanings and etymologies. • Allow longer lead-in times for casting, so that actors can get familiar with the text. • Consider potential earlier deadlines for learning lines.
Pantomime	• Schedule routines, business and more complex choreography earlier in rehearsals. • Offer more opportunities for stagger-throughs to allow the comedy to flow, from the mid-stages of rehearsal onwards.
Actor-musician shows	• Schedule for the music to be learnt early on, in order to enable actor-musicians time to work 'off-score' as well as off-book as early as possible. • Work with your creative team to explore early on how the instruments (literally, musically or symbolically) can be an integral part of the storytelling.
Musicals	• Offering opportunities to learn the music – 'the dots' – as well as any complex choreography sequences early on will allow consolidation time. • Be aware that there will be a high likelihood of needing to schedule split calls across different rooms: choreography, dialogue, company music, solo music, vocal or dialect coaching. Ensure time is regularly scheduled to integrate these elements, so that the piece can flow and be worked on as a cohesive whole.
New writing	• There are likely to be rewrites and revisions, ranging from the minor adjustments to wholesale rewriting of scenes or acts. Build in time for this and ensure there is time for re-learning lines and consolidation throughout. Do not expect the actors to do all (if any) of this work in their own time.

Regardless of style or genre, I always ensure that in each rehearsal of a bit or scene, there is time to run through the section prior to moving on. I prefer to overrun, rather than to let this key moment pass by. The actors need a chance, having worked through etudes[5] or broken down a section, to run through the work, no matter how clunky the result is, as a chance to test out their explorations and to immediately capture the spirit of some of this work. I always caveat this by saying something along the lines of: 'If only ten per cent of what we explored is in this piecing together, don't worry; it's a chance to see some new layers developing.' The actors are then able to go away and work on the section in whatever way they want, using whatever means or methods they trust, to reflect, consolidate and layer in the sub-rehearsal.[6] I will then ensure that there is a chance over the next couple of days to run the scene again, before we break down and explore further. Kate Wasserberg, Artistic Director of Theatr Clwyd, calls each version of the scene she is working on in rehearsal a 'draft'; subsequent drafts are almost inevitably full of more life and texture, and the term helps to reduce a striving for perfection each time the company delve into the scene. Always schedule a stumble-through or run-through ahead of time and communicate this with advance warning. Actors need to prepare for these physically and mentally and your production team will want to be there to get a sense of the shape of the scenes. By the final week of rehearsal, I aim for a run-through every couple of days, to build up stamina and to see the piece as a whole.

Other material factors also come into play when scheduling. Time is a key factor, as is finance, and the two are interdependent. When working with shorter rehearsal periods – which may frequently happen when starting out or when working in the commercial theatre sector – it is especially important to schedule how the precious resource of time is to be best deployed.

While I do not propose one method or one linear 'how-to' approach, much of what I am positing is hyper-pragmatic. There is no blueprint in existence that covers every single rehearsal period: each director should use what they will to develop their own rehearsal methodology, to move the rehearsal process forwards. Be aware that each actor may need differing approaches: Josie Rourke, interviewed in Part Three of this book, talks in some detail about this and the need to ensure that each actor is given what

---

[5] See page 110 for detail on etudes.
[6] The sub-rehearsal, as defined by T. M. Crawford, is the 'moment that occurs outside the specific organised schedule of the rehearsal, outside the direct interrogatory gaze of the director, or beyond or beneath the understood agenda of a rehearsal moment' (2015: 187).

they require. Be aware, too, that your personal directing methodology may not work for a given actor. It is essential for a director to be at least aware of a wide range of acting methodologies, in order to support one of the primary aims of rehearsal: that actors are enabled to embody their characters. There is no set chronology, either. Creativity is often messy and non-linear. Even Mike Alfreds, who has a robust toolkit of exercises and methods that explore world, text and character during each rehearsal, is quick to point out that there is no linear roadmap: finding the way is about using the exercises as and when required. This relates as much to practical challenges such as time, space or finance, as it does to creative ones. Scheduling for me is key since it creates a roadmap for the actors to follow. Recent research into neurodiversity has shown that for those with dyslexia or dyspraxia, for example, knowing what and when the destination is, is vital to doing the best work possible.

Textual interpretations and preparing a script

In *Inside the Rehearsal Room* director Richard Cheshire and I set out a detailed approach to textual interpretation called 'Unlocking the Clues to Create a World' (2022: 59–60) and we deliberately chose to use the term 'interpretation' rather than 'analysis'. As academic Anne Fliotsos argues in *Teaching Theatre Today*, using the term 'analysis' can create a reductive approach, sending a director into metaphorical digging in the dirt to find something in the text to back up their needs too early on. This may only reveal to them what they want to find and will reduce the possibilities. The word 'interpretation', on the other hand, suggests an opening up, considering the text as a field of possibilities and asking how the text might work on the individual instead. Linking this to the **'Why, why, why?'** exercise on page 43, we begin with many more visceral connections with the text, rather than imposing an intellectual or literary approach (although both of these are implicit within these methods).

Here it is worth mentioning the notion of 'ghosting', an idea put forward by academic Marvin Carlson in his book *Speaking in Tongues: Languages at Play in the Theatre*. 'Ghosting', in the context of a theatrical production, is the way in which previous performances or production concepts 'haunt' the decision making of the present moment. I often find myself having to stop early-career actors and directors when they talk about the way in which Juliet should be played, or the way in which *A Chorus Line* must be approached. To quote David Mamet in *True and False*, 'there are only lines upon a page' (1998: 9). The text must be returned to, and a production world developed from the architecture and words created by the dramatist. While previous productions may inform us, we should never be ghosted by them. As director Andrew Hilton states, 'we must be careful, as director, actor or costume designer, not to allow tradition to dictate responses and choices that should be made afresh with every new performance ... We must not be there before them' (2022: 139). Carrie Cracknell, formerly Artistic Director of the Gate Theatre and later an associate at both the Young Vic and the Royal Court, is acutely aware of this 'baggage', as she calls it. Cracknell has said that if there is – particularly in the case of the classics – a remembered way, or a seminal, successful production, she would encourage the acting company, when exploring their choices, to 'deliberately put that idea or concept in the bin ... and instead try and find our own moment, our own motif, and our own idea' (Waugh 2023: 8). In the light of this, below are several of my personal 'go-to' exercises, which enable me to move away from being ghosted to mint the play afresh.

Bogart's 'The Question' and Meckler's 'The Statement'

Director Anne Bogart, one of the founders of the influential Saratoga International Theater Institute in New York, says in her 2001 book, *A Director Prepares*, that she sees a question at the heart of every play that could be explored through the production. Think of your production as an enquiry about the play, with the piece being an exploration of this. Similarly, Nancy Meckler, former Artistic Director of Shared Experience, suggests in *Notes from the Rehearsal Room: A Director's Process* (2023), that for each production, a statement should be able to be made that captures the heart of that version of the play.

How to undertake this exercise:

You may wish to do both parts of this exercise, or just one.
   The Question. Work out what the question is that is being explored in this play. This frequently becomes philosophical, as an enquiry often is, and can be bound in moral, ethical, practical,

spiritual, religious, human choices. For example, if approaching James Fritz's *Parliament Square* (2015) the question might be: 'Is it ever right to take your own life for a political cause?'

The Statement. The statement that you formulate must contain mention of the protagonist(s) according to Meckler's rules. For *Romeo and Juliet*, she posits two potentials: 'Two young lovers from warring families pursue love in danger to their lives *or* Two families at war with each other are blinded by their need to dominate and end up destroying those dearest to them' (2023: 10). Work through the above, consider imaginatively how different the production worlds – and therefore design, tone and acting choices – might be, depending on the statement chosen. Now take the piece you are directing and work through these steps again.

Why it works:

All decisions taken as a company must, in some way small or large, be able to be filtered through either the question and/or the statement. These help you to frame the decision making, as well as having a pithy centre or heartbeat to easily communicate.

Key takeaway:

Take your time with this process: don't try to rush these exercises. Incubate, reflect and test these out in the early rehearsal stage, by working with your design and wider creative team and with your lead actor(s), if appropriate.

Locating the events

If I could pick one rehearsal method that has most significantly permeated the Western text-based rehearsal room, it is that of locating, honouring and playing the events of a scene. Events have been defined in manifold ways, but here are several helpful and concrete definitions that I use with students:

1 Director Katie Mitchell in *The Director's Craft*: 'A moment in the action when a change occurs and this change affects everyone present' (2009: 55). Note that Mitchell also states that *any entrance or exit* is an event.

2 Actor and practitioner Bella Merlin in *The Complete Stanislavsky Toolkit* : 'A piece of action without which the scene cannot take place' (2014: 202).
   3 Academic and director James Thomas in *A Director's Guide to Stanislavsky's Active Analysis*: 'Normally [things that] would or should not happen: unexpected arrivals or departures, discoveries, misunderstandings or misidentifications, breaches of social norms, accidents of nature' (2016).

Maria Knebel asks the actor to 'use the events as the starting point [to draw them] into the world of the play by the shortest possible route' (2021: 32).

How to undertake this exercise:

Use the above definitions prior to rehearsals to circle each potential event in pencil in your script. You now have some of the key architectural pieces of the story. Check through these: if they are events, then it would be difficult to remove these without destroying the fabric of the play. The scene could not move forward in the way that it does without this happening. In Part Three, Holly Race Roughan describes how the event then becomes 'inevitable' for the actor, if the actions leading up to that point are played well. These events become major stepping stones when entering the rehearsal room. You can work through scenes with the actors, agreeing on the shared events as per your early rehearsal work.

There will also be personal events for the actor: these are events which are key for individuals, but not necessarily for the scene overall. Remember that there will also be some 'invisible events', ones that have occurred before the action of the play, or between scenes. These events are still key for ensuring the action is played accurately. Move forward with these events by thinking about how each event could be 'storyboarded' as a key image as per a film. Your role as director then becomes about leading the company up to the event with that central image in mind. The company needs to move between events organically.

Why it works:

In the early stages of rehearsal, you can offer to the whole company the potential events of the play, ensuring that you hit the ground running. The events that you choose to privilege or foreground as a director help to shape and form your concept and world. Marry this with **'The Question and the Statement'** (page 54) and you will begin your rehearsal process with a solid foundation for the entire company, who can then collaboratively build their metaphorical walls and floors on this foundation and furnish it creatively as they will. Your aim here is to create the conditions for that creativity to flourish.

Key takeaway:
Here you are building out from the major architectural elements of the play. These are the stepping stones which the company can use to respond in the moment, organically building dramatic tension and climactic moments without forcing.

Casting processes

Casting is a major part of the rehearsal process. The director's role is to enable everyone else to do their best work, so it stands to reason that what is wanted is the best people for the role doing their best work. I suggest three key principles for casting:

- The casting must be inclusive and diverse. Positive action should be taken where appropriate to ensure this can happen.
- The casting breakdowns must be appropriate for the characters that the playwright constructs, or for the production demands.
- The casting should strike a balance between members new to the company and previous members.

Inclusive and diverse casting

Where there are few given circumstances in a play and a role such as 'Police Officer 1' is listed, then this is where positive action can be taken. Why should this character be a white male, even if cultural or historical norms have embedded this into our consciousness? To ensure diverse and inclusive casting, on grounds of sex, race, colour, ethnic or social origin, genetic features, language, religion or belief, gender identity, class background, age and/or sexual orientation (among others), directors must work with casting directors to ensure that there is a rich and diverse set of candidates in the audition room.

If the casting is around an ensemble – established or otherwise – this would be about taking positive action where there is a lack of diverse representation.

Appropriateness for the character and the production

Connected to the above, the character's given circumstances should be placed front and centre when determining the casting for that role. This needs to be balanced to ensure a diverse casting policy. Casting breakdowns should be written with an awareness of building out from the given circumstances and challenging norms, especially those that are a result of 'ghosting' by previous productions. Tonic Theatre is one organization that has offered a series of 'prompts' to help achieve this, available in their 'Theatre Casting Toolkit',[7] allowing directors to move away from looks or physical types.

The qualities of the character can prove a very helpful way of exploring casting breakdowns. Michael Chekhov is a key exponent of qualities, and I would encourage directors to explore contradictions within polarities, i.e. 'looking for an actor who can portray both shyness and confidence', rather than relying on physical or other norms. As discussed above, the production concept can also help to open possibilities to new narrative layers: recent examples include Sarah Amankwah, who is Black and female, playing the title role in *Henry V* at the Globe Theatre in 2019, or Ian McKellen playing the title role in *Hamlet* in 2021, at the age of 82. These are conscious casting choices regarding age, gender identity and colour. An ensemble playing style, where anyone can play anybody, can also be of value here. Michelle Terry, Artistic Director of the Globe, advocates for non-literal casting within an ensemble framework, which can support the liberation of the text from previous 'ghosts' as new storytelling choices and narrative possibilities are allowed to present themselves.

---

[7]The toolkit is available here: https://www.theatrecastingtoolkit.org/tools/.

Balance of casting

Playwright and director Charles Marowitz suggested that, following a period of researching the play for potential discoveries, an actor could experience information – via active rehearsals such as improvisations and exercises – more rapidly within an ensemble company, where shortcuts are made between actors and directors. Though the vocabulary of 'embodying' was not in common rehearsal room language in the 1990s, the concept seems to be the same: 'Many of the problems thrown up by the work in the theatre would either be solved or considerably reduced if the same director worked with the same actors over an extended period of time. After a while, a group intelligence is engendered which becomes greater than the directors' and the actors' intelligence combined' (1998: 8). Likewise, director Katie Mitchell's regular performers who 'kn[o]w her aesthetic and methodology' (Mermikides 2013: 160) have a head start in understanding how she operates as a director and how to help to achieve her vision. Lev Dodin, the Leader of Russia's Maly Drama Theater, has spoken about the shared collective experience of the works of Chekhov that exists at the Maly Theatre, because of the number of productions of his work that theatre has undertaken. He posits this as an explanation of how the actors came to share the view of the director on a production of *Uncle Vanya*, because the company had 'absorbed a good deal of Chekhov's world' (Innes and Shevtsova 2009: 49).

The benefits of an ensemble company are then certainly clear: the ensemble allows for a shared language and understanding and, therefore, a shorthand. However, I also suggest that while this is of benefit, it should not preclude a diverse ensemble. Nor should casting be a closed shop. A shared language can be built by the director from the casting stage onwards and during the first stages of rehearsal. Ensembles are built even within a single-production show, and even in cases other than a long-term ensemble, a director needs to think around building a short-term *ensemble feel* through a shared vision and language in the early stages. Casting must also ensure that audience members can see themselves represented by the company on the stage, so it needs to be built around telling the theatrical story for a target audience and ensuring the cast reflect these audiences.

In the 1990s, directors started to embrace 'colour-blind' casting, whereby there may well have been a diversity of company members, but characters were often essentially seen as white and there was no acknowledgement of cultural differences and/or the lived experiences of the individual cast member. Now, 'colour-conscious' casting, however, ensures that if a director casts a

Black female performer as Henry V, then this is how the character is played, with all characters responding to the character through this lens. Previously, through colour-blind casting, the rest of the characters would have potentially seen this character as white and male, with the performer sometimes depicting the titular character as such. Moving from blind to conscious casting ensures that diversity is meaningfully embraced as a narrative choice.

Underpinning the above is communication of ideas as well as expectations from the casting point onwards. Director Sue Dunderdale, founder of Pentabus Theatre Company and a freelance director, believes that this is the starting point of trust. The casting process is the primary stage for this and therefore 'the director must be clear and honest about the demands that creating the piece will make on the performers in the rehearsal room' (2022: 105). While Dunderdale expresses this in relation to devising processes, the principles remain the same.

Whatever the casting process employed, my audition process follows the below principles:

1 **Access**: Have actors been given what they need through any initial riders or communications in terms of physical or neurodivergent needs?
2 **Dialogue**: Is there the opportunity for both sides to ask questions? Is there time for everyone to get to know each other, for the director to communicate their ideas and for the actor to ask questions? This allows understanding in relation to the vision, concept and ways of working. I have been in certain situations where I do not have enough knowledge of the skills the actors have to make an informed decision, so do request time wherever possible.
3 **Criteria**: Are decisions being made against the criteria on the casting breakdown, rather than ghosted ideas of a part, which can often be based on physical attributes?
4 **Form**: If this an ensemble piece, can every individual show themselves to the best of their ability? If large dance or movement call auditions are necessary, is everyone being seen equally? Has it been ensured that there is enough time for acting, singing, music, dancing, musicianship or combat, for example?
5 **Inclusion**: Is there an understanding of cost in relation to longlisting, shortlisting and recalls? Can technology be used to move between these phases, perhaps via self-tapes, in order to see more people individually? Can auditions and recalls in person be communicated well in advance, to ensure that caring responsibilities can be met, and that transport can be organized (more affordably) in advance?

6 **Yes/no**: Equity, the actors' union, has encouraged directors, producers and casting directors to guarantee that actors will be informed about the results of their casting, as a matter of courtesy.

Gathering a creative team for the production

Directors need to think about who surrounds them when building the creative team. The recent production of immersive dance show *Free Your Mind*[8] by Factory International broke with convention somewhat and listed the creative team alphabetically, implicitly suggesting that the team creates and executes the vision collectively, even though the individual roles of director and designer remain central. As the hierarchy between director and creative team flattens, it is more important than ever that everyone finds themselves on the same page. This, as writer-director Tristan Fynn-Aiduenu states, is about 'plugging in' together: 'You, your team, your actors, are all plugging into this text' (Benjamin 2023).

Below are some of the key collaborators you may wish to work with. This list is by no means exhaustive – I've also worked with puppetry, illusion and military coordinators, for example – but will give you a flavour of the range of possible creatives.

Design team	This could include combinations of the roles below. Note, too, that many of these roles can be combined into one practitioner; set and costume design is a frequent combination, with lighting and AV design an increasingly popular combination. • The **set designer** coordinates the physical world that the characters/actors inhabit. They are responsible for the overall look of the world and the set, bringing together disparate elements into a unified whole. • The **costume designer** is responsible for all that the actors wear, ensuring their costumes are seen as clothing, which reflects or embodies time period, status, identity and position. • The **lighting (LX) designer** designs the lighting palette and moment-to-moment 'states' for the production, working closely with a programmer who inputs the lighting states into the board for the operator to run. The LX designer also decides on the lighting rig: where each lantern is positioned and how it supports the overall design and storytelling, in order to 'land' the design with audiences.

---

[8] More information about the show can be found here: https://factoryinternational.org/whats-on/free-your-mind/.

- The **sound (SFX) designer** creates the sonic world for the production. In musicals they will also ensure that the sound is well balanced between orchestra and performers, for example. They create all the spot cues (e.g. a doorbell) and effects. Sometimes the sound designer is also a composer, creating scenic underscores and transitions; if not, they will often source or commission these. They also work with venues and technicians to create the speaker placement plot to execute the overall design for the audience experience.
- The **video/AV designer** will create content where LED screens and projections (or, increasingly, virtual production technology) are used, in close collaboration with the set and lighting designers.

Choreographer	In a musical, pantomime, or play with music, the choreographer will decide on the steps and sequences to create the dance routines. Sometimes the role of choreographer will also subsume that of the movement director (below), or vice versa.
Movement director	A production may require movement, e.g. stylized moments or transitions, as well as support for the actors in their physical characterization choices, or the creation of a particular routine.
Composer and/ or musical arranger	The composer creates original music for a musical, play or pantomime. This may also include transitions and underscores. They often work closely with the sound designer to ensure a unified sonic world. The arranger (often the same individual as the composer) takes a pre-composed piece of music and 'arranges' the output in terms of orchestration, instrumentation (and scoring), tempos, styles and harmony lines for performers.
Musical director	Teaches the performers the songs, including harmonies and vocal styles. They will work closely with the arranger and/or composer to deliver the work, source and fix the band or orchestra, record backing and click tracks, conduct band calls and bring together all of these elements in the technical rehearsal. They may increasingly be called on to support vocal health in a coaching capacity as well as taking on limited compositional elements.
Fight director	Safely choreographs all fight routines, from a slap to a fully executed battle scene. Increasingly, the fight director's role overlaps with the intimacy director's role below as they originate from the same field, and all involve physical contact, consent and well-being.
Intimacy director	Intimacy directors help directors and actors to 'tell stories authentically and safely' (Ayshia Mackie-Stephenson 2021: 265) in relation to any scenes with physical contact that require intimacy. This may be anything from a kiss to a very intimate sexual scene. This ensures a desexualizing of the scene and professionalizing of the work. Marie-Heleen Coetzee and Kaitlin Groves explain, in *Touch and Consent: Towards an ethics of care in intimate performance*, that 'from our perspective, approaching intimate scenes with a range of techniques to create a "choreography" offers distancing mechanisms that draw attention to the fictionality of the interaction and heightens awareness of the personal/ professional interface' (2023: 112).

Stage One: Choosing and Establishing

Dramaturg — This is a very fluid role. There are dramaturgs who work solely with writers to help them create and tell the best version(s) of their stories: they support the writer with structure, dialogue and character, for example, supporting in the composition of the work. A production dramaturg, however, will research any contextual details (political, social, historical, religious or spiritual facts, in particular) and support the ongoing work in terms of having creative input into decisions about choices and moments. These are just two examples.

Well-being coordinator — Some theatres, including Derby Theatre and Theatr Clwyd, have now begun to bring in well-being coordinators to support actors in terms of mental and physical well-being. They may run check-ins and check-outs (or help the director to run these), especially if an actor is taking on a role that could particularly impact well-being (such as an evil-intentioned or tragic character). They may then signpost to further support and offer drop-in sessions outside of rehearsals.

Voice/dialect director — These may be different individuals, but the voice coach or director supports with vocal quality and technique in relation to the textual demand and the space. The dialect coach concentrates on supporting actors who need to affect accents other than their own.

Production/stage management team — The production and stage management team may include:
- The **production manager (PM)**, who oversees all production elements and acts as the conduit between all departments, keeping everyone on budget and on time.
- The **company manager (CM)**, who looks after the actors and creatives, ensuring the smooth running of the operation from a logistical point of view.
- The **stage manager (SM)**, who handles the day-to-day operations of the rehearsal room and leads the technical rehearsals.
- The **company stage manager (CSM)**: this role combines the management of the company and the stage management responsibility above.
- The **deputy stage manager (DSM)**, who is, for me, a director's key collaborator in the rehearsal room, creating the 'book' which records the blocking and technical cues. The DSM communicates rehearsal room decisions to all departments outside of the room. They then 'run' the show from the desk sensitively and technically, making sure the lighting, sound and other cues are brought in on time.
- The **assistant stage manager (ASM)**, who operationalizes many decisions, from prop creation to running the rehearsal room, coordinating props and running the show on the floor in production.

You will find many resources available online regarding the above roles. I also encourage you to think about whether you need to bring in someone as a creative team member or just as a consultant for a day, for example.

Video and projection designer Nina Dunn plays a light-hearted game of 'Whose Tool Is This?' early on, asking whether a production choice is being executed using the right 'tool': is a potential set design choice instead a video or light choice, or a could a video idea be realized instead using physical props or set? All technologies are merely tools to communicate creative ideas and storytelling beats.

Naturally, it is not always possible to have all these roles on a given production due to financial restrictions. It is down to the individual director to explore how to wrap these roles into their own role and process. As an example, everyone can take responsibility for dramaturgy, even without a dramaturg; a director can also ensure safe and consensual rehearsal rooms are run using some basic principles, if an intimacy director role is unavailable. It is not solely the role of the intimacy director to create a safe space. Intimacy and consent must be present in all rooms regardless of the play's content and the tone is set by the director. Many of the stage management roles outlined above are simply not feasible in small-scale companies, so consider how these can be rolled together to achieve similar results – without exploiting or overloading the team members you do have, of course.

Sustainability

As they are responsible for setting the tone, directors also need to weigh up how to ensure the theatre-making process is sustainable. In recent years, *The Theatre Green Book*[9] agenda has gone some considerable way towards creating a toolkit to enable theatre makers to make work sustainably. Director and dramaturg Zoë Svendsen took this work further in her 2023 report for the Donmar Warehouse, *Climate Conversations: Making Theatre in the Context of Climate Crisis*,[10] defining how we make work as part of undertaking climate dramaturgy. Svendsen's work 'builds on the foundations provided by the *Theatre Green Book*'s emphasis on collaboration and its emphasis that not only productions but also the operations and buildings that house them

---

[9]The scheme behind the publication is an initiative to create a sustainable way of working across all aspects of theatre, details of which are available in three volumes that cover everything from set construction to catering choices in theatre restaurants. More information can be found here: https://theatregreenbook.com/.
[10]The full report and recommendations can be found here: https://www.donmarwarehouse.com/wp-content/uploads/2023/07/Climate-Conversations-Making-Theatre-in-the-Context-of-Climate-Crisis-Report.pdf.

Stage One: Choosing and Establishing 65

have a key role in mitigating environmental impacts, exploring the multiple ways that a theatre can facilitate its creatives to achieve the *Theatre Green Book* standards creatively' (2023: 6). Climate dramaturgy goes beyond the story told and the onstage work. It is a holistic approach to how theatre is made, regardless of the story on the stage, asking organizational leaders to accelerate institutional change and 'therefore invites practitioners to look beyond their role, or the specific needs of the production, to influence theatres' practices in the longer term' (ibid.: 28).

As a director, ensuring sustainable making processes happen means being an advocate and champion for this. At the design stage, for example, Svendsen suggests 'inviting the creative team to hold an early stage "design concept meeting" to enable an anticipatory environmental exploration, to inform creative direction [as this] offers the opportunity for cross fertilization between the different elements of design (sound, light, costumes, set)' (ibid.: 40). What might this mean for the director? Svendsen articulates this clearly:

> Although a director might not expect to themselves engage with the pragmatic detail of minimizing the environmental impact of their production, their leadership shapes the culture of the production as whole, and as such, can empower others (or conversely, make it more difficult for them) to pursue climate care. As lead artist, who is contracted first and selects and leads the rest of the creative team, as well as the actors, the director thus has a crucial role to play in enabling the creative and production team to attend to environmental parameters. The director must then also give permission – and ideally inspiration – to the designer and to their wider creative team (sound, lighting, composition, video, and so on), to explore ideas in a climate conscious way. This permission empowers the rest of the creative team to pay attention to potential environmental impacts and be inspired to take avoidant action.
>
> (ibid.: 42)

Configurations and spaces: How these impact early rehearsal decisions

Directors and designers need to look at both the configuration of the stage space, as well as the architecture of the building in their early rehearsal stage of planning. Ideally, the configuration should follow on from the play choice (or the piece should be chosen because of the configuration, where a configuration is fixed). I believe that any play can be made in-the-round, for example, but I also believe that an end-on stage is more *conducive* to pantomime. I have seen farces in the round, pantomimes in promenade (where actors 'lead' audience members through a space) and musicals – which are traditionally end-on – as immersive experiences. The configuration is therefore a conscious choice, in terms of deciding on the actor–audience relationship with respect to the play/text chosen. A configuration may be fixed: for example, the New Vic Theatre in Staffordshire is a permanent theatre in-the-round. In that case, the director and designer must ensure that this arrangement can serve and enhance the play and the storytelling opportunities.

The **traverse** setting (with audiences sitting on two sides of the action) has a gladiatorial feel to it: each end of the configuration becomes a polar side, which can enhance the possibilities for creating tension and a 'tennis match' setting. **In-the-round** supports democracy: everyone is equal in the space, but can experience the production differently, depending on where they are seated. As an audience member, you may often feel as though you are eavesdropping on events in this configuration. **End-on** easily enables the majority of the audience to focus on the same part of the story at the same time – especially when framed by a proscenium arch – and this is often vital to the busier scenes of musicals and pantomimes. **Thrust**, which situates the audience on three sides of the action, can enable an intimate experience that the round can offer, but still offers the back wall that an end-on environment would, which can be used to create focused moments. With **promenade**, the audience are led around the space by the performers, moving from location to location for each element of the story. The increase of large-scale flexible arts **warehouses** as discussed by Elena Giakoumaki, a director of theatre design consultants Charcoalblue, is on the rise. These spaces can 'flex and expand to accommodate both the conventional and the unconventional' and where the 'entire building is ... the performance area' (2024: 15) to create a different audience experience.

In addition to considering the above configurations as well as the space itself, the director – along with their designer – must explore how the architecture and roots of the space or theatre can unlock storytelling possibilities. For example, when I adapted J. M. Barrie's *Peter Pan* for Selladoor Worldwide, for performance at the Blackpool Opera House, I worked closely with director Kirstie Davies and designer Jessica Curtis to harness the potential of this 2,800-seater space. Its heritage of variety and summer spectaculars, as well as the fact that Blackpool is historically connected to circus as an art form, allowed for a circus-inspired design, which took into account and made use of the height of the performance space and the architectural design. Designer Max Jones, too, starts with absorbing the space he is working in and seeing what the space can offer the production, rather than the other way around. Whether that space is a village hall, or the stage of the Olivier at the National Theatre, the configuration determines the relationship between the actor and their audiences and how they tell their story.

Linked to this is the creation of the groundplan, historically a two-dimensional bird's-eye view of the set and furniture in relation to the theatre building and stage. This allows the director, along with their designers, to explore where to position entrance and exits in relation to and with the furniture and other scenic arrangements. The creative team can use the creation of the groundplan to check that there is logically enough space, that the arrangement allows for possibilities to generate tension in the storytelling, and that there is a coherent approach to the design.

Creating a groundplan

How to undertake this exercise:

Take the opening of Arthur Miller's *The Crucible* (1953). Read from 'Act One (An Overture). *A small upper bedroom in the home of REVEREND SAMUEL PARRIS, Salem, Massachusetts, in the spring of the year 1692*' through the considerable background information and stage directions, to the point where the stage direction reads: '*MRS PUTNAM goes to the bed*'. You can use any edition; the text will remain the same, though the pagination will differ: I am using the Penguin Modern Classics edition from 2015, where this spans pages 13–21. Once you have read this, imagine you are creating the scene for an end-on (proscenium arch) staging, as per the original production. Note that Miller states:

> There is a narrow window at the left. Through its leaded panes the morning sunlight streams. A candle still burns near the bed, which is at the right. A chest, a chair, and a small table are the other furnishings. At the back a door opens on the landing of the stairway to the ground floor. The room gives off an air of clean spareness. The roof rafters are exposed, and the wood colours are raw and unmellowed.
>
> (2015: 13)

Position these key elements from a bird's-eye view before you read on, below. Consider how your positioning of the elements Miller describes will enable storytelling opportunities.

Why it works:

The original production positioned the door upstage centre, with the bed tucked in an alcove downstage right. The window was positioned stage left and the table and chair were situated upstage centre left, between the door and the window. Positioning the bed downstage right allows for Betty Parris, in bed, to be in a strong focal position for the audience; it also traps her. As the people of the village enter the room, the Reverend Parris, her father, is able to use the strong diagonal – which is always a powerful line to play on a proscenium stage – positioning himself between Betty and the guests, as he aims to keep control of the explosive situation developing and quash any ideas that his daughter might have instigated any of the supposed witchcraft.

Key takeaway:

The groundplan allows the director and designer to explore how the layout can enable dynamic and engaging image-making opportunities, create moments of tension, and help the story to be staged and told with ease. It also ensures that the director is thinking about the images that may develop naturally as a result of this, putting audience thinking at the heart of everything they are doing.

Research and development stages

Prior to rehearsals, many contemporary productions have benefited from a research and development (R&D) period. Of the professional R&D periods I have been involved with personally, most have been approximately a week in length, but they may be as short or as long as required – and as finance allows. There will ordinarily be a showing or sharing at the end of the period. This may be for audiences of potential producers, angels and backers, to see if the piece has 'legs', in terms of future investment, or it may be for the venue who will produce the work at a later stage, as well as any wider creatives involved, so that they can see the progress of the work. Sometimes, critics and other interested parties might be invited, to build interest in the work. Since these R&D periods do not form part of the official rehearsal period, they are process- and content-driven explorations, rather than concentrating on any final product, although naturally they inform the final production and its form. Such periods are part of the establishing phase and can have manifold purposes, often dramaturgical. They may also involve some or all of the following:

- **Creating material:** I have been part of an R&D stage which gathered actors and writers in the room as part of the development of a new musical, where a couple of songs had been written, along with a basic narrative structure. The writers were in the room as I led improvisations that allowed for dialogue and plot to be generated which, along with Post-it note exercises, shifted the narrative arc considerably. We also formed characters based on verbatim stories and the lived experiences of the cast, as well as undertaking collective research into the stories of the piece.
- **Shaping the draft:** I had adapted a version of *The Snow Queen* for national touring, as an actor-musician show. The first draft was complete, but the R&D period helped to completely reshape the second half, which ensured that the quest element of the story was sharper and more dynamic, with the director working through my re-drafts from the previous evening during the subsequent day. The composer and musical director also used this period to explore musical arrangements for the actor-musicians, as well as what narrative layers their instruments could offer, while the designer played with shapes and forms in the room.
- **Influencing storytelling possibilities:** In 2021, I directed *The Princess and the Pauper*, an adaptation of Mark Twain's 1881 novel *The Prince and the Pauper*, by Dave Simpson, which re-gendered the central characters. The piece had an inclusive cast of D/deaf and hearing actors, with British Sign Language (BSL) forming part of the musical numbers, key sections and narrative possibilities. The principal cast all communicated with BSL and with sign-song in musical numbers, as well as working with an integrated BSL signer throughout. The R&D allowed me, the cast (the majority of whom would go on to appear in the production), the BSL specialist, choreographer and the musical director/arranger to establish the logic of the piece, including who

signed, when they signed and for what purpose they signed. It also allowed for an exploration of how the conscious re-gendering and the incorporation of BSL could add narrative layers with purpose and meaning.

Director Tinuke Craig states that her aim 'isn't to make a rehearsal room fun, but it is to make it feel free and unencumbered' (Waugh 2023: 238). Craig's philosophy here aligns with the purposes of an R&D period. By not being obliged to focus on the end product, the creative team are liberated to explore and find possibilities without the background pressure of delivering to an audience. There may be several weeks or months between the R&D period and the main rehearsal period, allowing for re-writes or for designs to be worked on and frames of the production style and the world established.

By now, the director will have undertaken a considerable amount of work in their early rehearsal stage, working on why they want to direct the play and how they might want to tell the story. Stage Two allows us to venture out a little more onto the rehearsal room floor.

10

Stage Two
Creating and Forming

Chapter outline

First encounters with each other to build the ensemble	74
Theatre games	76
'Grasp': Initial collective encounters with the text and production	77
Warming and tuning up	80
Safe and inclusive rehearsal rooms	82
Access in rehearsals	85
De-roling and debriefing at the end of rehearsals	85
Creating a world for actors to inhabit	86
Exercises to begin building characters and relationships	88

If there is one principle that I adhere to unfailingly as a director, it is allowing ownership. The cast must own their work from day one of rehearsals (and even beforehand, as part of the casting process and any R&D work). As I leave the production – often after the press night – I need the actors to have taken this ownership and to have embodied their work, and for the creative and technical teams to be running the show with confidence. Producer Stephen Boden, joint CEO of Imagine Theatre, often talks about the director being primed at the start of rehearsals, like a fully charged battery. That charge – the prior knowledge and understanding embodied in the director and initial production team – needs to then be passed on. Navigating this charge changing hands is something you must build into the rehearsal period and, from day one, all the rehearsal methodologies employed should be with the express aim of ensuring this can be achieved.

This is not to say, however, that there is simply a one-way flow of information from director to actor. There are joint ideas, differing ideas, compromises, negotiations, bargaining, and agreements reached. Some of these processes are subtle and go almost unnoticed, while others are explicit and overt. Ideas must be tried out and the efficacy of these evaluated against the needs of the production and the scope of the frame agreed.

In the social sciences, 'routines' are interpersonal interactions, linking actions with the structures which house them. Axel Schmidt and Arnulf Deppermann's 2023 paper 'On the Emergence of Routines: An Interactional Micro-history of Rehearsing a Scene' explores how theatre rehearsals are sites for such interactive routines. If, as expected by the research, directors say far less as rehearsals progress and actors increasingly begin to embody their parts and take ownership, then directors need to structure rehearsals as environments in which a shared knowledge can be developed early on. This enables actors and directors to effectively coordinate with each other. As the tone setter of rehearsals, the director should make space for this, as 'common ground ... [is] accumulated over participants' shared interactional history' (2023: 277), which will mean that the director is able to instruct less and less as the rehearsal period progresses for those members of that company.

From day one, as well as enabling ownership, the work for a director is to support the actor in their embodiment of a role. The director's role is not to build a character for an actor to merely step into. Actor Steve Fortune is keen to point out that the strongest directors are those that suggest and guide, rather than dictate. Instead, it is to coach and guide and to make sure that the character creation – or as I like to describe it, the merging of the actor's self with the givens of the text – works within the frame of the production. To do this safely and inclusively will allow actors to play within that frame and will allow for the willing vulnerability that is necessary to take risks. Laura Rikard and Amanda Rose Villarreal reframe safe spaces as 'spaces of acceptable risk' (2023: 2) as 'no one is actually ever guaranteed safety' (ibid.: 6). The work places the focus on the leader of the group (i.e. the director) to ensure this is achieved, rather than a tacit assumption that this is happening and that it is solely the responsibility of participants.

I am often asked what it means to take a risk. For me, this is about where an actor can feel psychologically (as well as physically) safe, so that discoveries can be made, and progress can be achieved in the creation of dynamic, thrilling storytelling. Hierarchies in contemporary rehearsal rooms can be much more mercurial than previously, but Sue Dunderdale states that, even though a piece of theatre is created by everybody participating, this 'doesn't negate the need for leadership . . . There must be a centre point to the process – and that is the director' (2022: 104). Tom Dugdale, author of *Directing Your Heart Out: Essays for Authenticity, Engagement, and Care in Theatre* suggests that what is emerging in the current decade is the notion that the director is 'serving everyone else' (2023: 45), rather than being the controlling force.

I have referred several times above to 'embodiment' and this is a term that is increasingly brought up in the context of rehearsals and acting. Essentially, this is the actor's somatic encoding of all the information, given circumstances and work of the rehearsal room into their bodies. Actor trainer John Gillett describes this as the 'vocal and physical expression of the inner life and actions of the character, different from oneself but deriving from one's specific and common human make up' (2024: 16). This relates to the psycho-physical approaches that an actor needs to embody the text. Put crudely, what happens psychologically affects the physical body and vice versa. Actor and pedagogue Bella Merlin explains psycho-physicality as the way in which 'whatever I'm feeling inside can be conveyed to the outside world with ease, and whatever information I'm receiving from the outside world impacts on my inner experience' (2024: 76).

From day one, the director helps the actor to 'negotiate two worlds – the world of the play or character and the world of the performance' (Shipley 2023: 10). This is where, in my professional experience, nascent directors can sometimes lose track of things at an early stage. The play – the words and the world as conceived by the playwright – must be in balance with the world of the production as built and conceived with the designer, using whatever methodology or approach. Often, a classical work that has been transposed to a contemporary context sees the original play and world and relationships as secondary to the delivery of the production vision. Practitioners like Ivo van Hove, seen as a leading visionary director, aims to keep the 'words within the world' in balance.

Many of the exercises and ideas throughout Stages Two to Four are concerned with how actors make concrete connections to both the text and each other. The more work that you can accommodate with your actors whereby they lift their heads from their scripts and connect with each other so that they can perceive and communicate effectively, the better. You are planting the seeds for dynamic storytelling; for actors to make interesting, useful choices, that reach out over the footlights to connect with and affect their audience. As we will see in Part Three, many contemporary practitioners discuss how their rehearsal room choices affect their audiences.

Shomit Mitter, in his study of Brook's methodologies, believes that asking questions and empowering actors can enable a breakthrough, otherwise the director can result in infantilizing the actor's role, whereby 'the all-knowing director and the infantilised actor [paradigm] leaves no room for the more nuanced interpretations of director/actor exchanges' (Rossmanith 2000: 35). This is built upon by director T. M. Crawford fifteen years later, who lambasts the fact that actors are not part of the 'creative team' in current theatre terminology and thus infantilized by 'industry processes' (2015: 230). I believe that there must be a set of benchmarks that guide actors and directors towards the 'right' answers to verify a breakthrough moment, and for me this is about making decisions within the production 'frame' I posit throughout this book. Director Charles Marowitz wishes for directors and actors to move away from the concept that the rehearsal period is merely a child's treasure hunt 'unearthing only what had already been planted in order to be discovered' (1998: 5), by asking the question 'what [is] one looking for?' (ibid.) at the heart of rehearsals. This allows Marowitz's actors to search within a bounded and definite frame, as discussed in Stage One.

First encounters with each other to build the ensemble

The first day of the rehearsal period is often tricky, since it can be subsumed by genuine nervousness. Contrary to (many) portrayals in the popular media, actors are often vulnerable, and if the company has not previously worked together, then this first encounter is crucial. How a director sets the tone of this can ensure a happy, respectful and collaborative process. Greg Doran states that 'the first day of rehearsal is merely a way of getting to the second day of rehearsal' (2023: 2), thus identifying the compassionate approaches needed to ensure the team is psychologically safe and feels part of the forming team dynamic. So, how might this be achieved? First, directors should set up a warm, welcoming environment. This might include music, as well as lots of readily available tea, coffee and snacks. As people arrive, they should be welcomed by the director (with no physical contact unless consented to) and/or CM, and made to feel immediately at home. If actors are going to take ownership and feel that their contribution is valued, these initial encounters form the bedrock of an ensemble. Before encountering or working on the piece, or even introducing the production concept, some key initial introductions can promote an inclusive and less hierarchical environment:

- **Names and pronouns:** As everyone introduces themselves and tells everyone else their preferred name, I also encourage preferred pronouns to be included, as well as asking everyone to state what their role is in the production.
- **Access:** Any access needs should have been established prior to rehearsals. It may be that a quick self-description will be needed for blind or visually impaired individuals in the room. On the first day, it is not only the actors who are meeting, but often crew, administrative and marketing teams, as well as other venue staff. A self-description is a thumbnail sketch of yourself, perhaps two or three sentences long, and may include mention of gender, height, age, clothing, hair, colour, ethnicity and so on. So, mine might be along the lines of: 'I'm Rob; I'm in my mid-forties, my pronouns are "he/him", I have short, blondish hair and some light stubble and wear round, dark-rimmed glasses.'
- **Sign names:** If you have been assigned a sign name by a member of the D/deaf community you might also include this, if appropriate.
- **Ground rules:** My ground rules relate to mutual respect of ideas. If rehearsal is to be a safe place of constant transaction and negotiation, then how this is achieved must start from a principle of respect. I have several pillars:
  - I often say that there are no stupid questions: anyone should be able to ask anything, without fear or judgement.
  - The answer to a question or the means for unlocking a breakthrough does not always lie with the director.
  - All physical touch in rehearsals needs to be consented to and negotiated. (I will return to this later, including how to set up boundaries to create a safe and freeing rehearsal room.)
  - Everyone should feel empowered to speak up. If the director could do something differently to enable an actor to do their best work, then this should be safely articulated. This comes directly from work on compassion. In my early (pre)rehearsal conversations with actors, I ask if there is anything I need to be aware of, or any techniques that would support or help in their creative journey to doing their best job. Again, this returns to the need to ensure they are feeling confident enough to own their work and be part of an ensemble process.

- Everyone should work on impulse, even if these take us down a path we don't eventually take. Just as actors work on impulse, I will also, responding to actors in the moment.

Theatre games

Some directors swear by theatre games as a means of actors encountering each other, coalescing around something other than the text and allowing a glimpse into how people work in teams. I am personally not a game-player, but many directors are and a plethora of books of theatre games are available.[1] Here are a few to try:

> ### Counting up . . .
>
> **How to do undertake this exercise:**
>
> Actors stand (or sit) closely in a circle and close their eyes or pick a point in the room where they cannot see other people. The idea is that the group counts to 15, 20 or 30 (you may decide which). Somebody starts with 'one', another randomly says 'two', and so on. A person should not say more than one number consecutively and it must be at random; it cannot form a pattern around the circle in one direction, for example. If people speak at the same time, then the game starts again.
>
> **Why it works:**
>
> The group are really focusing on each other, listening to vocal impulses to speak and other clues. As it's quite a difficult game, there is a sense of euphoria when it is achieved, and it can remain a constant warm-up game.

---

[1] With younger participants, I highly recommend Samantha Marsden's *100 Acting Exercises for 8–18 Year Olds*, which is available here: https://www.bloomsbury.com/uk/100-acting-exercises-for-8--18-year-olds-9781350049970/. Jessica Swale's *Drama Games for Rehearsals* is also well worth a look and suggests games tailored to style and genre of piece: https://www.nickhernbooks.co.uk/dgrehearsals.

Key takeaway:

This game is excellent for inclusion, since nobody is ever 'out', so the game keeps the group together even when it fails.

Truths and lies

How to undertake this exercise:

Pairing up, each person has one minute to introduce themselves to the other, but has to drop one plausible lie into their introduction. After the paired sharing, everyone returns to the full group. One partner introduces the other: 'This is Bea, and they are . . .', recalling as much information as possible. The rest of the group have to guess the lie.

Why it works:

The participants are able to choose what they would like to reveal about themselves to the other person, giving ownership. It also moves from being an exercise in pairs to a group exercise, as well as being a fun detective game.

Key takeaway:

Both phases of the game, in pairs and as a group, encourage genuine listening.

'Grasp': Initial collective encounters with the text and production

Following initial encounters with one another through the meet-and-greet stage, the director needs now to build a bridge that leads to encountering the text and/or the production, to enable everyone to have a collective 'grasp' of the piece. 'Grasp' is a term used by Stanislavski and 'at the heart of grasp is the idea that you don't just communicate through words and gestures, but also through "invisible radiations of will, vibrations which flow back and forth between two souls [or performers]"' (Merlin 2014: 209). By focusing full attention on scene partners, grasp can be achieved. But I extend this to the text also, which should be in the company's collective grasp. There are numerous ways into this, including:

- **Themes and ideas:** Actor-trainer John Gillett explores these collectively on the first day of rehearsal. He undertakes this through collective work on a number of starting points, including 'place and period. The meaning of the title and character names, the primary or inciting event giving rise to the play ... and genre' (2024: 29).
- **Read-throughs:** This is where the cast sits around a table and reads the text aloud. Traditionally, actors play their own roles, but read-throughs can be done with actors taking any role, so that the play itself is positioned at the centre of the exercise. In *My Shakespeare: A Director's Journey through the First Folio*, Greg Doran explains how, during his time as artistic director of the RSC, he dispensed with a traditional read-through in favour of 'Shakespeare gyms', getting all the actors engaged with text through acting exercises using the Prologue from *Romeo and Juliet* or the opening scene from *Titus Andronicus*, for example. This allows for a democratic way into the classics, regardless of the part being played and allows for collective exploration. In contrast, director Sue Dunderdale always relies on a read-through to bring a company together, albeit that she uses it to explore the play, rather than individual characterizations. I rarely do a read-through on the first day; I personally find it can cause nervousness, or encourage showing off or bluffing, leaving one actor feeling inferior to another, if you have some that are already confidently off-book and some that are not. However, I may read the play later during the first week as a way of getting a sense of the whole and the polarities of the play. It's important that we know as a company where the play needs to finish and land with an audience, in order to get a sense of the polarities needed and how the piece is bookended.
- **Stumble-through:** A bold initial move is for everyone to be active in the space, script in hand, actively reading through the whole piece. This is often done with a playful approach, working out relationships and dynamics in the moment and relating to one another. This can be chaotic and messy, but the whole cast experience the play collectively.
- **Meaning read-through:** The actors read through the play, taking their own characters, with the stage manager reading in all stage directions. When there is a question about the play in relation to the world or a reference to something specific, then this is explored and answered using other textbooks, primary research or the internet. This allows the company to start putting together a picture of the world and

questions can be answered that are key to an understanding of the text. It is vital that the company know that this is not an exercise in acting but more like a fact-finding exercise or detective work. Aligned to this, I often have lots of Post-it notes to hand, so that the cast can write down any interesting points that could be worth exploring later.

- **Events read-through:** As above, the actors read through the text from the standpoint of their individual characters, identifying the major events of the scenes and agreeing on which are events shared between the majority of characters, as well as how these might relate to the director's early rehearsal decisions about events, discussed in Stage One. Breaking down the play into 'bits' (previously translated as 'units') can be useful here. Giving each bit a title using 'phrases that engage' (Shipley 2023: 11) provokes creative responses that arouse the senses.

- **Creative team introductions:** Often early on in the process, before any of the exercises above, there is a talk from the director, designer and wider creative team about the concept, vision and production. I aim to keep this to a minimum on day one, as most actors are already saturated with information and combatting nervousness. I therefore restrict this to salient points, most of which have been discussed at casting and in early rehearsal conversations with actors. On day two or three, though, I may have a more in-depth conversation, when some collective grasp work has been undertaken and there is the start of experiential and embodied work. A word of warning for the director: this is not an opportunity to show off, lecture or bamboozle everyone with prior research or to give a literary analysis of the play and share production histories. What is said here must inspire, igniting interest for practical exploration and action.

- **Safe spaces statement:** The UK actors' union Equity encourages the 'safe spaces statement'[2] to be read out at the beginning of each rehearsal period, which is a commitment to run a rehearsal room free of bullying and harassment. This also discourages 'bystanding': in the same way that everybody is responsible for health and safety, they are also

---

[2] https://www.equity.org.uk/advice-and-support/dignity-at-work/creating-safe-spaces/#safe-spaces-statement.

responsible for the well-being of all company members. Do explore the work of Rikard and Villarreal, however, in their repositioning towards 'spaces of acceptable risk'.
- **Model box and costume showings:** It is crucial to share any initial designs at a very early stage. Sharing the model box (a 1:25 scaled-down version of the whole set and scenographic space) allows the actors to begin to understand how the concept has been formulated visually and grasp the dynamics of the playing space. Actors inhabit worlds when embodying their characters and this – along with the costume design showing – becomes a crucial stage of the process. Costumes, for actors, are their characters' clothes. Often in a contemporary play, actors will have some input into their clothing through the rehearsal period and can articulate sensitively to designers their body issues, with suggestions of how these might be considered in the design and making processes. Sharing and showing the costume designs, and then bringing as much as possible of the costumes to wear in the rehearsal room, supports the embodiment process in an inclusive manner.

Warming and tuning up

A warm-up is key to the rehearsal process and needs to be relevant to the task undertaken. I prefer the alternative term that Russian acting practitioner Nikolai Demidov uses, which is 'tune-up'. The actor's instrument must be 'in tune' with the work ahead. As Demidov states, when 'iron has been heated, you can forge it … you can't forge cold iron' (Malaev-Babel and Lasinka 2016: 558). It's key that the warm-up or tune-up needs to be relevant to the work ahead. There is no point playing a boisterous theatre game brimming with competition to then sit down for two hours analysing the text. The tune-up should naturally segue into and relate to the main body of rehearsal. There may be use of movement, body and relaxation techniques, or vocal limbering and strengthening. A concentration- or energy-boosting warm-up may be key, dependent on the mood or energy of room, but the director must be flexible and not fixed on driving through a set of pre-prepared exercises, if these do not feel right in the moment. Just as actors must be in the moment with their scene partners, directors should be attuned to the energies and rhythms of the room and the atmosphere within, as well as knowing what is coming next.

Some tune-ups essential to musical theatre – or indeed anything requiring song and dance – are vocal and physical warm-ups. These are often non-negotiable and are needed to ensure that vocal and physical health is considered. Traditionally, a warm-up for singers began with a series of scalic and arpeggiated patterns; however, understanding of physiology and vocal anatomy has moved on considerably in recent years.

I frequently work with the musical director, vocal coach and arranger Daniel Jarvis, who always recommends that a warm-up be tailored to what is needed collectively in the room, as well as individually. For many, this means focusing on the vocal folds (cords), as they are ultimately responsible for creating the contact that produces the pitch, tone and quality of the voice. Contact of the folds can also relate to the breathing mechanism, because the vocal folds need to meet effectively in conjunction with the air flow. It can therefore be helpful in a warm-up to spend some time loosening, engaging and placing attention on the coordination of these muscle groups. Warming up by straightaway giving full voice to a song with five-part harmonies can be counter-productive: this may feel like warming up but, as Jarvis notes, such an approach is more likely to tire out the voice before even beginning, since it can lead to pushing volume and placing greater effort into the abdominal wall. This increases sub-glottic pressure (the pressure beneath the folds), which can add strain to the sound by inviting the larynx to close down (constriction). This can also lead to ineffective closure of the vocal folds, which may result in an undesirably breathy tone and shorter phrase lengths, which in turn can lead the performer to push even more. This is why warm-ups for Jarvis often start without using the keyboard or piano, but rather begin with the company limbering up the body and voice through a deliberate series of stretches and muscular exercises as part of a systematic approach to enhance the functionality of the entire vocal system. He then leads to connecting appropriate breath with voice, prior to any singing. Jarvis suggests exercises such as sirening – holding the 'ng' sound of the word 'sing' and gently exploring the range of pitch the voice naturally offers – and focusing on voiced fricatives – the 'z' and 'v' sounds – as two examples of safe warm-up practices. Only then does the company move on to more sung and fully engaged exercises, tailored to the demands of the session. It is probably worth adding that while a multitude of sung exercises can often be crucial in developing technique, it should be considered as to whether they are necessary in a warm-up to prepare the performer for the voice work they are about to engage in.

My long-term collaborator choreographer and movement director Laura-Ann Grecian suggests a number of physical warm-up principles dependent on the context. Like Jarvis, she emphasizes the needs of the room, the individuals and the work ahead for that day. For any performance, Grecian suggests that the initial warm-up for actors should relate to mobilizing all of the performer's joints (e.g. shoulder rolls and spine rolls) after moving the body by walking and/or moving in the space as appropriate. This ensures that there is a slight increase in heartrate. For dancers, in addition to the above, moving onto cardio-vascular work is vital, finishing with stretches prior to any dance rehearsal.

In relation to both the physical and vocal warm-up ideas above, without a musical director, vocal coach or movement expert, then the director must potentially encourage the actors to warm up efficiently and effectively using the principles outlined by Jarvis and Grecian. Numerous alternatives are, of course, available, as are a myriad of books offering suggestions for both vocal and physical warm-ups.[3] As a director, one crucial tune-up cognitive exercise is that I ask the actors the following questions:

- What worked yesterday for you?
- What would you like to build upon?
- What is one thing you'd like to do differently, or explore today?

Safe and inclusive rehearsal rooms

'Check-ins' are now becoming part of the rehearsal process, allowing for a space that is a bridge between the real world and the world of the rehearsal. These can equally be thought of as an extension to the tune/warm-up, or indeed part of it. Also, as part of the early parts of rehearsal, Australian director and intimacy coordinator Andrea L. Moor is clear that

> consent-based actor training incorporates safe consensual agreement of touch, appropriate support in dealing with challenging material, non-biased casting, appropriate recognition of gender, safe acting practices, safe cultural

---

[3]Among the many texts available, I would suggest Jeannette Nelson's *The Voice Exercise Book: The Warm-Ups*, available here as an audio text: https://www.nickhernbooks.co.uk/the-voice-exercise-book-the-warm-ups-cd. Some excellent physical warm-up ideas can be found in Jackie Snow's *Movement Training for* Actors, available here: https://www.bloomsbury.com/uk/movement-training-for-actors-9781408128572/.

practices, diversity of representation in teaching and directing staff and clear guidelines for discussion and complaint. In a nutshell, consent-based actor training ensures the safety and agency of all actors in training.

(2023: 89–90)

While Moor is explicitly discussing actor-training here, these principles should extend to all professional rehearsal environments. Improvisation in rehearsal, for example, often leads to physical connections without any consent being negotiated. For free impulses to be allowed, intimacy needs to be respected, as then actors can play within safe boundaries. Consent can only be given by an individual. A director or creative may give permission for physical contact to be had, but this is certainly not consensual. Where there is a scene that requires physical contact or intimacy (from a simple handhold to a kiss, to scenes of sexual content), then consent-based work is paramount. Directors should be aware that if there is scripted material which involves intimacy, then this should be scheduled far in advance, so that there are no surprises. Actors can prepare for this and consider how they wish to approach the scene looking at the moment of intimacy, how the characters relate to one another and what any stage directions suggest, bringing ideas to the table through the lens of how their character would approach intimacy. This should be handled by the director in the same way they would if initiating a discussion to how a character views or responds to violence in a fight call, or anything else in relation to the world around them. This paves the way for approaching these moments as choreography, with the director checking in (following the exercise outlined next on page 84) that everyone is comfortable with the situation and each other. Directors should work with their performers and stage managers to ensure the set choreography of these moments is locked in as written in the book by the DSM. At no stage should any of this be improvised, nor left to impulse, as boundaries must be set and respected. As outlined in Stage One, at the casting stage, the director must articulate any contact or intimacy requirements as per the script, or indeed within the wider production concept. Marie-Heleen Coetzee and Kaitlin Groves (2023) state that 'ethical professional touch involves three key aspects that are encapsulated by a broader frame of beneficence and nonmaleficence' (Fuller 2006): first, an understanding of what ethical and/or appropriate touch is; second, an understanding of what kind of touch is inappropriate and unethical; and third, clarity of intent and boundaries and openness between those touching (2023: 106).

New Zealand academic and director Hilary Halba also ensures a check-in in rehearsals as a space to articulate either general or specific concerns, while all the time knowing that this is undertaken within the environment and framework of a rehearsal room, rather than a therapeutic milieu. Halba describes her approach to negotiating consent in relation to intimacy, needed in both scene-work as demanded by the script, as well as in rehearsals:

> I need[ed] ... to obtain information on how the actors were feeling about the show. I normally ask the actors how they are feeling about the scene(s) and any concerns they have around the intimacy. I normally take the actors aside individually and ask them these questions, so that they feel like they can speak freely. Despite the open Zoom setting, I still decided to ask the cast and crew how they were feeling about the intimate scenes: 'What are your fears and/or concerns?' ... In order to build Consent and Choreography from the Five Pillars,[4] I asked: 'What will feel safe and respectful to you?' I also focused on Context, another one of the five, asking an actor, 'What does your character do?'
>
> (2021: 266)

Negotiating consent in rehearsals

How to undertake this exercise:

Gather the scene partners for the scene in question, and have each person individually describe where they are comfortable to be touched or have a physical connection made. The others in the scene listen without judgement or interruption and then repeat back what they have heard, to ensure they have understood correctly. This is, however, not fixed, and the exercise can be repeated at the start of each session or day.

Why it works:

This exercise can be done very quickly, yet can have enormous benefits in terms of physical and psychological safety in the work.

---

[4] The Five Pillars of Intimacy in Production are components for the safe and ethical creation of intimate content in theatre, TV or film, and comprise Context, Consent, Communication, Choreography and Closure. More information is available on the Intimacy Directors and Coordinators website: https://www.idcprofessionals.com/blog/the-pillars-of-intimacy-in-production.

> **Key takeaway:**
> Consent is agreed and boundaries set respectfully, giving the actors agency in their approach to physical touch and contact, whether for improvisation in rehearsals (or training), or for scenes that require physical contact or intimacy.

Access in rehearsals

An inclusive casting process should also enable the director to identify any access needs that may be essential when working with their company, such as sign interpreters or rehearsal room lighting requests. The access riders that production companies receive can also help with this. The language that is used in the rehearsal room is often cued by the director, specifically in terms of the acting process. This unifies a company implicitly and allows a shared language. The same principle is to be applied to the language used when working through exercises in terms of inclusivity. One such case is in relation to ableism and not making assumptions. Bella Merlin honestly reflects on her unconscious bias as she discusses training actors via Zoom during the Covid-19 pandemic, speaking about the need to adapt her language to that of journeying around the room, even with their eyes, instead of talking about walking, or assuming feet could be firmly planted. This led to, as she puts it, a 'radical overhaul of vocabulary' (2024: 77). In Stage Three, I posit some exercises to enable inclusive rehearsal processes, drawing on some of the latest thinking and research around working with neurodiverse actors, as well as offering approaches that directors can use when making adjustments to their processes.

De-roling and debriefing at the end of rehearsals

As a director – and particularly when working with actors on tackling an emotionally or psychologically sensitive role or scene – you should factor in some time and space to decompress and return across the bridge from the rehearsal (and any demanding characterization) to the real world. This honours the rehearsal space as a workplace and forms part of a moral responsibility to the individual actors, so it is vital that the process must allow for some time for this approach. Hilary Halba's suggested exercises for this include, among others, some 'phased relaxation ... identification of five things the actor can see [or] exercises where actors name each other with their real names (rather than their character names)' (2024: 51).

Debriefing, however, is more of a company objective approach, often reflecting on the day's work, articulating any discoveries or breakthroughs, or things to work on next. I often do a debrief in miniature at the end of the day and pick this up the following morning, particularly if the company have been undertaking some sub-rehearsal research or have incubated ideas or questions overnight; this is especially the case following a weekend's break. While the tune-up (as described above) is about setting personal tasks and goals for the day, the debrief is an opportunity to share reflections, ask questions and (p)review the work in progress, both as an ensemble as well as individually. These exercises should be in addition to cool-ups and warm-downs for the voice and body.

Creating a world for actors to inhabit

The director must unify a company around a shared vision. A major part of this is establishing the world of the production (aligned to the world of the play or piece) and building the world together for actors to inhabit. This performance world is key for academic Richard J. Kemp, who states that 'humans exist in physical, social, and cultural environments and are intricately entwined with those environments, simultaneously acting on and being acted upon by them' (2023: 2). The performance world is created by this relationship being in harmony with the text, the world of the play (and/or the original conventions attached to it), as well as the world of the production and design. Actors can then play actions in relation to the given physical, social, political, cultural, societal and spiritual world that encloses them. These actions then extend to relating with and to other characters and their given circumstances. As a result of this, an actor's character emerges through the 'physical actions [which] both express character and also create character by temporarily altering an actor's sense of self' (ibid.: 9).

Put simply: play the action and the character will emerge through what the actor experiences.

So, the director's role is to keep ensuring that the actors play their actions within the logical world of the play, musical or panto, to allow for organic characterization.

The words *are* the world

How to undertake this exercise:

The cornerstone of building a physical, concrete world is grounded in the words of the play. Take the whole play (or an act or scene) and ask everyone to pull five words from it that jump out and resonate with them. These should be words that pique interest, arouse creative curiosity, or otherwise speak to them personally. Write these down on separate sheets of paper. Each company member places these down on the rehearsal room floor, so that there is a scattering of words. Ask the actors to move around the space, stopping off at different words. They should then allow the word to work on them: encourage the actors to drop the word into their imagination and see how it lands naturally.

The word should be allowed to work on the body and voice. Does the word stimulate a need to move in any way? If so, this should be allowed to happen; the impulse should be embraced and allowed to inform the movements of the body.

Next, the word should be explored vocally, starting quietly and then taken into full voice. The actors should continue to move around the space.

Afterwards, discuss the impact of the words and how they affected the performers, as well as how these words conjure up and support the world of the play.

Why it works:

The actors are not intellectualizing the words of the text, but actively analysing them from the gut, forging visceral and psychophysical connections with the language and its texture. The director can then unpack key themes, ideas, characterization and relationship concepts following the exercise. Discussions may take the company into fresh creative areas as a collective, rather than settling with the director's preconceived ideas, or they may strengthen prior decisions by adding nuance.

Key takeaway:

The words of the play are the foundation for the world of the production that the characters (actors) inhabit.

Exercises to begin building characters and relationships

The final part of this chapter consists of a series of directorial and rehearsal exercises that provide a way in to developing characters and their relationships with others.

Actions, wants, needs, objectives, tasks and supertasks

Characters need and want things from moment to moment (their immediate 'action') as well within a scene (their 'want') which feeds into what is driving them throughout the piece (their 'supertask', previously referred to as their 'superobjective'). This is a key part of the Stanislavskian technique.

How to undertake this exercise:

Let's take a short section of one of Lady Macbeth's speeches in *Macbeth*:

> LADY MACBETH   Art thou afeard
> To be the same in thine own act and valour,
> As thou art in desire? Would'st thou have that
> Which thou esteem'st the ornament of life,
> And live a coward in thine own esteem,
> Letting 'I dare not' wait upon 'I would,'
> Like the poor cat i' th' adage?
>
> (*Mac* 1.7. 39–44)

Here Lady Macbeth is convincing her husband Macbeth to kill the King of Scotland, Duncan, who is staying at their castle that night, so they can claim the throne of Scotland for themselves, as prophesied by the three witches.

First, try to work out the intention of the scene moment. This is the overall objective/intention/task/motive (often interchangeable terminology for the same thing) in the section being explored. This is in response to an obstacle, either internal (such as pride or fear) or external (such as another character with a counter-objective).

Objectives change when they are achieved; if they become impossible to achieve, due to external forces, then the character may change tactic. They are not always to be found in the lines themselves: the line is the last part of the process which starts from the impulse for the need to play an action and speak, and the spoken word may be a lie, or a cover, for true thoughts and feelings. We might say, then, that Lady Macbeth's overall intention is 'to get Macbeth to murder Duncan'. The action is then determined thought by thought: up to a full stop, exclamation mark or question mark. The actor and director can work out their thought-by-thought processes, which feed into achieving this objective. Lady Macbeth's obstacle here is external: only a few lines earlier, her husband has delivered a soliloquy to the audience where he resolves *not* to kill Duncan.

Examples of potential actions are given below in brackets:

LADY MACBETH [*To patronize.*] Art thou afeard
To be the same in thine own act and valour,
As thou art in desire? [*To belittle.*] Would'st thou have that
Which thou esteem'st the ornament of life,
And live a coward in thine own esteem,
Letting 'I dare not' wait upon 'I would,'
Like the poor cat i' th' adage?

The supertask (or overall driving motivation) is the driving force behind all the above. We might conclude in rehearsals that Lady Macbeth's supertask is to achieve ultimate power. Now, move on to working out the difference between the character's wants and needs. As director Declan Donnellan states in *The Actor and the Target*:

> 'Need' makes it clear that the target has something that we cannot do without, whereas 'want' can imply that we can start and stop wanting with a concentrated effort of will. 'Want' I can turn on and off like a tap, 'need' turns me on and off at its will . . . If we merely want, it isn't so shaming not to get; but not to get when we need is humiliating.
>
> (2005: 62)

So, this might be as simple as 'I want to go out clubbing tonight, but I need to revise to pass this exam tomorrow'. With a 'want', an individual should be able to switch off, but a 'need' propels the individual to make a decision and the consequences of not achieving the need could be catastrophic for them.

Why it works:

All of the above examples are transactional. They are about changing the other character/actor in the scene, placing the focus on the scene partner(s) and the dynamic relationship, rather than a more individualistic approach concentrating on oneself. In my experience, individual characterization develops through their relationships(s) with others, as how they act and interrelate *is* the basis of an actor's characterization. Working out the 'need' (imperative) versus the 'want' (objective) of a scene can raise the stakes and create, in my experience as a director, a dynamic energy, which heightens the storytelling. The late playwright Peter Whelan once said to me that you shouldn't look at the characters as a director or writer, you should look *between* the characters: at the energies flowing between one person and another and how what they need can change these energies and make for dynamic relationships.

Key takeaway:

Perhaps you're thinking: 'How will I remember the differences between wants or needs? How does the action relate to the intention? Does the action feed into the intention? How do I play the supertask?'. Don't panic! Keep things alive and don't allow the process to become too academic. Bella Merlin states, 'I don't get too hung up on terminology. My main intent (objective? task? problem? desire?) is to stir the actors' imaginations' (2023: 91).

Much of this work is often intuited by actors. As a director, I will often use some or all of the above explicitly to 'unlock' a moment if we have become blocked which then leads to honouring the scene's events.

Given and imagined circumstances

How to undertake this exercise:

The given circumstances of the play are part of a director's bedrock. These are the undisputed facts from the text that you can return to. I often undertake lists of these for both the directorial overview and character by character.

As a director, work through each character, writing down:

1 What the playwright says about them;
2 What they say about themselves (and any reasoning);
3 What they say about others (and any reasoning);
4 What others say about them (and any reasoning).

Start to explore the above lists to create a picture of the relationships and dynamics between characters. Katie Mitchell sees the text as the mediator of any conflict between director and actor, which means that the facts within the pages of the play can be used as a basis for discussion. These lists could be created jointly with the actors or created individually and then shared in the rehearsal room as a topic for discussion, or as a springboard for hotseating.[5]

These lists should be in addition to the factual lists created by the director as discussed in Part One, and Stage One of Part Two. From the lists created – and working alongside your actors and creative teams – you can then begin to build imagined circumstances on top. These might be more related to the world of the production, rather than the world of the play; they will also allow you to explore layers and complexities not always apparent in the original text.

Why it works:

The given circumstances are the raw ingredients for creating a dynamic production with characters rooted in the world of the play. It is often impossible to determine a playwright's intention, living or dead. A well-known (living) playwright I worked with was keen to stress to me that they didn't fundamentally know what the play meant, or indeed what certain elements represented. They were determined that these meanings were for the production's cast and creative team, as well as audience, to determine. This offers another way into interpretation. Building the imagined circumstances on top

---

[5] A traditional exercise where an actor (in role) is asked questions about themselves, their lives, their motivations and otherwise, by directors and actors. John Abbott's *Improvisation in Rehearsal* explores how hotseating can be undertaken in numerous ways, including character-to-character, as opposed to actor-to-character, and reframes this as 'Centre of Attention' (2009: 126) with the aim of reducing stress, relating it more to character intentions and personalities. This aims to be more creatively useful and scenario-driven for the rehearsal room. Details of the book can be found here: https://www.nickhernbooks.co.uk/improvisation-in-rehearsal.

of the given circumstances gives a solid foundation to choices you make as a director in rehearsal with your actors. If there is a gap between your thinking and the actors' thinking, then the given circumstances allow for a return point for discussion.

Key takeaway:

A simple list can form the foundation for creative discoveries relating to character and relationships.

Moment of orientation

New characters coming into a scene often constitute an event as discussed above, since the presence of a new person affects everyone in large or small ways. Watch a group of friends in a coffee shop or any social environment. One person joins (or leaves) and dynamics shift. People change places, allegiances alter and the status between individuals and across the group shifts. In plays, where stories are heightened and conflict is often rife, this can afford a major gear change in mood and relationships between characters.

How to undertake this exercise:

Ask the actors to explore a scene either around the table, or in action on the rehearsal room floor. At the start of the scene and each time a character enters or exits, allow time to explore these new moments of orientation. Prior to beginning the scene, ask them to give full attention to their scene partners, in a metaphorical 'grasp' as outlined above and think internally about the relationship and status between one another, voicing this subsequently in a whisper. Encourage the actors to allow these inner thoughts and feelings about one another to affect their bodies and breath and allow this to radiate from themselves.

Direct the actors to be patient as their scene partners finish the exercise, while keeping them in grasp, and then begin the scene when everyone is finished. Whenever characters enter or exit, undertake the same exercise as above: departing characters should also speak their thoughts on exit.

Once you reach the end of the scene, play the scene again without stopping at these moments, but encourage the actors to attune to these moments in the exercise and keep them alive. Remind the actors that they need to decide whether they want to externally radiate these feelings through non-verbal communication and body language ('I want you to know that I like you') or not ('I need to hide the fact that I despise you'). Explore this exercise later in the rehearsal period and see how the actors have deepened their thinking and added layers.

Why it works:

Texture and detail are created in terms of relationships and individual characterization; nuance is therefore achieved, as these major events are honoured, keeping these moments alive. As a director, you can also hear what the actor/characters are thinking and feeling and you can side-coach by feeding in extra thoughts based on the givens in the text, or discuss afterwards if there were any fundamental elements missing.

Key takeaway:

Relationships and interrelationships are constantly changing, and this exercise allows time for the actors to negotiate these complex moments, exploring how much is (or is not) revealed and why.

Opposites and polarities

Practitioner Michael Chekhov advocates for a deep exploration of polarities in texts, as well as how actors might play these. Director and acting coach Sinéad Rushe states that when using Chekhov's technique, 'the more contrasting we can make our beginning and endings, the more sharply focused the performance will be' (2019: 93).

How to undertake this exercise:

Work with your actors to see how the beginning of the piece differs from the end. How might you move towards the end from the beginning? How does a speech start and end? How do characters interact when they are polar opposites and want very different things?

You could read out lines, sections or a speech and then ask the actors to write or draw their thoughts, feelings and observations about this from their character's points of view.

Discuss findings and reactions collectively and pull out useful or interesting elements to work on. As an example, I recently read out the opening and closing sections of Shakespeare's *A Midsummer Night's Dream* to an acting company. These sections of the play are literally polar opposites in every respect. The actors who didn't know the play were shocked at the darkness of the opening scene, especially with Egeus attempting to force his daughter Hermia to marry Demetrius, using the law to threaten her otherwise with the penalty of death. This is in complete opposition to the fairy world at the close of the play, bookended by Puck's self-effacing address to the audience. We discussed how the acting company could commit to the playing of these polarities and the rich tapestry of each section and atmosphere.

When exploring a scene or a speech, watch as a director whether the actor has truly moved from one polarity to the other and is playing these polarities.

Why it works:

You can use this to support the actors to find the polarities and opposites and encourage them to play these. This enables journeys to be played and for there to be tangible changes and dynamics, as well as tension that rises and falls.

Key takeaway:

Understanding the nature of the end of the play/scene/bit allows the actor to get a sense of the whole and the journey they have to make.

Inner motive forces or psychological drives

Another exercise I explore with my actors relates to inner psychological drives, as used by Stanislavski and later practitioners such as Michael Chekhov, with Bella Merlin describing these as 'the most useful tools in the whole toolkit' (2014: 162).

How to undertake this exercise:

Ask the actors to respond, initially out-of-role, through different dominant centres in turn: these centres are thought, emotion and will (or action). Begin by asking the actors to start exploring 'thought' and placing this in the head. The actors are to explore the room through the 'thought' centre: first by walking, sitting, standing, crouching, rolling and then by undertaking activities such as viewing the world around them, or picking up and exploring a personal object. After this, they can begin greeting one another and then – if a consent exercise has been undertaken – they can start to physically connect with one another. After five or ten minutes, let this go.

Discuss the exercise.

Actors often respond that many questions or philosophical thoughts entered their head regarding what they were doing and why they were doing it. They often observe that the room was filled with a slower, pondering, inquisitive atmosphere.

Then ask the actors to explore again but using 'feeling' and placing this into the torso. Undertake the same steps above using this centre. Encourage the actors to repeat the same activities in the same order, to ascertain any similarities and differences. Again, after five to ten minutes of exploration, stop and discuss the exercise. This will often elicit reflections about emotional connections with objects.

Finally, have the actors explore once more, but using 'action', with the centre shifting across to the legs, hands and feet. Undertake the same steps above with the 'action' centre, repeating the same activities. After ten minutes or so, stop and reflect. The discussion here often centres around rapid responses, working on impulse and more playful and exploratory approaches.

Now ask the actors to think about their dominant inner drive from the character's point of view. This will naturally shift with the polarities and at different moments in the character's journey. Play around physically, using the steps above, and allow words of the text to be spoken. Ask characters to meet and connect through these forces. How do they motivate behaviour and connections with their world? You might even think about 'scoring' a text or a monologue of what the potential inner motive forces are.

Why it works:

As a director, you are able to encourage boldness in choices, as well as exploring oppositions between characters.

Key takeaway:

This exercise places the actor at the heart of their own characterization processes and can quickly get an actor into a place of 'action' and exploration, rather than there being too much thinking and discussion around a table. As Tom Dugdale states: 'You don't need a table to do table work' (2023: 104).

11

Stage Three
Building and Encouraging

Chapter outline

The world: Working within the wider conditions	99
Active analysis as a directorial tool	109
Blocking: Some different approaches	114

During the middle stages of rehearsal, the director's role is to keep an eye on the growing emergence of a form. From early content explorations, a physical shape should now be coalescing. This means that, in essence, the director – or indeed any visitor to the rehearsal room – should be able to see:

- an embodiment of the roles, with the characters beginning to take shape and relationships being established between them;
- a physicalization of the text: whether the piece has been formally 'blocked' with actors being positioned onstage, or whether there is a more organic process, whereby the natural and impulsive need to move is affecting the physicalization as well as the proxemics, there should be a shape arising (and I will discuss blocking and the physical shaping of the play in more detail during this part of the chapter);
- a sense of the rhythms and cadences of scenes, acts and of the whole piece;
- rising and falling moments of tension: this often centres around the events and whether they are being honoured;
- a story being told with an element of clarity: for me, this last point underscores and underpins all of the above.

Gwenda Hughes, who was Artistic Director of the New Vic Theatre in Newcastle-under-Lyme when I was beginning my career as an assistant director, aimed to have worked through the piece at least once by this middle stage, going on to work through it again to add depth and richer textures. This has remained part of my practice. While Kate Wasserberg often likes to stumble through a rough draft of the piece at the end of week one, other directors may have conversely explored content in depth by this middle stage, focusing less on the production's form and instead investigating the relationships, given circumstances, events and internal dynamics of the scenes. Whichever process is followed, actors will be looking to the director at this stage to either sharpen the emerging form, or to encourage them to begin to mould the content exploration into a shape that can be shared with the audience.

Returning to Axel Schmidt and Arnulf Deppermann's model, there should ideally be a 'shared knowledge' (2023: 274) by this middle stage that has come through the exploration of the scenes and the piece as a whole. If the building of scene work in the interaction between actor and director has been working effectively, there should be a 'mutual anticipation of future behaviour' (ibid.: 275), with fewer negotiations between actor and director as everyone gets to know each other well. This is a measure of an effectively performing rehearsal room, as there is less discussion or delay, but more of a sense of flow in the room, since a shared knowledge and way of working has been developing throughout the first part of rehearsals. To use a social sciences model, this 'routine building' should now be evident, with the director (or musical director and choreographer) saying less and less as the performers embody their characters and take ownership of the scenes.

Directors need to monitor whether the actors need a new challenge in this middle stage of rehearsal. Any repetition of a scene should not necessarily be about locking things down too much, but should be about exploration and layering, even while consolidating. In terms of adding a new challenge to the rehearsal process, the director needs to work out what rehearsal method is required, so as to continue to build and add nuance and detail, rather than concentrating on cementing a form at this stage (though this can come later, if needed). Keeping an eye on whether actors are repeating *without* adding a layer or exploring a new opportunity is key to the director's role in this part of the creative process.

A brief sidenote here: director Katie Mitchell underlines the importance of where and how you might sit in the rehearsal room as a director. I, for example, like to sit at the end of a table rather than behind one, so that I am able to get up and move about if necessary, but still have a flat surface on which to write or keep my script just to the side of me. I find sitting behind a desk can implicitly create a parent/child dynamic between director and actor which can create an unhelpful power dynamic. I also try to be fairly neutral in my body language if I am uncomfortable with progress, not wishing to radiate that there are issues or problems, though I know I don't always achieve this! Stefan Norrthon and Axel Schmidt go even further, in their interactional study of communication between director and actors in a rehearsal room, noting how gestures can communicate the 'internal state, [and] attitude' (2023: 342) of the director, which becomes part of the shared knowledge and therefore tone of the process. Understanding the gestural language they implicitly use is therefore important for all directors. Norrthon and Schmidt argue that at a later stage, instructions get shorter, references are more implicit and negotiations decrease (ibid.: 366–7).

At this stage, for the director, it is worth checking on the health of the director/actor relationship. As a form develops, it is important that the director does not suddenly panic and resort to a more declamatory mode, or one akin to a parent/child relationship, especially as the pressure of opening night draws closer. Nothing loses respect for a directorial figure more than when their approach changes abruptly. As theatre maker and researcher Tamur Tohver states, 'directors can only achieve their goals *via* other people, guiding and encouraging them wisely' (2023: 341). As a result, it could be easy for compassion to disappear and to jettison the responsibility of being the tone setter in favour of something more results-driven. Tohver realized that when he was directing, he needed to be 'supportive of the actor in every way' (ibid.: 342), seeing directing as a coaching role. Maintaining this approach throughout is essential for a healthy director/actor relationship.

The world: Working within the wider conditions

Throughout this deepening middle phase, the world that has been established should continue to be built and enriched. The director also needs to maintain an awareness of whether their performers are working within the logical given world of the play, or if they are straying too far from the path.

Everything forms part of the world, especially the acting choices, the actions of the characters, the words spoken by them, and why the characters do what they do. But the world also forms in response to the music, sounds, atmospheres, images, props, settings, furniture and clothing within the production. Director Carrie Cracknell uses her rehearsal period to work with the actors to embody 'the conditions of the world the[ir] characters are in' (Waugh 2023: 10). As a director, I ideally want to build the world with as many of the scenographic and design elements as possible in the room as we enter this middle stage. Costume is often key for the actor, as it is the character's clothing. For an actor to be able to be (literally) in their character's shoes – let alone their whole attire – can be invaluable for understanding how the character presents themselves to the world and how they perceive the world around them. Andrea L. Moor adds to this, asserting that 'actors should be able to give their consent [to] what costumes they are comfortable wearing and what works best for and on their body. Costume plays a vital role when working on intimacy [and sexual scenes] and additional support may be needed to ensure bodily boundaries are respected' (2023: 94).

Props and furniture, too, can frequently act as extensions of a character's personality. Substitute props are all well and good, but to have the actual props or furniture within the rehearsal room can enable a greater ease as the production moves into the technical phases. More importantly, how a character interrelates to their surroundings (whether they are, for example, comfortable, uneasy, weary or frustrated with their material environment) is key. We sit in a stranger's chair very differently from our own. Financially and logistically, having all elements in the room in this way is not always possible, but I encourage this approach wherever it is feasible. Ask and see what you can get. Your actors will almost certainly thank you for it!

At this stage, actors may need more challenge and the addition of more layers, if things are becoming a little stationary and as skills increase. As Nikolai Demidov states, the director 'needs to knead and warm up the play if it has lost the temperature of its first reading' (Malaev-Babel and Lasinka 2016: 558). Below are a few exercises to ensure the production continues to simmer.

Pressing issues

How to undertake this exercise:
Ask yourself as a director, what are the issues putting pressure on the scene from all directions and affecting behaviour? This is about working within the wider world from the givens of the play and

these issues or factors could be social, historical, political, religious, spiritual, or a combination of some or all of these. Bella Merlin defines a 'pressing issue' as a 'subject that underlines a dialogue, propelling it – either secretly or implicitly – in a particular direction and . . . it's the preoccupation which can drive a character's objective' (2016: 79). These may also become obstacles to move around or smash through. Now, work out with your actors:

- if there is an overall pressing issue for all the characters in the play, or in a given scene. In Federico García Lorca's *The House of Bernarda Alba*, for example, this might well be the strict Catholicism of 1930s Andalusia, which affects everybody's actions, whether they are subsumed by it, or rebel against it.
- if one actor's character has an individual pressing issue separate to the rest of the characters. To take *The House of Bernarda Alba* again, this may be the unseen character of Pepe el Romano. Some of the characters are so affected by this individual in terms of desire and longing that it impacts their every waking moment. For the maid, la Poncia, her personal pressing issue could be that of maintaining honour, with an awareness that the townsfolk are watching.

You could ask the actors to imagine these issues as an image, or as a metaphor, or to picture these things specifically. For actors with aphantasia,[1] you could ask them to draw their pressing issues, or write them down in a way which matters to them. Now ask the actors to imagine these pressing issues filling their bodies from their toes to the tops of their heads, so that they are eventually consumed by these thoughts. Ask your actors to play the scene again with these pressing issues at the forefront of the scene. After playing the scene, discuss thoughts, feelings and observations and determine what you would like to keep exploring as a company, as well as what was useful from an outside-eye perspective.

---

[1] Aphantasia is the inability to create mental imagery; though the condition was identified in the late nineteenth century, it remained largely unstudied until a revival of interest in the early 2000s. The idea reached a wider audience in 2020, when social media posts asked the reader to imagine a red apple and rate the depiction they had in their 'mind's eye', on a scale from 1 (photographic visualization) to 5 (no visualization at all). There was considerable surprise from participants who discovered that their ability (or inability) to visualize was not universal.

Why it works:

As the actors return to the scene, there is often a new crackle of electricity between characters or radiating between actors. The **stakes** of the moment (see Stage Four, page 124) are often raised and, as with all the exercises in this text, it is not about rejecting what has gone before, but building and layering.

Key takeaway:

This can often re-anchor actors at this middle stage of rehearsals to the world and the givens of the play and/or production.

Shared improvisations

How to undertake this exercise:

There are often events that characters share in the offstage world of the play that need to be explored. These might occur prior to the start of the play, or between scenes or bits. They could be key moments that affect the onstage lives of the characters. Work out these key moments and create a shared picture with your actors of location, circumstances, objectives, obstacles (inner or outer), time scales and pressing issues. These become the shared imagined circumstances that emerge from the concrete given circumstances.

Set up a space for your actors and define the parameters for a structured improvisation to create an embodied, shared experience of these moments. Make sure the events of the moment are honoured and that the wants and needs are played against the obstacles of the moment. Afterwards, discuss what was useful (or where the improvisation might have veered away from the circumstances discussed beforehand). If it is helpful, replay the improvisation.

Why it works:

You have enabled space in your rehearsal process for a shared embodiment of key events. Too often actors work out prior events (or those that occur between scenes) individually at home. They then can get stuck within their own interpretation of events. Although their interpretation is often completely valid, it may work counter to that of the other actors, or to your thoughts or feelings, so this exercise ensures that everyone is 'on the same page'.

Key takeaway:

Events do not always live within the boundaries of the selected life of the play and should be collectively explored as a company.

Keeping the character's journey alive

How to undertake this exercise:

The world doesn't have to cease to exist when an actor leaves the stage. Often when working on a more realistic or naturalistic piece, it is possible to keep these worlds alive. If you have a rehearsal room large enough and the play is in real time, you can mark out or create the offstage worlds: indeed, I have done this using other studios in the same building. When the actors leave the stage, they can then keep their world alive through silent (or quiet) improvisations as other scenes take place, prior to re-entering.

Why it works:

The world of the play remains alive and there is an unbroken throughline of the journey of the selected life of the characters. This enables the actors to remain within the world, particularly during run-throughs.

Key takeaway:

This can be as simple or as sophisticated (building whole sets and offstage worlds in miniature) as you want or need it to be. It may simply be that the actors have their own space in the room to imagine, draw, write or think through the wider world and the events that take place between scenes. You do not need much in the way of resources to keep connected to the world of the play.

Timelines and pressures

How to undertake this exercise:

Our modern lives are bound by time pressures. We may have twenty minutes to complete an essay and submit it; forty minutes to buy a birthday present for a family member, or indeed, as I once had, fifteen minutes to make a life-changing decision for somebody else. I once observed director Kate Wasserberg remind an actor that their character had been secretly in love with another character for a year. It was clear the actor hadn't embodied this, instead playing the dynamic of a throwaway crush. This simple note saw the actor heighten his feelings and his desire to protect the other character in the scene. In the same rehearsal period, Wasserberg led her cast in establishing the timeline of the play. At one stage, several characters worked out that they had not slept much in a 48-hour period, sharpening their understanding of why their characters were on edge and volatile.

Ask your actors to work out timelines of what they know within the play and the timelines of events or relationships prior to the play or, linked to the exercise above, between scenes. Ask them to play the scene(s) again with these timelines in mind. Indeed, the time pressure may end up being a pressing issue in itself. Discuss your findings collectively.

Why it works:

We are frequently so bound in our everyday lives by time pressures (or, indeed, lack of time) that we can often take this for granted when working on a play. People who may otherwise be calm and composed can suddenly become irritable or stressed once time pressure is placed upon them.

Key takeaway:

This exercise can reveal how time can affect behaviour and raise the stakes of achieving an action.

I will pause here to remark that you will probably have noticed by now that I always like to ensure that there is space and time to reflect and collectively discuss thoughts, feelings and observations from any rehearsal method. For me, this is about building the world collectively. The exercises below now move into deepening characters and relationships.

Character lists and opposites

How to undertake this exercise:

In the '**Given and imagined circumstances**' exercise in Stage Two on page 90, there are a number of lists that you can create with your actors. These lists can, however, inadvertently 'lock in' the characters too early, in terms of qualities and characteristics. During the middle stages of rehearsal, encourage your actors to make choices and decisions that create a more fully rounded yet complex character.

Ask your actors to make a list of character qualities, but through finding moments in the piece where there are contradictions, making sure all the while that these are anchored in the givens. The title character of *Othello*, for example, has moments where he demonstrates great tenderness towards his wife, only to – and I will provide another spoiler alert – murder her in the play's final act. Roy Cohn in Tony Kushner's *Angels in America*, to take another example, is both a manipulative, unscrupulous power broker and (arguably) a scared, self-loathing victim of circumstance.

Ask the actors not to blur the edges of these qualities but to play the opposing dynamics of these qualities as they emerge, honouring the differing and divergent colours on the palette. Explore which sides of themselves they choose to present to different characters and why.

Why it works:

Often audience members discuss how a character feels 'dangerous'. This isn't necessarily about physical danger, but rather means that the audience is unsure as to how the character might respond to a given moment. Ensuring characters are complex and contradictory can create great drama. Even in pantomime, the adorably warm Dame character, always an audience favourite, might suddenly verbally (and physically) lambast her foolish son, or decide to sell the family pet (cow or goose) in the most coldly mercenary way possible. As author Philip Pullman so eloquently puts it: 'It's probably better to think about good or bad actions rather than good or bad characters. People are complicated' (2017: 118). You can also link this work to the '**Opposites and polarities**' exercise in Stage Two, page 93.

Key takeaway:
Great characters are contradictory and can create elements of surprise for their audiences.

Waking up . . .

How to undertake this exercise:

Ask your actors to find a space in the room and lie down (or find a viable alternative). Have them keep a pen and paper or an electronic device close by, so that they can record thoughts and feelings. Then ask them to pick a key moment in the play that affects the life of their character, as a major turning point or event. Either through an imaginative storyboarding, or through words and drawings as an alternative, encourage the actors (in character) to trace the story of their day from the moment they wake up (including with whom they wake up, or by whom they are woken, if anyone), through their morning rituals to the major event or moment you have asked them to encounter, including everything and everyone they encounter during the course of that time.

Encourage them to think (in character) about how they feel about the other people they meet. This is a non-verbal, solo exercise, so actors can move around the room embodying this without disturbing their colleagues, or they can simply remain in their own bubble. When they reach the major moment, ask them to write and draw their thoughts and feelings about what is happening and why.

Ask them to focus on three key questions. What becomes different about this day in their lives? Are there any anomalies in their usual routines? Do they meet different people on this day and, if they do, why?

After the exercise, discuss their findings and the usefulness of these as a company.

Why it works:
Characters are made to consider their lives in relation to their environment and people they encounter or know.

Key takeaway:
The actors are encouraged, in character, to think about how this day is different to the other days in their lives.

Inner monologue work

How to undertake this exercise:
I always, at some point midway through rehearsals, like to get a sense of what the actor in role is thinking and feeling about a given moment. This is an extension of the exercise '**Moment of orientation**' in Stage Two, page 92, which I will often use when we are stuck and at a bit of an impasse. In the playing of a moment, a bit or indeed an entire scene, ask the actors to commit to speaking their inner thoughts and feelings aloud constantly in the scene (occasionally adding in a line of dialogue for good measure). The inner thoughts must be committed to as fully as the lines themselves. What characters experience, perceive, think, feel and eventually say may all be very different. Push your actors to make these conscious inner thoughts and feelings about one another to affect the body and breath, allowing this to radiate from them to their scene partners naturally. This might be about giving themselves permission to share their inner experiences outwardly.

Afterwards, discuss these elements and what was useful or not so useful. As a director, you may side-coach and add ideas and thoughts that the actors may not have considered. Repeat the exercise if you feel there is more to discover.

Finally, ask the actors to play the scene again, encouraging them to keep alive the inner spirit of what they have been investigating. As with the '**Moment of orientation**' exercise on page 92, remind the actors that they then need to decide on whether they wish to externally radiate these feelings through non-verbal communication and body language – 'I want you to know that I like you' – or not: 'I need to hide the fact that I am falling in love with you'.

Why it works:

As a director, you can check in on whether your actors are genuinely continually listening and in dialogue with one another, or attuned to non-verbal clues as to how their scene partners are behaving.

Key takeaway:

You have created an environment where inner thoughts, experiences and feelings are just as important as the quality (and/or quantity) of the lines an actor may have. Everyone's inner being should be crackling with intensity and bubbling with life. The lines spoken by the character are therefore the last stage of the process.

Characters 'in' the scene

How to undertake this exercise:

This exercise works well with the full company when you are at a point to stagger through the whole play. It could, however, be easily adapted to be a standalone exercise. Moving away from the 'blocking' of the scene, ask your actors to create a wide circle of chairs so that the action can be played in the middle, without furniture and without worrying about any blocking that has been worked on so far. During the stagger-through, if a character's name is mentioned, but that character is not physically present in the scene as it appears onstage, the actor playing that character should make themselves present in the playing space. Assuming the company has undertaken the consent exercises outlined on page 84, the actors can interact with the characters they mention or discuss, either directly or indirectly. The character that is not in the scene needs to be open and should react non-verbally within the scene as the improvisation dictates. Actors can talk to, refer to, or physically connect (safely and consensually) with these new characters in their scene. Persuade the actors to connect with how they think or feel about these individuals at the moment of connection.

Why it works:

Without much work, this stagger-through can add an additional layer of meaning in terms of character relationships. The exercise can ensure a dynamic connection with the characters who have not been written as being present in the scene, yet who are ultimately vital to the relationships depicted. This expands the overall story world and keeps it alive and brimming with possibilities.

Key takeaway:

The lives of all characters in a play are intertwined. When not actively in a scene, the actors can nonetheless engage them imaginatively as if they were present.

Active analysis as a directorial tool

Later in his career, Stanislavski developed a process now known as 'active analysis' as a tool for creating work. This is a rehearsal methodology in its own right, placing action at the forefront of the work with the lines spoken being a by-product of this. At the heart of the process is the idea that the actor never takes their script onto the rehearsal room floor, allowing for a genuine connection between performers that is not inhibited by reading the script. The process essentially involves moving from reading and discussing the scene, to non-verbal and then verbalized improvised scenes and finally to a word-perfect version of the scene. Working throughout on intuition – the 'sixth sense' according to Stanislavski – is central, with the actor balancing what they are genuinely 'experiencing in this very moment with dynamic listening' (Merlin 2023: 82). Bella Merlin's work on active analysis in terms of concept and detailed practice is very much worth reading, as are Jean Benedetti's *An Actor's Work: Konstantin Stanislavski* (2008) – which is a contemporary translation and interpretation of Stanislavski's own texts, *An Actor Prepares* and *Building a Character*, Maria Knebel's *Active Analysis* (2021), who trained directly with Stanislavski, and James Thomas's *A Director's Guide to Stanislavsky's Active Analysis* (2016).

Active analysis

How to undertake this exercise:

There are some key principles that underpin active analysis, but many variations on its theme. Here I offer my approach, in eleven steps, which is composed from several iterations:

1. Ask your actors to do a 'slow read' of a scene. Sitting opposite each other, the actors drop their heads to look at their script, assign a line, look up and deliver this to their scene partner. The scene partner 'receives' this line, considering how to respond once the next line has been assigned. The key rule here throughout is that an actor should never be looking at the script when saying their line or when receiving a line from the other character in the scene. It is about maintaining a genuine connection throughout. You might need to encourage your actors to take their time with this exercise.
2. Work together to decide on the events in the actors' scripts and then mark these by drawing a circle around them in order for them to be easily identified.
3. Break the scene down into workable 'bits' (each 'bit' should contain an event or events). Draw a line to separate them and give them a title.
4. Take one of the 'bits'. Do another slow read as in step 1, above. Discuss the events and the shifting dynamics between the characters. Maybe identify a key intention each.
5. Undertake a silent etude (essentially an improvised sketch or draft of a scene), thinking about how the physical 'push and pull' of a scene may express itself non-verbally. This isn't about miming (or pantomiming) the scene: it should be a realistic back-and-forth, non-verbal exercise, with actors moving only when there is an impulse to move.
6. Re-read the scene and then discuss the non-verbal etude. How close was this to the key action of the scene? Were events and givens honoured? What was missing?
7. If you think it worthwhile, you could repeat another non-verbal etude here.
8. Next, undertake an etude of the 'bit' where actors can use their own words that express the dynamic, arc and events of the scene. If words from the writer come into play, this is fine, but this is not an exercise in memorizing the lines. All lines must come from a place where there is an impulsive need to speak.

Silence is fine and all words spoken must be justified. This is a new layer, with the impulse to move being kept alive. Note that this is not done within the playing time of the bit; a ten-minute etude of a thirty-second bit is fine, as long as the actors are exploring and connected to the inner dynamic of the bit.
9 Re-read the scene and discuss the verbal etude. How close was this to the key action of the scene? What resonated or 'worked'? Were events and givens honoured? What was missing? Why? Which words were close to those of the playwright and which were not?
10 Repeat steps 7 and 8, above, as many times as required, until the scene or 'bit' is a word-perfect version, as per the playwright's script.
11 During this back-and-forth iterative approach, I also explore and layer in some or all of the following, where I feel it appropriate:
- Furniture or stage layout, which should be introduced when the actors are moving naturally from the content exploration to more of a natural shape or form.
- Encouraging the actors to sharpen their intentions in relation to what they are doing, why they are doing it and who they are doing it for. This ensures that characters are thinking about their actions in relation to their futures (rather than creating a backstory).
- Related to the above, encouraging the actors to consider what problems their characters might be trying to solve, who might be their allies in achieving a solution and who might be their obstacles? I also prompt actors to consider their inner obstacles, too.
- Encouraging the actors to take into consideration the long-term aspirations and hopes of their characters.
- Ensuring the actors are connecting to and with the pressing issues in the scene.
- Exploring whether the characters have any secrets in the scene and what these might be, as well as how they might affect their behaviour.

Director Mike Alfreds might term each one of the above prompts a 'point of concentration' (2010: 183). A point of concentration is essentially a given circumstance; by playing these one by one, it 'give[s] the performance richness of texture, complexity and resonance . . . add[ing] colour and juice to the relatively spare linearity of actions and objectives' (ibid.). In essence, these layer in the given circumstances each time the scene is played. Each time a new point of concentration is introduced, this is at the forefront, but is stacked upon the previous one which remains in the playing of the etude, embodying the givens layer by layer.

Why it works:

Etudes are 'a method for doing actions' (Shevtsova 2023: 8). Active analysis asks that actors carry out 'etudes in their own words to own them and be the authors of their texts before they learned the words of "others" in order to make others' words their very own for a role' (ibid.: 11). Words and lines come last in the active analysis process: there must be a need for words and, as Tom Dugdale argues, a director and actor must ask what makes it 'utterly necessary' (2023: 11) to give voice to a line. Concentrating on what characters do, rather than what they say initially, gets to the heart of the story. On an inclusion level, actors may be less worried and anxious in terms of learning lines. This process ensures actors know why their characters are saying the lines they do: many actors I know who have gone through this process are surprised at how easily the lines 'go in' as a result. Active analysis allows you and your actors to excavate, going beneath the surface of a scene to understand the internal dynamics, the relationships between characters and the need to connect and communicate through and leading up to the core events. All of this is experienced moment to moment. Finally, actors embody where the need to speak comes impulsively and the emotional texture of a scene develops naturally as a result of the doing. The physical acts affect the psychological and emotional parts of the actor, removing the need for personalized 'emotional memory' techniques. This safeguards the actor, as the trigger for the emotion comes from the scene's circumstances, rather than from the actors.

Key takeaway:

Although led by a director as a process, academic Sharon Carnicke states that active analysis 'offers a collaborative process of work in sympathy with contemporary efforts to break away from patriarchal and authoritarian hierarchies in the arts, because it envisions the director as the leader of a creative ensemble, rather than as a "benevolent dictator" who controls all aspects of the production' (2009: 133). In other words, your actors rightly become genuine co-collaborators.

Throughout all of the above, some side-coaching from the director in the moment might be useful to encourage and stimulate, as might side-coaching during the reflection and unpacking of the exercise. For Hilary Halba, side-coaching 'provides a rudder to steer the through-line of etudes, and a further safety-net' (2024: 48). As an early career director, I felt that I was being rude if I interrupted an improvisation that I felt was not useful. However, given that everything explored needs to have some creative value within the frame of the production, then side-coaching can allow everyone to stay on the right track and ensure that time is not wasted, particularly in frequently truncated rehearsal periods. I now understand that side-coaching – when sensitively done – is part of a rehearsal methodology, as opposed to an unwarranted intervention. An adjustment in mindset was all that it took for me to confidently embrace side-coaching. The key is to side-coach where appropriate: examining moments where an outside voice may nudge the etude or exercise back on track within the frame of the production, relating to the moment being explored. This might be done by throwing in a reminder of a given circumstance, such as a time pressure, a textual fact or a previous event. An imagined circumstance may add a texture that is not manifesting itself organically. Often, side-coaching is useful if you have identified an actor's potential misunderstanding of a moment, or if something is absent and needs foregrounding; in this case 'dropping something in' can prove beneficial, as there may potentially be a genuine and useful discovery to be made. If things are totally off track, then stop, regroup and start again. As a director, you need to know when to sensitively intervene in order to be useful, rather than simply interjecting: otherwise, as Tom Dugdale states, you are 'pulling the rehearsal over to the side of the road. The longer your pit stop, the harder it is to get back on the road' (2023: 23).

Underpinning all of this is the need to free the actor from having their head stuck in the script and being in a place that does not enable dynamic listening. There are other approaches that the director can employ in the rehearsal process, under the umbrella title of 'dropping in'. This essentially frees the actor to connect and respond to their scene partner without holding a script in their hands. There are several methods, but here I offer two of my favourites, which I have used in the past, dependent on resources:

1 **Shadowing:** Each actor in a scene is allocated a 'shadow' (another actor, or a member of the stage management team) who will read their lines to them. The 'shadow' does just that, literally following the main characters closely, as they move around the space and feeding in the character's lines as quietly and as neutrally as possible. The actor, once

they have their lines assigned to them by the 'shadow', can then connect with their scene partners. They never interact with their shadows.

2 **Projecting:** The lines from the script are clearly and boldly projected onto several walls of the rehearsal room. The stage manager controls the pace of this, responding to the actor's rhythms and needs, as would an autocue operator. This allows the actors to read a line from the projection and then respond to their scene partners, while giving full attention as to when and how their scene partner is communicating with them.

While undertaking either of these variations, it is important that the actor perceives how their scene partner is delivering the lines. They must receive and interpret both the tone and the non-verbal communication (i.e. the subtext) as well as the spoken lines. Both will affect how they deliver their next line in return.

Blocking: Some different approaches

All directors know that the final piece will have to have a physical shape and a form. This takes into account the proxemics of the characters and the haptics employed. The proxemics are how close (or distant) characters physically are to each other and their physical surroundings, while the haptics are the type and quality of the physical connections made between characters.

'Blocking' is a term which traditionally referred to the practice in which the moves of the characters were worked out in advance of rehearsals by the director, who then guided the actors through these moves during a couple of days early on in rehearsals. One problem with this approach can be that few moves are motivated by the character's actions, nor do they originate from a place of needing to speak or move in response to the character's intentions and relationship to their environment. The actor's impulse is completely removed from the process, as is the necessity to move and speak engendered by an impulse, following the active analysis process outlined on pages 109–12. I personally sit somewhere in the middle. Having established the groundplan (as in the exercise on page 67 on *The Crucible*), I can then support actors in their responses and remain open to their impulses. In this way, I find that a natural physical shape emerges as the 'blocking'. Occasionally I may need to suggest moves or side-coach in order for the story to be told clearly for an audience, and to ensure that the stage does not become 'unbalanced' with the majority of the characters congregating in one area. There can therefore be a balance of stagecraft and impulse in the blocking process, and the two are certainly not diametrically opposed. Being attuned to the genre and style of the piece can help a director to formulate which approach they might take. A musical, pantomime or other piece on a large scale, or with a large cast, may require some forethought as to entrances and exits and basic stage 'traffic'. Indeed, resident and associate directors working on, for instance, revivals of megamusicals may be given blocking arrived at by the original creative team to replicate. A three-hander realistic play set in a single location like a living room may need less directorial blocking than will a full-cast scene in a classical text, where an audience need the physical shape to read the story. This also ensures that the focus is where it is needed to be for the majority of the audience.

This leads me to the point that directing, for me, is partly about creating a series of images that audiences can focus on, allowing them to receive the story clearly and dynamically. This isn't to force the manufacture of images in the rehearsal room as if you were creating a composition for painting, although recreating famous compositions from visual art is a useful exercise to undertake to flex the image-making muscles. Rather, it means ensuring that the images that are formed are interesting and support the storytelling.

To pull together the key principles of Stage Three, it is the collegiate and enabling director who offers suggestions through asking trigger questions, selecting rehearsal exercises and using metaphors or stories as a vehicle to unlock an actor's creativity, who ultimately realises the goal of allowing the actors to take ownership of the creative process. Rather than infantilizing actors, directors, as the tone setters of rehearsals, are able to use an adult-to-adult method of transactional analysis,[2] which permits the actors to embody their own ideas and concepts. Underpinning all of this is the importance of the director having an acute awareness of recognizing verbal and non-verbal signifiers when a breakthrough is occurring in rehearsals. A director is then

---

[2] In very brief terms, transactional analysis is a psychotherapeutic theory devised by Canadian psychiatrist Eric Berne in the 1950s to explain human behaviour. While drawing on some established principles of psychoanalysis from figures such as Sigmund Freud, Berne's innovation was to suggest that insights into an individual's personality could best be obtained by an analysis of their social transactions with others. These interactions can (in simple terms) be seen to correspond to three archetypes: child (dependent and intuitive), adult (rational) and parent (critical and nurturing). Berne's bestselling book, *The Games People Play* (1964), popularized the idea of transactional analysis among a wider audience.

able to work with the breakthrough moment for the benefit of the overall production.

We will now move into the later stages of the rehearsal period, where the director is bringing the production to its eventual destination: an audience.

12

Stage Four Shaping and Layering – the Final Stages

Chapter outline

Off-text exercises	123
On-text exercises	126
Run-throughs and giving notes: When and how to approach them	130
Dealing with differences and smoothing over conflict	131

At this stage, the director's eyes very much become those of the audience. A form should have emerged throughout the previous stages, and dynamic storytelling should be unfolding in the rehearsal room. Ideally, there should now be a committed ensemble working to tell the story, led by the director. A symbiosis between dynamic listening and a willing vulnerability should be in evidence, all underpinned by an inclusive work ethic. A director should now be looking to see whether the embodied storytelling of the actors is beginning to radiate psycho-physically with their audience in mind. This does not need to be fully formed on entering Stage Four, but as the audience anticipates opening night, what is developing needs to demonstrate that the ingredients are combining to enable the company to then enter Stage Five (outlined below) with ease.

By the end of this stage, the actors must have confidence in the story form they are going to share with their audiences. The director, conversely, must have enabled their actors to take ownership of their work. Academic and director Tamur Tohver shared with me that this is the period where I, as a director, already focus on making the story run as a whole. That is, when going to the actual stage, there would be no questions about the specific artistic solutions of certain roles – how to perform what, exactly. The same goes for the entire scene. In a sense, this is the period when I, as a director, prepare the actors to 'let go' of me. Mainly so that they already feel their freedom.

(2024)

At this stage, there may be more notes sessions taking place. In their study of over 160 theatre rehearsals, Axel Schmidt and Arnulf Deppermann identify that notes offered by directors may be both verbal as well as demonstrative (in the broad sense that notes may be more physical in their starting point). Many physical demonstrations 'depict and do not describe' (2023: 7) and these physicalizations may be metaphorical or symbolic and accompany verbal notes. I am aware that I often use metaphorical language in rehearsal – 'Think of this more as pushing a heavy boulder uphill', for instance, or 'Release the tension like you've suddenly opened the floodgates' – accompanied by physical demonstrations or gestures. This may be a simple hand gesture, bodily movement in the space or, indeed, a series of movements indicating a rhythm. This is all to 'convey how [the line or scene] is to be interpreted' (ibid.: 8) by the actors. If ownership is to be achieved, then a literal demonstration that the actor is expected to copy and repeat exactly should not be an option. Occasionally, if I feel I have crossed unwittingly into something which feels akin to demonstration, I will immediately apologise and exclaim something along the lines of 'Don't copy me!'. I then encourage the actor to work within the spirit of what I was communicating and give the room a more exciting offer. When teaching introductory directing I will set the directors a challenge: they are never to use the 'demonstrating a move or giving a line reading' tool from their toolkits. Though at first some are shocked by what appears to be a fairly draconian restriction, they soon begin to find this liberating, enjoying the discovery of how methods and techniques enable the actor to own and embody their work.

So, what is the director looking for at this late stage? Here is my list:

- The work should be **compelling** and hold the attention of the audience. In the same way that a well-written, deftly plotted novel becomes a page-turner, or a series on a streaming platform entices its viewers to binge-watch, a theatre production needs to keep audiences in their seats, as well as excited to return to them after the interval. For actor Sean O'Callaghan the director is crucial in reminding the company of

the original seed from which the production emerged, as well as their initial responses to the story and the first impulses that drive the rehearsal process; this becomes increasingly important as a form emerges.
- The story should be **clear and understandable**.
- The **events should be honoured throughout**. The moments leading up to any major event should be in place and should become inevitable for the arc of the story and the actors, but should not be inevitable for the characters at the start of the scene: this distinction is key. Sean Holmes directed Edward Bond's play *Saved* at the Lyric Hammersmith in 2011. The play provoked significant controversy in its original production in 1965, not least because of its being refused a licence by the Lord Chamberlain, who was responsible (until 1969) for effectively monitoring and censoring plays on the British stage. The play also somewhat notoriously features a scene in which four characters abuse a baby, culminating in them stoning it to death. In an interview with the *Guardian* newspaper, Holmes recalled Bond's advice to the actors about such moments: 'There was one evening rehearsal when we did the famous ... scene. He asked if he could lead it. He took everyone through it and explained that no one at the start of the scene is going to stone a baby. No one has even thought of it. There are 60 or 70 events in those 10 pages that result in the stoning' (Fisher 2024). So, while the actions are inevitable for the actors playing the scene and the lead-up is clear, the characters need to play moment to moment, action to action, layer to layer. As Holmes states: 'One thing leads to another and suddenly we're in hell' (ibid.). Dramaturgically, the architecture of the scene is then being embraced and played through these series of moments.
- **Actors should be playing moment to moment**; the director may need to help scenes back on track if actors are unintentionally 'endgaming', by which I mean playing the end result of the scene or the play ahead of time. Linked to this, the director needs to make certain that actors are playing and thinking *on and through* the lines – rather than thinking *before* the line – which enables the company to be in the moment. Thoughts should be turned quickly between lines, to then be played on and through the line. If the playwright has given them to the actors, then pauses and silences should be honoured. As highlighted in Part One, even Shakespeare directs actors as to where to pause.

- As a result of the above, at this stage actors should be playing **turning points**, while **climaxes and moments of tension** should be coming across to the audience and being experienced either emotionally or intellectually. If this is not the case, the director must undertake a degree of reverse engineering, returning to the moment-to-moment actions that lead to the events as previously outlined, otherwise climaxes are not being organically owned or reached.
- Even in a well-known story, there should be **elements of surprise**. If the story is well known, then these come from the sense that there may just be a different outcome: Hamlet might actually plunge the knife into Claudius, or Snow White might actually refuse the poisoned apple. The director should be looking to see whether what I call the '**choice doors**' are in front of the characters. Maybe, just maybe, the plot could take a different path from the one that we know so well. Greg Doran terms this a 'crossroads' (2023: 125) moment. If the director is working on a new piece of work, it shouldn't always be obvious which 'choice door' the character might take. Sometimes it can be, if the text indicates that it should. Andrew Hilton, former Artistic Director of Shakespeare at the Tobacco Factory Theatre in Bristol, states that 'we should pause in rehearsal to ask an important question, one we should ask repeatedly, but in my experience rarely do: "What would happen next, if what *does* happen next *didn't?*"' (2022: 17). Hilton, as an experienced director of classical plays, aware that many audience members enter the theatre knowing the play's story, is right to position this simple question at the heart of the rehearsals. Answering that question enables the actors to keep the story fresh, dynamic and alive to the moment.
- **Characters should be multi-dimensional and complex**, with the **relationships between characters** being clear and nuanced.
- As an outside eye, the director should ascertain whether the **energies, moods, tones and atmospheres of scenes, acts and characters are clear and appropriate.** These can often shift accordingly, with the pace and cadence of the scene also changing as a result.
- The director should be attuned to the **scene's rhythms and cadences**, when starting to undertake **run-throughs** during this stage. On several occasions I have noticed that scenes run in isolation have had appropriate tempi and rhythms of their own; however, when scenes are run together, there has been a merging of these, with the next bit, scene or act picking up the rhythm and tempo of the previous one. That said, this is often due to misplaced energies during early stagger-throughs

and run-throughs;[1] in this case, a gentle reminder of trusting in and returning to the earlier work is to be embraced. This is frequently a general note, with a reminder that it is not about the need to 'start again' or 're-rehearse', but simply to trust the earlier discoveries and explorations and consciously to reconnect with these, ensuring that all the colours on the palette are being deployed and all the rhythms of the score are being played. I often relate this to the way in which a novel may contain a series of chapters. All of the chapters are part of the same narrative, but all of them contain their own different and idiosyncratic energies and rhythms. Turning the pages of a book is a useful metaphor for ensuring that there are clear gear-changes of rhythms. In Lorca's *Yerma* (1934), for example, the very first scene sees the tempo increase between Yerma – who is unable to have children – and her husband Juan, which has developed into a fully stichomythic[2] rhythm by the end. When Juan leaves, the next bit contains a poetic and longing song with a different tempo, undercut and changed again by the arrival of Yerma's pregnant friend Maria. Ideally, such rhythms would develop organically through the earlier stages, but a director's role is to ensure that these are defined by this part of the process. Tension naturally accrues through finding the rhythms of the piece: the final act of *Macbeth* is full of short scenes and the rapid flipping from one scene to the next accelerates the action to its inevitable and tragic conclusion.

- At this stage, as much of the **design world** as possible should be brought into the room, especially if this has not been possible up to this point. Clothing, furniture, actual props rather than substitute ones, AV, music and sound, underscoring, as well as lighting, can – if it is within the bounds of possibility to incorporate them – enable the

---

[1] In *Inside the Rehearsal Room*, I posit that it is not always healthy to use the catch-all term 'run-through' and that there are four potential iterations of this. The first is 'piecing together' what has been done in the room during that call and on the scene. This allows the actors to consolidate what they have been exploring. The second is a 'stumble-though', piecing together sections and bits, stopping and starting along the way. A 'stagger-through' comes next, functioning as a low-stakes run-through, aiming to stagger through the piece, only stopping if really required, to see what the company has built so far. Finally, the 'run-through' proper comes nearer to the end of the process and is as close to performance conditions and energies as possible, ideally with much of the scenographic world in the rehearsal room for the actors to play with.
[2] 'Stichomythia' is a term that derives from ancient Greek drama but is now used of any verse drama where sequences of single alternating lines (or even half lines) are given to alternating characters. It is particularly suited to scenes where characters are tense or are in conflict, especially if lines are cut off or interrupted by one or other character (though it is conversely equally effective for more prosaic things such as question-and-answer sequences).

actors to build and react within the world of the production. The director should check that the **world is unified** and that the inner world of the actors and rehearsal meshes with the outer world of the design and scenographic elements. If this is not yet the case, then there is time enough to make changes to any of these elements.

The above list is by no means exhaustive but it does ensure that the director is metaphorically in the audience member's seat all the way through rehearsal. Audience thinking is crucial at Stage Four, as the director is beginning to bring the production into landing with its audience: knowing how it is likely to be received and being able to pre-empt the reception of the piece is crucial.

Throughout this stage, the director is also ascertaining which elements of the form need to be established, worked on or refined, with choices made in the earlier stages being solidified. As Hilary Halba notes, it is incumbent upon the director to ensure that the concepts of play and exploration are embedded within the later stages of rehearsals. While a form is settled upon, it is certainly the case that embracing 'off-text exercises' such as etudes and improvisations can prevent the company becoming trapped in a vicious circle, merely locking things in for the sake of repetition. There is a fine balance to be achieved: what is created must be able to be reiterated through the nightly repetition of telling the story, but at the same time the moment-to-moment action-reaction-decision cycle must be able to be constantly adapted, within the given circumstances of both the play and the production. It is this latter that keeps the production fresh and creates an ongoing, effervescent frisson of moment-to-moment playing, as well as a liveliness and ease of storytelling, embracing both imagined and given circumstances within one unified world. The director must understand what needs to be locked in with perfect repetition – often for reasons of health and safety, or for a specific, choreographed stage picture or effect to be achieved – and where there is room and space for adaptation and play.

Regardless of which end of the spectrum you are working at, notions of playfulness should run through the process and here I will use Miguel Sicart's definitions. Sicart is the Head of the Center for Computer Games Research at the IT University of Copenhagen and states that playfulness can 'open the possibility of who we are ... playfulness brings the essential qualities of freedom and personal expression to the world outside play' (2017: 29–30). For Sicart, play is often constructed at a fundamental level with rules and guidelines (such as those of a board game), whereas playfulness is more of a state of mind and a way of being. Therefore the director, as the tone setter, must ensure that as the form settles, playfulness is maintained within the DNA of the work, since the 'beauty of play resides in the tenson between control and chaos' (ibid.: 84). The control, in a rehearsal context, is the form that is created with the chaos residing in the exploration of the content: the words, sounds, ideas, characters and relationships. I encourage my actors to remain alive to the spirit and energy of this chaos and playfulness, which sometimes gets lost as opening night looms and the form puts down its roots.

There should be a balance between 'off-text' and 'on-text' exercises throughout the entire rehearsal process, including during this late stage. On-text exercises are about layering and adding detail using the playwright's words and might relate to work on points of concentration. The exercises for Stage Four have methods for both approaches and are intended to add layers and encourage more detail and nuance, rather than aiming at any fundamental reworking of the foundations. Ideally any major changes (such as those involving characterizations or relationships) should have been picked up prior to this stage. It is also important to think about the timing of these exercises. As actor David Bowen notes, actors can be conscious and nervous of time at this stage and the imminence of technical and dress rehearsals means they need to be confident in performance. That said, this is also a key stage where fresh routes can be explored, if there is a benefit to this.

Off-text exercises

Talking and walking your way in . . .

If your actor is playing a moment of orientation (as described in Stage Two, page 92) in a scene, but as a director you feel that they are not bringing their immediate circumstances into the scene with them, then this exercise, developed by the late, great voice practitioner Kristin Linklater, affords an opportunity for the company to develop this further. This is particularly good for work on monologues, soliloquies and solo songs.

How to undertake this exercise:

Before the actor enters a scene, ask them to move around the space in character, muttering their inner thoughts in relation to their previous immediate circumstances, why they are entering that space and what they wish to achieve. When the actor feels that there is a connection, they then enter the scene and begin the speech or dialogue. When I undertook this exercise myself, playing Egeus in *A Midsummer Night's Dream*, with Linklater side-coaching, I was asked to move around the space muttering my inner thoughts about coming into the court to begin the speech that begins: 'Full of vexation come I with complaint / Against my child, my daughter Hermia' (*MND* 1.1. 22–3). Egeus is entering here to demand that Thesus, the Duke, force Hermia to marry his choice of bridegroom, Demetrius, rather than her true love Lysander. The ultimatum Egeus gives is that unless she obeys him, the law should be invoked, and his daughter sentenced to death. It is not the cheeriest start to a comedy! I was encouraged by Linklater to start from mumbling prior to moving into full voice. My movements – which could have been realistic or symbolic/stylized – involved pacing around the space, as if tensely charging down corridors to find Theseus. I exploded into the scene and delivered the ultimatum to the court.

Why it works:

The physical embodiment of the immediate circumstances – which I consider to be within the past twenty-four hours of the character's life, up to the moment the action commences – ensures an immediacy in the playing and allows for a strong connection with the moment of orientation. While this starts with improvisatory, off-text approaches, it must segue into the text with ease.

Key takeaway:

This allows you to 'hit the ground running' in a scene through a psycho-physical embodiment.

Raising the stakes

So often at this late stage, I feel that the stakes of the scene, or the piece, can be too low. Great plays and musicals (and stories in general) take a slice of life at its richest and fullest, where individuals are making (relative to themselves) monumental decisions or where external events are impacting on them. You often hear directors asking actors to 'raise the stakes', but what does that actually mean?

How to undertake this exercise:

The stakes of a moment relate to how much and what there is to win for a character achieving their objective, as well as how much and what there is to lose for a character if they do not achieve it. Ask your actors to work out what there is to win and lose at any given moment, particularly in relation to the lead-up to the events in a scene, or in relation to the concepts and ideas in the exercise '**Actions, wants, needs, objectives, tasks and supertasks**', in Stage Two, pages 88–90. What a character stands to win might be a person, a job, love, security or power. What they stand to lose might be dignity, pride, confidence, honour or social standing.

Ask the actors to think about what is to win and lose and play the scene with these in mind. Encourage the company to think about *relative* stakes. It may be that your actors are struggling to locate the stakes: resist blaming your actors for this, especially if a piece is far removed from their lived experiences. Work with the company to find them by encouraging a discovery of the green shoots of these stakes. Stakes need to be explored from the perspective of their characters; through this lens, the behaviours, wants and needs of the characters always have stakes, regardless of personal opinion. The actor's role is to be the guardian of their character and at this late stage the director needs to check that everyone remains on the side of their character, rather than sitting in judgement upon them, consciously or unconsciously. The actor playing Iago in *Othello*, for example, must stand behind the choices their character makes, regardless of their opinion of Iago's motives and actions.

A couple of variations on this exercise include the following:

1 At any stage 'freeze' the action and ask the actors to say out loud what it is their characters what to win and what it is they are afraid of losing. If the actors are struggling to identify what these are, suggest some ideas to play with.
2 Play around with a scale of one to ten, where level ten is 100-per-cent dogged commitment and pursuit of 1. above, in order to raise the stakes of what the characters need to win. Level one might just involve occasional glimpses of this, but the need to win must still be present in the mix.

Why it works:

Locating the stakes can ultimately ensure dramatic and compelling storytelling. Seeing characters invest in pursing their wants is accelerated by the stakes being raised. This exercise offers a framework in which to understand and experiment with 'raising the stakes'. In every scene, the character has a crisis or crisis-in-miniature and exploring how they solve this (or fail to solve this) ensures that the stakes remain relatively high.

Key takeaway:

It is rare that a piece of drama has low stakes. There are stakes to find in every moment of the drama; playwrights do not write anything by chance, so every word matters, and every character reveals themselves by what they say (or do not say) and what they do.

On-text exercises

Thinking forwards: The 'what for?'

How to undertake this exercise:

At this stage of rehearsal, your actors need to be in a place where they are 'future-thinking' and driving the action forwards in relation to achieving their wants and needs, thereby raising the stakes. Keep an eye on whether the actors are thinking forwards, rather than backwards. Check whether the actors are following the path, rather than being distracted by the woods around them. It can sometimes happen that the actors are thinking about *why* they are doing something, which could root them in the past, rather than the future. Thinking about what the character wants to achieve in their future can sharpen present actions.

Ask the actors in role, 'What are you doing this for (and for whom)?' This ensures that characters are thinking about the horizon, how they might get there and with what intensity or quality. Imagining or thinking through their future selves is another approach to this exercise. It could be easy for example, for the actor playing

Tom in Tennessee Williams's *The Glass Menagerie* (1948) to mainly explore *why* he acts in the way that he does. It is clear from the text that since he was a young man, he has desperately needed to escape the dingy apartment in St. Louis where he lives with his histrionic, faded Southern belle of a mother Amanda and his mentally fragile sister Laura. The reasons why he needs this are not least his dead-end job and a desire to follow in the footsteps of his father, who left the family many years before. For the actor, focusing on this 'why' can mean playing a generalized mood about past events. What is more thrilling is to explore the question of 'what for?' All the clues to answer this are in the text: he wants adventure, a new life and a change; to be a writer and traveller, as well as, in his own words in Scene 4 of the play, 'a lover, a hunter, a fighter'.

Why it works:
The past informs the present, but it is the future – the 'what for' – that drives our actions.

Key takeaway:
This is a simple reframing of the age-old rehearsal room question of 'why?' The simplicity of this reframing at this stage can unlock key discoveries, adding layers of richness.

The mixed-up rehearsal

I would like to offer my grateful thanks to David Bowen, for permitting me to reproduce this exercise here.

How to undertake this exercise:
With the entire cast present on the first day of the final rehearsal week, choose one or two short scenes. Mix the actors up: ignore who is cast as what, including any gender specifics, since anyone can play anything here. With text in hand, ask the actors to play the scene but without copying anything they may have seen being done during the rehearsal process. The original cast, as well as any other actors not being used, observe the scene.

Following the 'mixed-up rehearsal', have an open discussion about what was observed or felt. Think especially about what nuances, mannerisms, tones, interpretations and/or choices expressed or made in the 'mixed-up rehearsal' were different from the explorations so far? Ask if any of these differences might prove a useful addition to the scene or role(s). Guide the discussion to avoid unnecessary negatives ('I wouldn't play it like that' or 'That's not what my character would do') as this may undermine an actor's confidence.

Replay the scene(s) with the original cast. Have they introduced anything from the mixed-up rehearsal? Has it helped create a clearer understanding of the scene/role(s)? There may not be immediate changes, but small nuances and differences may be kept at the back of the mind and may appear as the performance develops.

Why it works:

This exercise puts the play back at the heart of the rehearsal process. By this stage, the company are rightly embodying their roles. The mixed-up rehearsal can liberate the actors and possibly unlock new possibilities.

Key takeaway:

Each individual actor has their own interpretation of the role(s). Here, actors can develop their skills and understanding of a piece by experiencing other actors at work.

Atmospheres

Practitioner Michael Chekhov believed that atmospheres located within scenes and from characters can direct the actor. This exercise plays around with what this looks like from a director's point of view.

How to undertake this exercise:

At this late stage, you are examining whether the atmospheres of the world are being created. The atmosphere should, in the shared space and time of the theatre world, be felt not only by the characters, but by the audience, allowing them to viscerally experience the production. Exploring atmospheres is not about playing a mood or a tone. This can be a dangerous thing, since playing an imagined Chekhovian, Pinteresque or Shakespearean mood or tone can lead to generalized acting and a very dull evening indeed for the audience. What atmospheres can do, however, is to support and sharpen the dramatic storytelling and these are the atmospheres that each individual character might radiate. Some characters have more of a default atmosphere that they appear to carry around with them, while others constantly shift and change theirs. Often, the situation is somewhere between these two poles.

Ask your actors in role, to think about the atmospheres their own characters radiate at a given point in the play. Think of this inhabiting the kinesphere[3] like a bubble: the kinesphere is the area around the body that can be reached by your outstretched limbs. Don't force this: allow it to radiate naturally from you. Ask the actors, in role, to meet and to come close to each other without physically touching, but to potentially be within the kinespheres of each other. Is there a conflict of atmospheres? Do the characters yield and become absorbed into another character's atmosphere, or do they resist and hold onto their own?

Similarly, explore the atmosphere of the space. Take a scene set in a specific location; here we will return to the opening scene of *A Midsummer Night's Dream*, set in the court of Theseus and Hippolyta. The actors in that scene imagine the atmosphere to be oppressive, tense, conflicted, even though the scene starts with a discussion about marriage.

This can be done in numerous ways (and with eyes open or closed). Within the space, create imaginatively – and individually, since everyone's associations will be unique to them – what the air feels and looks like, in terms of textures and density. What colours would the space be? What sounds or music might be in the space? What objects might be scattered around? Encourage the actors to enter the space and explore within it, individually. How do they sit, walk, stand and move? How do they pick up objects or undertake activities? How do they experience the space?

---

[3]This term, often used in dance, is rooted in Laban's practice.

Then, when playing the scene, allow the actors to experience the atmosphere created. Do their characters sit comfortably, allied to or absorbed into the atmosphere of the scene? Or do they have an uncomfortable awareness of the atmosphere as they attempt to consciously pull away from it? Do they try, through their own personal atmospheres, to change the atmosphere of the space, of another person, or even of a group of people? How are the lines spoken changed or affected by the atmospheres radiating from themselves or by the ways in which the atmospheres of the space, the place and others work on them? Take time afterwards to discuss the experiences of the atmospheres on themselves as actors and from the perspectives of their characters.

Why it works:
Beginning with working abstractly and finishing up 'on text', this exercise enables you to ensure that a further layer of reality is added to the playing of the scenes. It also works towards allowing your audience to be affected by the atmosphere of a moment. Once generated, these atmospheres should encompass the whole auditorium, rather than just the playing space.

Key takeaway:
We are all affected by the atmospheres of a particular space, place and/or individual(s). Allow this to be a key feature of the scene and storytelling.

Run-throughs and giving notes: When and how to approach them

The actor Nick Barclay describes how this final stage is, for him, about finding the rhythm of the piece: through running an act, a scene or the entire play. This enables Barclay to 'see the whole picture ... and to see whether all the work of the previous weeks is there and that it's all coming together' (2024). This is also the case from a producer's point of view. Naomi Symeou, currently Head of Theatrical Production Development at the Really Useful Group, advocates for running in this final stage for several reasons, including building stamina, but more importantly to ensure the actors start to appreciate and embody the whole journey integrating thought, action and emotion. Actor Neil Roberts also advocates for run-throughs in this period, needing to embody the source material. Roberts also wants the director to still allow space for creativity, to avoid the production become too set.

In terms of noting these run-throughs, actors should 'not ... be over-noted. Drip-feeding is far better than drowning' (2024), according to actor Christian Patterson. This is echoed by Nick Barclay, who looks for a 'light touch' (2024) from his directors in the notes and working of scenes, as the bigger picture is now emerging and actors are being allowed to metaphorically 'fly'. Actor Emmanuel Olusanya describes how he looks for the director to allow further investigation and discovery while anchoring this within the established world and the dynamics between the characters. This enables the actor to keep the work fresh and connect with their character, while working within the production's frame.

Notes given by the director at this stage need to enable the actors to fly, as explained above: they must therefore be enabling rather than crushing, encouraging rather than restricting. Barclay also makes clear that it is critical at this stage that extra details can be explored and the exercises above are all about sharpening choices and adding detailed layers, rather than reworking from scratch. Actor Steve Fortune, who has performed in numerous musical theatre productions as well as non-musical drama, believes that when directing a musical, as well as running the acts and whole production, the director should allow their collaborators time to 'clean' the production: for example, the musical director should be given time to sharpen and work complex harmonies, while the choreographer should be given time to tidy and clean the moves. Sue Dunderdale warns that notes sessions should not become merely didactic, as it is 'disturbing [to see] talented actors ... reduced to an audience, receiving the wisdom of the director' (2022: 143). Rather, a notes session should be a genuine dialogue, through the process of continued creative endeavours. This also goes for notes given at the dress rehearsal and previews, as well as any noting of the show that might be necessary upon your return(s) throughout a longer run.

Dealing with differences and smoothing over conflict

Different ideas can constitute conflicts of opinion, but these are rarely insurmountable and need to be redefined as creative differences. Emerging directors can often – understandably – find it challenging to differentiate between personal and professional opinions, but recognizing this distinction is key to resolving conflict and knowing how to navigate these discussions.

Going back to the text and initiating open and honest discussions can often result in differing ideas finding a middle ground. As a director, it is incumbent on you to be able to instigate professional conversations if there is a difference of opinion. My advice: go back to the text and earlier rehearsal work on shared given circumstances to see if there's an answer. If the answer isn't immediately apparent from the text, ask the actor how useful the decision is in relation to the story world. I once had a conflict with an actor who wanted to propose a different sexuality for a character; this didn't sit easily within the givens of the play, and we discussed this openly and honestly from the perspective of usefulness in relation to the world and production, underpinned by the text.

If a situation escalates into something more than a creative divergence of ideas, then remember that the director is part of a wider team. Ideally, any earlier tensions would have been ironed out directly, or indirectly, by engaging with collaborators such as well-being coordinators. If you are a student director, then immediately talk with your course leader or instructor in this case: you are not responsible for managing behaviour in an educational context. If you are in an amateur or community environment, bring it to the attention of the committee. If you are a professional early-career director, then discuss this immediately with line managers such as artistic directors or producers. There are numerous HR processes which can be implemented, and as a director you must not feel that simply because you are the tone setter and leader of the room that you are the ultimate manager.

When discussing this final stage of the rehearsal process with actors, it is abundantly clear that it is a delicate one. For Christian Patterson, this is the 'culmination of the joy of discovery before going into the tech ... I need to trust the director and feel that they have trust in me' (2024). Taking risks has been a common thread throughout this text, and this notion is supported by Patterson who states that 'I need to be able to fail without fear' (ibid.). At this late stage, taking risks in run-throughs and uncovering new levels of detail as the piece comes together requires an open and supportive approach. The fear of being judged by their director is anathema to an actor's process: more than ever, during this brittle final stage, as everything begins to coalesce, the actor needs support, love, guidance and compassion.

Mervyn Millar, former Artistic Director of Handspring, and part of the original creative team behind the National Theatre's *War Horse*, defines a good director as one who can create a rehearsal room that is safe, where 'people can propose half-formed thoughts that might turn out to be silly, or pointless, or crazy – without them being crushed. This culture benefits more than the work. It encourages those performers and collaborators to be bolder, more playful and more confident in themselves – so they are developing as artists alongside the development of the work' (2018: 324). To reach this stage, however, actor Chrissie Perkins believes that it is crucial that all the creative team are in alignment with the vision throughout a rehearsal process and that they clearly communicate this with the cast. The director must also be gracious in giving the other creatives the appropriate time they need, especially when pressure increases as the dress rehearsal approaches. Actor Dominic Meir alludes to the need for a director to support the actor as they move to the next stage (technical, dress rehearsal and opening) and to create the conditions for that to happen. From a place of play and creation, the director can help move the actor 'towards the space we are playing in' (2024). It is rare to rehearse on the actual stage, or for all the design elements to be present in the room. It is for the director to find ways to scaffold and support this period, as the actor will now have one eye on the playing space and opening night.

13

Stage Five
Delivering and Entrusting

Chapter outline

How to run a technical rehearsal: The principles	138
Running a dress rehearsal	146
Previews, first nights, press nights and beyond	148
Advice for shorter time periods	151

Actor Gracie McGonigal explains that by the time she is into technical rehearsals, the whole company should be enabled by the director to learn and continually evolve, even if the production is 'locked in'. Being locked in does not mean that the elements of the production are immovable and fossilized; rather, the director needs to support everyone in continuing to find and discover additional layers and qualities as the production makes its way from the rehearsal room to the stage. That said, there must be a degree of consistency as the company begins to finesse the product that will be shared with each new audience at every performance. Tamur Tohver is keen to point out that from the latter part of the rehearsal period onwards, the director is also letting go of the company, echoing the notions I expressed earlier about enabling the company to fundamentally own the work.

The final run-through in the rehearsal room will most likely have been attended by the artistic director of the theatre (or someone in an equivalent position) and/or the producer(s): this is often termed the 'producer's run'. As a director, by this time, I find myself craving some notes from the viewpoint of a respected outsider. Following the run, the producer(s) or artistic director will then usually offer the director notes – observations both of things that are working and things that require more work – and it is vital to be open and receptive to these fresh viewpoints. An outside eye can enable the director to 'see the wood for the trees', as it were. I find that these note sessions almost invariably give me a much-needed creative boost at this late stage. In my early years as a director, I was wary of these sessions; however, these notes come from a place of care about the product and the company, and now I relish the moment when someone outside the rehearsal room – who is often someone that I admire and respect creatively – can provide me with fresh perspectives. If you are a student director, or you are establishing your own company or even working as an ensemble where this isn't part of the process, my advice is to bring in someone you trust to be an outside eye and invite them to offer opinions about the work. Whether you want them to give notes to you personally or to the whole company is your call.

McGonigal is keen to stress that as the company emerges from the final stages in the rehearsal room, actors should continue to feel that they are supported and nurtured by their director in continually developing their scenes. This is especially important in the final stages of the rehearsal, as is the way in which the director speaks to actors and gives notes following the dress rehearsals and early performances.

A professional company now physically moves out of the rehearsal room and into the theatre space for a week – possibly two – of technical and dress rehearsals, as well as preview performances and opening to a live audience. If you are working in a student, small-scale or community capacity, these stages will still happen; however, the time scale may be considerably compressed and may even be condensed into a matter of a few hours in situations like the Edinburgh Festival Fringe. On pages 151–2, I will work through the key steps a professional production will ordinarily take and then offer some hints and tips as to how to compress these steps into shorter time periods, should the need arise.

The technical period, in which all production elements are put together, is about leading with energy and working to make quick and informed decisions. Decisions will be made constantly, with some elements cut and some new ones added, with some initial ideas changing and adapting, as the director with their team respond instinctively to the work being pieced together. As a director, you will find yourself making both creative and technical decisions throughout this stage. Ideally, these will be made in consultation with colleagues, but there may be occasions where it is down to you as director to make a decision and implement it, since your role involves having an overview of the complete picture. Even if the director takes a unilateral decision, they must still collaborate with their teams to realize it.

Most importantly, the director must be transparent when articulating the reasons behind the decision, to ensure that everyone is on board with it.

Ideally, many choices made in the technical stage will have been pre-empted at production meetings and in the rehearsal room. As a director, I like to be clear in rehearsals about why we are doing things in a certain way, if it relates to a production element the company physically cannot work with in rehearsals. Production meetings and daily rehearsal notes should prevent any major last-minute changes, but in my experience, adaptations are inevitable. There might also be completely new elements that will have been impossible to work with in the rehearsal room, including automated scenery, revolves, pyrotechnics and flying (both of scenery and cast). All these need to be put in place safely and calmly.

The director will also need to be highly supportive of their actors. As Meir suggested earlier, this is particularly important in the transition from the rehearsal room, given that most productions work in separate spaces and without the luxury of the design elements. That said, the director's key collaborators during this period are their creative teams, technicians, programmers, production and stage managers and crew: they must have the full focus of the director. The actors have been immersed in the world of the story and building the production for several weeks, but the teams the director is now working with – who may sometimes meet for the first time on the day that the production moves into the auditorium – need full attention. The director knows the show intimately by this stage, but many of the team will not, since it is not always financially possible to have them attend all rehearsals and production meetings. Team members will have been reliant on their heads of department for information, as well as the rehearsal notes from the DSM. The director, working alongside their immediate creative team of designers, choreographers, fight directors, musical directors and so on, must ensure they explain what is being sought and – more importantly – why. If the director has empowered the actors during the process in the rehearsal room, they should now be able to solve any problems by taking ownership of their own roles within the technical period, rather than waiting for the director or CM to supply them with every note.

I want to point readers again to the 'Reset Better' charter that I mentioned in Stage One. Conceived during the pandemic by the Production Managers' Forum (PMF) and now expanded into a cross-industry working group, the core aim of this initiative is to operate in a post-pandemic world with a better balance struck between work and personal life. The charter itself states: 'We will strive to achieve five-day work weeks, an end to three-session days, encouraging and embedding job flexibility/sharing. We will plan better. We will be smarter.'[1] Many theatres, drama schools and universities have signed up to this pledge, with technical periods taking place over longer periods of time so as to eliminate evening calls wherever possible. There are increasing efforts to schedule individuals to work for five days (even if there are six days of activity) and to send out weekly calls in advance, to enable people to plan their working weeks. Think how you as a director can work within the principles of the 'Reset Better' charter, more details of which can be found in Stage One, page 49.

How to run a technical rehearsal: The principles

Band calls, sitzprobes and soundchecks

Any production with music – especially musicals and pantomimes – will need time allocated for the music prior to the main technical rehearsal. In the first place, the band or orchestra will need time to rehearse the music together and to integrate any live elements with recorded tracks, as well as getting used to any in-ear monitors or 'clicks' (which are used like a metronome, to ensure that recorded and live elements synchronize). It is often the case that the full band will not be in place until the later stages of rehearsal, so they need time together. These sessions are led by the musical director: the director needs to enable these sessions to happen but should otherwise refrain from interfering!

Following the band call, a sitzprobe[2] can be scheduled, where the actors are fitted with microphones and get a feel for the full sound they will be singing with. In rehearsals, they may have been accompanied only by a piano or a basic arrangement. Unless working on an actor-musician show, or with

---

[1] The rest of the charter can be accessed here: https://www.productionmanagersforum.org/wp-content/uploads/2021/04/The-Reset-Better-Charter.pdf.
[2] The German *Sitzprobe* literally means 'seated rehearsal', although performers will rarely sit down in practice. If the performers are onstage, they may move around to check that they can hear themselves and the band from the different locations on the stage from which they will be performing. Sound monitors should be available around the space so that actors can hear each other and the band, especially the keys and melody. The Italian opera term *prove all'italiana* is occasionally still used in place of sitzprobe.

considerable resources, it is rare for the full band and/or finished tracks to be in the room. Actors need time to acclimatize, so this is an important part of the process. If the sitzprobe is held onstage, the sound engineer is also able to explore basic levels in the playing space, ensuring that the band is properly mixed, with appropriate sound levels for each individual instrument and with vocals heard over the level of the band. Frequently, however, the sitzprobe will take place in the rehearsal room with free-standing microphones. This part of the process is often a thrilling one for the director to be part of, but it is the musical director's session and unless there is something urgent, I will allow them to lead. The director then can listen to the entire sound world and I have often picked up on additional performance clues during this period. Parts of the arrangement or orchestration – particularly in complex works such as Sondheim musicals – can inform an additional acting choice. Similarly, hearing the fully underscored transition into a musical number might suddenly offer a deeper sense of the mood and tone, which could provide hints as to how the lighting, for example, could change at this point.

If a sitzprobe is not possible, but microphones are to be used in the production, then a quick 'mic check' will often be required before the technical rehearsal proper commences. Here, the sound technician can fit personal microphones onto the actors, ensure that the microphones are working correctly and in the right positions, and have the actors deliver a few lines, so that they are happy with the sound levels. After individual checks, the technician will sometimes ask for group dialogue or singing to check the levels and balance across the company. As with all the above stages, the director needs an awareness of what they are for and of what they will entail, but should allow the relevant technical teams to lead on these, ensuring that there is time in the schedule for these crucial steps.

Plot sessions for lighting, sound and audiovisual elements

Prior to the actors arriving onstage to slowly piece all the elements together, several plotting sessions are usually scheduled. This is where the lighting (LX), sound (SFX) and audiovisual (AV) elements – including projections, LED walls, animations and other technologies – can be 'plotted' into the lighting and sound boards which run the technology. These will be controlled by the operators, but prior to this there may be several programmers who literally programme the lighting states, AV sequences and sound levels into the boards. Programmers are highly skilled and work closely with their respective designers, who will frequently have preferred collaborators that understand their styles and ways of working, and therefore how to work at speed efficiently and creatively. The plotting sessions offer an opportunity for the designers to incorporate some states and levels into the sound and lighting boards, prior to the technical rehearsal.

As a director, I will always check with my designers as to whether they need me present for the plotting sessions. Often, designers like to have the first plotting session with their programmers to themselves; if long-term collaborators are involved, the director can completely trust this to their creative team. There would have been many meetings and discussions prior to this stage; wherever possible, designers will have attended several run-throughs that allowed an opportunity afterwards to liaise with the director. If this is the case, then the director should certainly allow the designers to get on with plotting what they need to. If the lighting programmers have been unable to programme the intelligent (moving) lights into the boards prior to this stage, they will also need to do this during these early sessions. Similarly, sound designers can ensure that stacks of sound cues are in place in their QLab (or equivalent software).

For technically complex pieces, I prefer to plot everything all together, ensuring that sound, LX and AV integrate and speak to each other. Timecoding may require extra time prior to plotting, since this is a system whereby lighting cues are synchronized with music, AV and sound, rather than everything being individually cued by the DSM. This is particularly useful in, say, a rock-and-roll number, where numerous lighting states may need to be fired on specific musical beats. Where a production has fewer sound cues, I will plot these separately. As a director, I never like to call people in only to leave them to hang about and wait: respecting the team's time is important.

Working from the top of the show, we then build these technical elements before the actors arrive. The designers often use headphones ('cans') to communicate with their programmers and operators, as the DSM sits nearby, writing all of the cues into a fully annotated script ('the book'), so that they will know where to instruct the technical team and crew to initiate cues (or, in theatre-speak, to 'go'). The creative team need space to bring their skills and expertise to the production and the director should try not to micromanage, but support and encourage, giving notes where useful and ensuring that all the elements are unified. What the director will be looking for will depend on the production: a realistic play may need key lights in the

LX state (where the light must look as if it is coming from a realistic source, such as a window or lamp), but these must blend with the additional atmospheric and tonal qualities of each lighting state to create and add narrative layers. A musical may demand more varied states throughout (even multiple states within numbers), with ballads requiring more atmosphere and production, or finale numbers potentially requiring heightened vibrancy and colour. Regarding sound, there may be momentary realistic elements that are heard through speakers placed on the set, such as phone or doorbell effects (sometimes called 'spot effects'), through to more stylistic effects, drones, underscores and soundscapes. Levels and intensities will need to be basically set for each cue, as will the location from which the sound will emanate. Timings will need to be established, too: whether the effect is in isolation, or a crossfade; whether it is prolonged or a quick 'snap up'. Again, the designers will guide the director in terms of what they believe works best within the frame that has been established. If working on a piece with musical numbers, I will always bring my choreographer into the plotting sessions, since they will often want to contribute to the overall look and feel of the numbers they have been staging.

As a director, I spend a lot of time with the team considering the first experience that the audience have when they enter the auditorium, before the story actually begins. This sets the scene for the world into which they will be transported, transitioning from real life into the life of the production. Director Robert Icke points out that he places the audience at the heart of his directorial process, over and above everything else. In an interview for *The Stage* newspaper, Icke explains how he does not take his audience for granted, but wants his theatre to '[excite] the audience and [for] everyone to lean forward in their seats' (Gardner 2024: 13). The plotting session allows the creative team to think about the first encounter that the audience have with the world in terms of an experience: does this encounter offer a flavour of the style, genre, mood and atmosphere of the piece through the production values? This is key, since some members of the audience may potentially be sitting in their seats for up to half an hour before the show starts. This pre-show experience might even be designed to deliberately be at odds with the show itself, to make a startling impact, or to lull the audience into a false sense of security.

I do not always plot things in order. In a play that follows a psychologically realistic path, I may do. Plotting out of order needs consultation with your designers and is often more useful for stylistic pieces, musicals or pantomimes. For example, if the production features a major transformation such as the end of the first act of the pantomime *Cinderella*, or a key 'show-stopping moment' in a musical such as the rain sequence in *Singin' in the Rain*, this allows time and space to put all the component parts in place freshly, without rushing, as well as giving the team a more concrete base for entering the technical rehearsal with the cast. Simpler scenes can then potentially be augmented and built during the rehearsal proper. By the end of the plotting sessions, something should ideally be programmed into the boards and sound stacks for each cue and state for the whole production. These can then be changed, built upon and augmented when the actors are present, performing in costume. Throughout all the plotting sessions, each lighting state will have ideally been programmed and created along with the scenic elements, including the set and furniture, so often the stage management and flying crew are called upon to undertake the scene changes. This also allows for a scene change rehearsal before the technical rehearsal. If there is the luxury of time, the team are sometimes able to squeeze in an additional scene change rehearsal and this is invaluable if a complex and detailed set has been designed.

Technical rehearsals

The technical rehearsals bring all the production components together with the acting company. Working slowly and methodically through the production from start to finish allows everybody to build the show in sequence, getting to know its practical rhythms and the traffic of people and scenic elements, both on- and offstage. As the jigsaw assembles, the technical rehearsal finalizes who is doing what at any point. It allows for rehearsal of the scene changes and the perfecting of the production overall: it is here that the director ensures that each ingredient is perfectly prepared and blended to be delivered to the metaphorical plate simultaneously. Personally, as I know the guts of the production mechanics, I tend to run my own technical rehearsals from the auditorium, supported by my PM and the CSM from the side of the stage; in turn, both will liaise via headphones with all departments, working out the logistics and supporting with any problems that need solving.

Prior to starting the tech rehearsal, I ensure that everyone receives a full introduction. It will often be the first time that some roles on the stage crew or roles like follow-spot operators will have met anyone on the team and building an inclusive environment where everybody's contribution and role is recognized is crucial for a harmonious technical period. Everyone is a cog in the storytelling wheel. The director can then set the mood for a supportive, collaborative technical period. After these introductions, I set out the principles of how the technical will be run. Mine are very practical and as follows:

- We will all be building the parts of the show slowly, safely and methodically. There will be lots of stopping and starting, but that's entirely OK.
- We will all ensure that we are patient, kind and considerate to one another, especially during the first session, as we all find a new rhythm. This is especially true of getting into the show and through the first scene, which is notorious for taking some considerable time. While we have targets to meet, we need to support each other and work collectively.
- The actors can solve problems for themselves as much as possible, liaising with the PM and CSM if there are any issues that affect other people, or any health and safety considerations.
- The actors should wear full costume for the technical rehearsal. This is as important to the design team to see what works under lights and with the set as it is for the practical purposes of seeing how feasible any quick changes of costume may be.
- The DSM is essentially 'out of bounds' to the actors. This can be somewhat tricky to navigate at first, as the DSM has been a key ally of the actors throughout rehearsal and a constant conduit for communication. However, at this stage, the DSM needs their full concentration to focus on running the technical and building the 'book' of cues. Questions about breaks and scheduling, as well as other concerns, should now be directed to the PM and CSM to answer. The DSM now effectively becomes the production's conductor, deftly orchestrating events and sensitively cueing all elements of the show, in order to ensure the production's rhythms are maintained.
- It will often fall to the CSM or director to call 'stop' (and sometimes with surprising frequency) to pause the action to allow time for the creative, stage and technical teams to fix issues as they arise. Actors, too, must feel empowered to stop the technical rehearsal, since they must feel comfortable and safe in a scene, and they may encounter issues with costume or set. When 'stop' is called, the actors should remain physically where they are onstage. When everyone is ready to start again, the CM or DSM will provide a line from which the action

will resume; this may rewind through half a page or so of script. There will then usually be a 'thank you' from the CSM or director, which is the equivalent of the call of 'action' on a film set.

- We will always stop before a scene change or a quick change of costume. This allows space to check that everyone is comfortable with everything so far and ready to move on. We will then rehearse the scene change, without costume changes. Once we are comfortably through the scene change, we will then repeat it, layering in the costume elements to time any quick or complicated changes. Before moving on, I check that all departments – including the actors – are happy and gauge whether we need another attempt at the section.
- The actors are encouraged to keep one eye on their creative choices while their key focus is on technical elements. If they remain open to possibilities and discoveries, there may be more to find, even at this late stage.
- If it is a musical that we are rehearsing, then a vocal and physical warm-up may be required. The company need to be physically and vocally prepared so that sound levels can be set to where they would be in the show and to check whether all dance moves can be undertaken in full in costume. A short warm-up is essential to meet the vocal heath needs of the performers. The actors should also be reminded to keep warm and to look after themselves during periods of time that they are not being used (which may be prolonged at points where scene changes need to be re-run).
- It will be made clear anything that will require special space and time during the tech. This could include fight calls and intimacy coordination. We will also make clear if any sequences will be worked on out of sequence and, if so, for what reason.
- Encouraging the actors to sit at the back of the auditorium, or in the circle or balconies during the technical rehearsal when (and if) they have periods of time free offers the company the chance to get a sense of the playing space, as well as the techniques needed to fill the room physically and vocally.
- The director should let the company know that they will try, as far as possible, to move around the auditorium to be the eyes of the audience to resolve sight lines and focus issues.
- The director should also give a rough sense of where they would preferably like/need to be by the end of any given technical session, so that everyone has a goal to work towards.

- Finally, this is a time for the director to metaphorically wave goodbye, as they will next properly see the actors in the dress rehearsal. The company won't be running the piece in its entirety or in real time until that dress rehearsal, which may in some cases be a week away. There is little point, then, in concentrating too much in relation to the acting at this stage. Nevertheless, if space and opportunity present themselves, the director might be able to find time to tidy up/work on little sections, or to give some notes.

Following this, the PM or CSM must be given time to brief the company, too, as there will be health and safety issues to be discussed and demonstrations that need to be held; these might relate to pyrotechnics, illusions and effects, trapdoors or other scenic elements. Finally, a walk around the space is undertaken, led by the PM or CM, so that the company can see any backstage props tables and quick-change areas. Actors can also start to think about backstage traffic and travel, such as the backstage mechanics of getting from one side of the stage to the other. I often accompany the actors here so that I understand what is possible and what is not.

And then the technical rehearsal proper begins.

As a director, always keep your primary focus on the creative and technical teams. Communication is key. They may have seen only one or two run-throughs and you cannot expect them to know the production as well as you do. It is imperative that you keep communicating what you are trying to achieve and *why*, if something isn't working, not just *how* you are trying to achieve it. In return, listen to their needs and questions. I was involved in one production at a venue where I didn't know the team, nor did they know me; during the technical rehearsal, we all struggled to achieve one of the production's effects. We went and sat in the auditorium as I articulated verbally what I felt the effect should look and feel like from the perspective of the audience. With this visualization and the subsequent collective discussion among the team, we were able to achieve together the magical look needed for that moment.

Always keep an eye out for creative opportunities during the technical period. Breakthrough and 'aha' moments can happen here, too: the technical isn't merely a case of cementing rehearsal room decisions. I've had many exciting moments when I have seen spatial opportunities to rework something, from the proxemics, set and lighting of the Prince-to-Beast transformation in *Beauty and the Beast*, to working more closely with light, sound and the actors' positionings in the scenes set on the moor in an adaptation of *The Hound of the Baskervilles*.

Alongside the PM/CM, it is the director who fundamentally makes the call as to whether everybody is ready and happy to move on to the next scene or bit. The director's role is to ensure that everyone stays calm and focused while moving forwards and to ensure that any unforeseen challenges that face the creative teams do not affect the actors. Asking what the reason for the wait is, when there is a pause, allows both the director and the actors to understand and appreciate how long something might take, and to gauge whether there are other things that can reasonably be worked on during this time.

Always remember that your waiting period is someone else's working period.

At the end of the final 'formal' technical session, I request some expansion time in the schedule, prior to the dress rehearsals commencing. This is not always possible, but – if the time is available – it can be used in any of the following ways:

- an emergency technical session, if the technical rehearsal overruns;
- an opportunity for lighting and sound designers to continue to plot or shape the states and cues;
- an opportunity to undertake further 'dry runs' of any scene changes;
- a call for specific actors and crew to run any particularly demanding and complicated sequences;
- an opportunity for stage management and crew to work through their snagging lists.

Alternatively, where needed, this can provide a much-needed additional session 'off', for everyone to rest prior to dress rehearsals.

Running a dress rehearsal

I always plan at least two dress rehearsals. The first dress rehearsal is the first time we aim to run the show as it will be presented in front of an audience, combining all elements together. Actors are in full costumes, with any wigs, hair styling and make-up as they would be under show conditions. This dress rehearsal is often 'closed', meaning that there are no outside eyes as it offers a low-stakes opportunity to run without the pressure of visitors and enables the run to be stopped if necessary. Stopping the show should not be done lightly, as many things can be fixed at a later stage; it should only be done if it is a matter of health and safety or other unavoidable necessity. It is crucial for stage management, the costume department, the crew and the actors to start to embody the flow of the show, and to get a sense of this the show needs to run in real time. Sometimes this first run is called a 'tech-dress' to take into account that there may be some stops and starts.

The second dress rehearsal should not be halted, unless it is a matter of health and safety. During the first dress rehearsal, the actors will be concentrating on technical elements, as well as their entrances, exits, quick changes and backstage traffic. As a director, I am also more focused on the technical aspects here as the production teams are, for the first time, piecing together the jigsaw of the production in real time and they will often be focused on getting through this. In contrast, the second dress allows more of a sense of flow, as everybody becomes more familiar with the production mechanics. This is where I refocus my attention back on the actors and their journey through the story. From speaking to actors over the years, the second dress is when they believe they can genuinely start to reconnect with their rehearsal room work.

So, when is it best to give notes in this period? After the first dress rehearsal, I will frequently go through technical and production notes with the various heads of departments. Often, they will have their own notes sessions with their teams, and I will always offer a caveat before giving my notes, along the lines of: 'I know you will know some of this, but I'm just saying what I saw and experienced.' The team has only had one opportunity to run the production through and these notes need to be given honestly, but with care and compassion. Even where the principles of 'Reset Better' are in play, everyone is often tired coming out of the technical rehearsal and into dress rehearsals and giving the production their all. A director does not need to be heavy-handed when talking to the team about elements that have not run as smoothly as they might.

I rarely give actors notes after the first dress rehearsal. They are finding their feet with the storytelling once again, as well as layering in additional elements and it may have been a week since they last ran the production at show speed (and that was likely to have been in the rehearsal room). I may give some broad notes, mainly about reconnecting with rehearsal discoveries and the final run-through, as well as any relating to health and safety concerns. The actors need a second opportunity to run the piece to begin to bed in, especially as the second dress rehearsal will often be an 'open' one, with friends or volunteers of the theatre in the space, as well as producers and artistic directors, who will be giving the director notes, too.

Following the second dress, I try to schedule an appropriate time prior to the first performance to give notes. For the production team, this is often straightaway since they need time to undertake any technical amendments. With cast notes, the actors need an opportunity to rest after the dress rehearsals, but there also needs to be sufficient time to allow them some space to reflect on and consolidate any amendments prior to opening. The notes given at this stage should preferably feel similar in tone and quality to those given in the rehearsal room. I have now started to try to find an open space to work notes, rather than giving notes around the table, so that we can work physically if needs be; however, this isn't always possible. Actors will also have their own notes. However the notes session is organized, ensure that it remains a dialogue, as discussed in the stages above, and allow your co-creatives such as musical directors an opportunity to give and work their notes. This is why a practical space is often useful.

I will also find actors to give individual notes, as something that may be quite a major change is best communicated to those individuals first. This allows for much more of a private conversation. A confidential chat is often much appreciated, particularly if there is something sensitive or personal to be discussed.

Directors will also receive their own notes from the producer or artistic director. Again, I welcome these openly, as I, too, may be sufficiently tired from the intensive technical period to be fully objective, so this chance for feedback and an alternative perspective is much appreciated.

Previews, first nights, press nights and beyond

Previews are deliberately designed to allow a company to have an audience prior to official opening and offer space and time in the day before an evening show to continue to work on the production. Preview periods might be anywhere from one day to several weeks, depending on scale, finance and need. They can be used for amendments and adjustments, as well as allowing the show to bed in; the price can be substantially lower for audience members as a result. The press does not attend, to allow the production to gain its momentum and confidence, which means that the creative team and cast can experience their work in a low-stakes environment, ascertaining audience responses and reactions. A director, working with their teams, might decide on one or more of the following courses of action after each preview performance:

- Working with the writer to explore cuts, rewriting and restructuring of scenes or other elements, or even add in new scenes and elements. Some new musicals will use this period to cut some songs and replace them with others. In some remarkable cases, I have even known preview stages to introduce new characters. The writer may need time to undertake these changes and the director needs to negotiate as to when it is reasonable to deliver these amendments. The wider creative team will also need time to rehearse and work new elements: it may be too much to ask for an entirely new number to be choreographed for the second preview, but feasible for the third.
- Looking at cuts or trims needed to sharpen the storytelling, if the work is an existing one. This is the task of the director; occasionally with a classical play I have changed odd words when it has become clear that the audience are not grasping what is being said, when it is important to a crucial plot point.
- Re-rehearsing will obviously be necessary in the case of all the above. Equally, the director may want to call additional rehearsals, not necessarily to make changes but to bed in work, sharpen and consolidate.
- Working with designers and potentially the cast, the director may need to re-plot and run any scenic elements technically.
- The director may not call a rehearsal or alter anything, but give and work notes prior to another preview, to gauge what the audience's experience and reactions are. It is often too hasty to make any significant changes based on one performance.

How directors arrive at these decisions will always be a balance of the head and the heart, the subjective and the objective. I personally try to sense whether the audience are captured and held by the story. Are they bored? Shuffling? Losing interest? Are there laughs where I was expecting there to be? Is the tone or pace working? Is there an emotional connection to the piece? Are there reactions in the places I had anticipated there would be? These are just some of the prompts I use to sense what I might do the next day. It's crucial that the stage management and crew are aware of any changes and – liaising with the PM and heads of department – have sufficient time to ensure that any changes suggested do not have any other unintentional knock-on effects that the director has not foreseen. As a director, you must check that everyone is happy before cementing any major changes.

If there are no previews, then the first night will invariably have higher stakes. A director may not have time to make fundamental changes, but responding to the audience's reaction and responses to the piece is still key. The director can sharpen, deepen and change bits through notes sessions and there may well still be space in the schedule to do some more minor reworking.

At some point in the first week a press night will be held, which is intended to include representation from national and local press, trade papers and media outlets, as well as (increasingly) social media critics and bloggers. More and more as a director you will need to be aware that while there is an official press night, critical opinions from audience members (both those who offer opinions professionally and recreationally) can proliferate online throughout the run, thanks to social media. These opinions can dramatically inform audience expectations and influence ticket sales. Bear in mind, too, that scheduling may dictate that the opening night may well also be the press night, raising the stakes higher still. Throughout all of this, the director's duty is to support the actors and creative team as the production is shared with an audience. Whether it is a question of a quick notes session, or the wholesale re-fashioning of an entire act, a caring, considerate and collegiate approach is required.

Returning to a run of a show as a director can be an uncanny experience. The production should now be owned by the company (both cast and crew) and the director becomes more of a guest at the party. A well-timed and judicious notes session, with the director now being a fresh outside eye, is welcomed if handled well. If changes have been made in the director's absence, then ascertaining why this is the case from the CM and the cast is important, if this hasn't already been made clear from the show reports[3]. The director's notes must be in the context of how the production is bedding in. Some variations may be because of notes given by an artistic director or producer during the early performances; they are at liberty to make changes and often the director is contracted only for the first couple of shows, so will not be on hand later in that first week. The director should not take this personally, since the show does not belong to them by this stage as the piece beds in, evolves and develops. Where it is more than reasonable to intervene

---

[3] After each production, a report is compiled by stage management, with running times, crew names and notes of illness and health and safety issues. The reports have a section for each department (lighting, set, costume and so on) with notes about anything that did not run as expected or intended, as well as any cues missed, costume malfunctions, requests, audience reactions and other elements. Each department will monitor the notes and act upon them accordingly. As a director, the first thing I look for is the running time. If, for example, it is expanding, I aim to ascertain whether an element of the show is dragging and, if so, why this might be.

is where the changes made fundamentally sit outside of the production frame established in the early stages of development.

Advice for shorter time periods

Resources being what they are, there are often one or two, rather than four, plotting sessions. There may only be one dress rehearsal, and the preview and press night may well be bundled up with the opening night. In the context of productions in drama schools, universities and community contexts, there will likely be a short run, with the director remaining throughout the run to keep working on the show. In some contexts, such as the Edinburgh Festival Fringe, the technical and dress rehearsals may be combined (and compressed) and followed by an opening night on the same day. In such scenarios, the director should hold their nerve, keep collaborating and communicate with their cast and crew about how the time will be used. I always work backwards from opening night and cut my cloth accordingly. Above all, a director needs to be compassionate, and having a reduced technical and opening period brings with it additional challenges.

Following are some practical hints and tips to help with shorter time periods:

- Combining the plotting with the technical rehearsal allows you to plot the lighting, sound and other elements as you go.
- Plotting any complex elements in advance allows you to get ahead if you have a limited plotting period; the simpler elements can then be plotted during the technical rehearsal.
- Undertaking a 'cue-to-cue' technical, moving in and out of each technical cue, allows you to concentrate on quick changes and scene changes, as these might not have been rehearsed in advance. Additionally, select sections you won't need to tech and can skip past.
- Prioritizing retention of the band calls, sitzprobe and soundcheck where possible, if rehearsing a musical or pantomime, will pay dividends.
- Ensuring you are focusing on both technical elements and acting journeys if there is only one dress rehearsal will allow you to note both.
- Never cutting corners with health and safety elements is paramount: these trump everything. Keep everyone physically and mentally safe and include necessary fight and intimacy direction.

- Working out what battles are worth fighting, and what you are willing to let go is important when there is limited time for notes and reworking. Think about an order of priority and work out what you need to achieve.

Part Three

Interviews with Leading Theatre Directors

14 Tamara Harvey
15 Holly Race Roughan
16 Josie Rourke
17 Roy Alexander Weise

14

Tamara Harvey

TAMARA HARVEY *began her career as a directing intern at the Shakespeare Theatre of New Jersey and went on to become an Assistant Director at Shakespeare's Globe under Mark Rylance. In 2015, she was appointed Artistic Director of Theatr Clwyd. In June 2023, she became Co-Artistic Director of the Royal Shakespeare Company in tandem with Daniel Evans, former Artistic Director of Chichester Festival Theatre. Having regularly collaborated in the past, the two had applied for the post together. This interview was conducted just prior to her taking up that post.*

Which practitioners, practices, methodologies or techniques do you draw upon as a director?
I think the most constant influence, probably, is the director Tim Carroll,[1] whom I assisted early on, when he and I co-directed *Hamlet* for The Factory. I use a lot of exercises that he was using, or that stem from those exercises. The methodology – or the philosophy – behind what Tim does is how can we ensure that the performance is as alive as rehearsal? How can we ensure that we are discovering in the moment? Continuing to play, continuing to keep ourselves and each other off-balance? Rather than trying to recreate something that we discovered once in a rehearsal room and have flogged to death ever since. There's a term he uses that I love, which is 'WWIBL', which stands for 'what would it be like?'. And the notion behind it is: 'What would it be like, if we said it, and meant it?' And the idea that, fundamentally, if you strip everything else away, what you're trying to do is say the words in a way that has meaning. And where you mean them.

---

[1] From 1999 to 2005, Tim Carroll was Associate Director of Shakespeare's Globe, where he was an exponent of original practices. His productions of *Richard III* and *Twelfth Night* transferred to Broadway in 2013. He has also worked with the Factory Theatre Company in London, known for pop-up performances, where the only props used are those brought by the audience. He has been Artistic Director of Canada's Shaw Festival since 2015.

I think also that we can stray quite easily into: 'What's the right choice?' I mean, in terms of how we play this scene; in terms of the actor's intention. The other constant for me is that there is no 'absolute' version; there is no 'right' version. What we must figure out is what the most *interesting* version is. And often, we're only going to figure that out by trying it out. So, let's try it lots of different ways, because what I do strongly believe is that you can only figure out so much by talking about it, or by sitting around a table. Ultimately, you're going to discover more by standing up and doing it in the space. And I think that's one of the reasons that the most exciting work I've ever seen is by companies that have rehearsed and worked together for years. The one I'm thinking of in particular is the Maly Theatre of Moscow.[2] I saw a show of theirs that they'd rehearsed for seven years, and had been performing for twenty, by the time I saw it. You could tell that they'd gone through all the most predictable choices they could possibly have had in about the first year of rehearsal and got to somewhere so thrilling and so alive, that it felt as though you were watching something for the very first time – even though, when I saw it, it had been going on for twenty-seven years.

I'm wondering what happens for you when you recognize that things are getting potentially repetitious? Are there things that you do to unlock that? I'm very interested in that notion of it being for the first time, whether it's Shakespeare, pantomime, Chekhov or new writing.

Well, I think what you've always got in your *favour* as an actor is that there is someone else in the space who will change what you're doing, if you focus on them. So, whether that's the actor playing opposite you, or whether it's the audience, if you make sure you focus on the other person or people in the space, that will always shift things, just as it constantly does in life. And sometimes that can be the tiniest thing: the way that they blink; which word they blink in the middle of. You don't have to be looking at them: it might be that you hear something different in their breathing that can change and shift what you're doing. So, I think that there is something important about

---

[2] The Maly Theatre was established in Moscow in 1806, and rapidly gained a reputation for producing classical heritage plays. The repertoire has, in the past, included work by foreign dramatists such as Shakespeare, Molière, Pirandello and Schiller, but gradually shifted to more native writers, from Alexander Pushkin and Denis Fonvizin to Mikhail Bulgakov and Vasily Zhukovsky. By 2009, the Maly employed a company of over one hundred professional actors, touring as far afield as South Korea and Italy. Long runs have typified the Maly's repertoire: Schiller's *The Maid of Orleans*, which premiered in 1885, held the stage for eighteen years.

focusing on the other person – the other people – and what you're trying to do to them.

The other thing that I am influenced by is the notion of actioning. Whether you call it 'actioning', or whether you call it 'intentions', that's a tool I use – though again, I kind of guard against the notion of actioning every single line, or every half-sentence.

And I do sometimes just say, 'That is brilliant, that's working, so let's put it in our back pocket and try something else.' Sometimes, it's as simple as just suggesting a different thought. So, you know, throwing in points of concentration,[3] I find quite useful for changing things up, as well. I'm going to use *Robin Hood* as an example, as it's the last thing I directed at Theatr Clywd, and because I firmly believe that pantomime is as glorious – if not more glorious – an art form as almost anything else we do. So, for example, in a scene with Robin and Marian, it may be that his point of concentration is Scarlet: how does that change things? There are always a million things that you can change up, although I did once, as an assistant director, have an actor in the company who wanted a different point of concentration for every show. As the show was running for about three months, I was running out by the end!

Is that something you engender from day one of rehearsals, this notion of points of concentration?
It depends on the company and the piece. As you were asking that, I was thinking of an actor I worked with, not all that long ago, who was really thrown by the idea that things might be different every night. So, with that particular actor, I didn't push that, because that's not going to help anyone, if someone's feeling unsafe onstage and if that's not the thing that will help them in rehearsal and performance. Then, I think it's just counter-productive, to try to get them to do that. I find it tough if *none* of the actors in a company are interested in changing things up and keeping things fresh in that way, but if you've only got one or two, then all the other parts can keep moving around.

---

[3]Points of concentration are central to the methodology of practitioner Mike Alfreds as outlined in *Different Every Night* (2008). In simple terms, they are factors that can affect a character, their objective and the scene they are in. An environmental point of concentration is something from the outside world that may affect a character, such as the weather being hot. An individual point of concentration, using Alfreds's example, may be that a character has just been released from prison for theft, which may affect their behaviour when shopping, or when near authority figures. Points of concentration can, in this way, add layers to a scene and encourage the actor to think in more depth about how to play a scene.

Katie Mitchell[4] **talks about being explicit in the audition process: i.e. 'This is how I like to work; do you want to come on board?' Is that something you talk about at the audition stages as well, for people that you haven't previously worked with?**

Again, it depends on the piece. Continuing to use *Robin Hood* as an example, there are so many other things at play in that particular show. It's pantomime but with actor-musicians, and there are a whole load of songs to learn before anything else can happen; then there's a whole load of choreography. The scenes themselves are a relatively small part of the whole and the most important thing is that the audience will be having the best time of their lives. That might be particular to that art form, but maybe that's something we should be thinking about with every show we ever do. But with pantomime, they're having a really joyful, hilarious time. So, there are moments in that where it's a clear rhythmic element we have to achieve. For example, if you enter on that line, and pull out the prop on *that* line, it *will* get a laugh. And if you don't, it won't. And so that needs to stay the same and we can find other moments to play.

When I was doing auditions for that production, I didn't really talk about my methodology. But I think, even when I don't, the way that I am in the room and the notes that I might give in an audition hopefully give people a sense of how I work. Often in an audition you're giving a note purely in order to see whether the actor is willing to play and to what extent you speak the same language and if you can find common ground. And quite often they'll try it and then say, 'Oh, I'm not sure I got that,' or, 'I don't know if I quite delivered that note.' And then I'll often say, 'Who knows? I mean, we'd figure that out, wouldn't we? There is no "right". I don't know if that's the right note, but it's just about trying.' So, there are probably phrases that I use in an audition to give the sense that I am going to be looking for someone who's just up for trying and then falling and trying again, rather than specifically saying, 'Here is the way I'll be working.'

What I do try to ensure is that I have a smorgasbord, for both me and the actor to draw on. Also, if an actor has used a similar technique and has a different phrase or word for it, then brilliant! I'm never interested in insisting that my terminology, or my way of working, is absolute.

---

[4]Katie Mitchell's *The Director's Craft: A Handbook for the Theatre* was published in 2009. Originally directing for Welsh National Opera, Mitchell continues to direct for various opera houses, as well as the Royal Shakespeare Company, Royal Court and National Theatre. Her production of *Waves* at the National in 2006 blended theatre making with live video. She has also worked at Hamburg Schauspielhaus, Toneelgroep in Amsterdam and Bouffes du Nord in Paris, among others.

So you respond to an individual actor's need, yet, at the same time, pull a company together to work as one?
I think it's fundamental to the way that I work and also, as you've intimated, really tricky, because we might end up with two actors in the room with totally different working methodologies. And then the director must be a bridge. I think the other thing that can be tricky is where the play or the scene is weighted. I had a project recently where there was one very large central role and then a couple of other smaller roles. And inevitably – and necessarily – the person playing the big central role has the right, I think, to dictate a little how the room functions. But then part of your job as a director in that moment is to make sure that the other actors – even if moment by moment in the rehearsal room, they're not necessarily getting what they want – have space in the rehearsal process for them to work in the way that they need.

You've spoken about creating a safe and ethical space, one which considers everybody's needs in that room, either in terms of the planning of that schedule and/or in terms of how you work on the rehearsal room floor. You've spoken, too, about scheduling in advance, for people with caring responsibilities, making sure that there's that space for incubation and not filling every second of the day with work-time.
It's really important to me. I think, maybe, it's becoming easier as an artistic director to ask that of others. More people are really pushing the notion that we're all adults, we all have lives: we all need to be able to juggle those lives alongside whatever we're doing in the rehearsal room. We need to be respectful of other pressures in life, so I think perhaps that conversation has become a little bit more prevalent, though not necessarily as prevalent as I'd like.

You've often spoken about not being interested in emotion for the sake of emotion, but interested in the emotional by-product. How do you tackle emotional scenes in the rehearsal room?
My feeling about characters – and around character backgrounds as well – is that if an actor says to me, for example, 'Do you think really I had a very difficult relationship with my father and that's what I'm bringing to the scene?', then my response will always be, 'Does it make the scene more interesting? Does it give you a whole load of other things to play? And still allow the scene to be true? Let's make sure we're not bending it wildly out of shape. If it does work: fantastic. But, let's also try the version where you had

a really brilliant relationship with your father. Let's try both and see which throws up a more interesting version of the scene.' I don't really believe in absolutes for the sake of absolutes. The number of different ways to play a scene is infinite, and the choices that we make in the rehearsal room should keep as many of those different possibilities in the air as we can.

Do you do work on character backstories?
I'm open to having the conversation and to test in the room how they affect the scene, the work onstage. But I am unlikely to get the actors to write down every aspect of their history as an exercise. I think hotseating[5] can be useful, sometimes. And I think, again, it comes down to this idea of being responsive to the actor's individual needs. If I'm working with an actor for whom it is fundamental that they work out the intricacies of their backstory and if part of what they need is for me to hear that and share it, then I'm up for that. I would probably schedule a moment outside of the main call to do that, because I think the playing of the scenes is the business of everyone in the room and because I think part of the way that you make discoveries and part of the way you get to the point where you can be completely alive onstage is by saying the words as much as possible.

When do your actors need to learn their lines by?
My ideal would be that everyone turned up on the first day off-book. I absolutely don't believe in the argument that says, 'But I might learn it in a certain way and it'll get stuck!' If that's true, then we're doomed, because there's going to be a point in rehearsal where you know it and if you're telling me that you can't make any changes once you know it, then we're totally shot!

I think it's slightly different for new writing: with some writers, the rehearsal draft is basically the Bible and you might change a couple of words; with others, the play will change massively in rehearsals. But I think the sooner you get off-book, the more freedom you have. I do get frustrated when the rehearsal room is treated as an extension of the learning process; when all I'm doing is being a glorified line-partner and we're having to work our way agonizingly through the scenes. If we take a four-week rehearsal

---

[5] As noted in Part Two, page 91, hotseating is an exercise whereby a character steps out of the drama to sit in an appointed chair (the 'hotseat') in front of the rest of the actors. A director will sometimes facilitate as the actors question the character. The questions can feed into the motivations, beliefs, background, experiences and behaviour of the character, as well as events in their life (as depicted onstage, or taking place offstage). The exercise is designed to encourage exploration of character, but is also a good exercise in improvisational ability.

process, for example, I certainly think that as you're heading into week three and you're coming at the scenes for the second or the third time, you should be off-book. But it's really noticeable to me that the actors that I admire most tend to turn up, day one, off-book. I think what's tricky is that I would love to be able to say to every actor I work with, 'Turn up, day one, off-book.' But, if you're going to do that, then I think you must pay them for their time before rehearsals and then you get into a situation where the finances are impossible. So, it's a balancing act, isn't it?

Let's talk about your work on classic plays. I really liked how honest you were in an interview[6] while you were directing *Uncle Vanya*; you said something along the lines of, 'Oh my gosh! It's Chekhov! And there's an *expectation* around doing this play.'

I think there is an 'extra bit' with classic plays, around making sure everyone understands what they're saying, which I think you can't take as a given, perhaps, in the way that you would with a new play. So, for example, we're just rehearsing Laura Wade's *Home, I'm Darling* again, because it's going on tour. With that play, I would say that with ninety-eight out of a hundred lines, the actors understand what they're saying; they understand the words on the page. That just isn't true with a Shakespeare play, for example. I think it's really important to spend time making sure that the words become as familiar as any contemporary word, and that even if 'incarnadine' in *Macbeth* isn't an everyday word – by the way, how *do* you pronounce that? 'Incarna-*dyne*'? Incarna-*deen*?' Anyway, even if it's not a word that we use every day, that you get to the point where it feels as though it is. And so, I do exercises around the repetition of words, where the actor opposite you can repeat back any word you say, if they feel the need to hear it again, if they just don't feel like it's landing. And you have to say it again and then they can repeat it back at you as many times as they like and you *have* to keep saying it, until they stop repeating it, which is the point at which they're happy that they've kind of got it. It's twofold: everyone speaking knows what they're saying; everyone listening understands what's being said to them, because that can't be a given.

And then there's something really important to me around the verse form and knowing where the rhythm lies and where the line-endings are, even if you choose to ignore them. I think of it a little like jazz. A jazz musician will have played scales hundreds and hundreds of times. They may then play

---

[6]Harvey was interviewed by Rosemary Waugh for *Exeunt Magazine*, hours before the premiere of *Uncle Vanya*, co-produced by Theatr Clwyd and Sheffield Theatres in October 2017. The full text of the interview can be found here: https://exeuntmagazine.com/features/tamara-harvey-interview/.

around with them, to the most wonderful extent, but they know where they are; they know where those notes are. And I think it's really important with the verse to know where you're stretching it, where the tension lies. If you're choosing to emphasize a word that the verse doesn't naturally ask you to emphasize, then you should know that you're doing that.

There are a thousand clues in Shakespeare, and by examining the verse form, you'll come across all those clues. I think there's an interesting thing that happens sometimes, where if you completely ignore the verse – particularly the lines and the line-endings – you might naturally fall into just going sentence to sentence, or punctuation mark to punctuation mark which is, of course, not at all lifelike, in terms of how we speak. Actually (and increasingly so, throughout his later plays) Shakespeare's line-endings give you that kind of unfinished thought, or that breath in the middle of a sentence. So, I think there's a whole load of stuff around the meanings of the words, and the verse form, that is necessarily different.

How do you cultivate the actors' relationships with their audiences?
I am not someone who ignores the fact that the audience are going to be there. I don't try to pretend that we're doing this just for art's sake; that feels disingenuous to me, because theatre is fundamentally about storytelling and about sharing that story. But at the same time, I think it's very dangerous to assume we know how the audience is going to respond. Once you get into previews, the audience start to tell you stuff. And what's always fascinating about previews is that sometimes the audience will react completely differently from one night to the next, and you'll think that you've got something and then you haven't!

With regard to audiences, too, I don't like to write programme notes, because I think the work *is* the programme note. And I also think that one of the extraordinary and beautiful things about theatre is that if you have one hundred people in the audience, there will be one hundred different opinions as to what that play was about, or what it was trying to tell you. And I think that sometimes, we tend to see that as a bad thing, but I think it's an amazing thing.

One of the things that I guess has shifted slightly for me is having people in the rehearsal room more often. And I think it's a balance. Daniel[7] and I

---

[7] Daniel Evans was appointed Co-Artistic Director of the Royal Shakespeare Company in June 2023, in tandem with Harvey. Previously he was Artistic Director of Sheffield Theatres, where he directed productions including *Oliver!* (2013) and *Flowers for Mrs. Harris* (2016). From 2015, he was Artistic Director of Chichester Festival Theatre, where he directed *Me and My Girl* (2018) and *Local Hero* (2022), among others.

were talking about this recently, because we differ slightly in this. Of course, it needs to be a safe space and the actors need to feel like they can fail and all of that might seem to be at odds with having people in, but I think it's really important that everyone in the company feels that they are part of the work. There's also something important for me in trying to ensure that the moment when you go from the rehearsal room to the theatre isn't a massive shock to the system, which – if you've had a really closed room – I think it can be. Whereas if you've had people in and sitting around – not all the time and not indiscriminately – as part of the process, then that moment that you go into the theatre is not quite as horrifying.

15

Holly Race Roughan

HOLLY RACE ROUGHAN *is Artistic Director of Headlong Theatre and was formerly Associate Director of Kestrel, a theatre company that works within the criminal justice system. As a director she has worked at Shakespeare's Globe, Chichester Festival Theatres, the Royal Court, the Liverpool Everyman and Leeds Playhouse, among others. She has previously worked in an associate and assistant director capacity for the National Theatre, the Royal Shakespeare Company, the Royal Court and the Royal Exchange in Manchester.*

Could you talk me through your pre-production process, from why you choose a particular project or play, to the process of design and how you create the world, to why you do what you do, prior to entering a rehearsal room?

I frequently direct and commission new plays, which means that I'm often involved at the very inception of an idea. So I go on a long journey with a play, which means that by the time I get into rehearsals, I may have worked with a playwright on anywhere between three to eight drafts. The play will be in my bones by then. Because of that, by the time I reach rehearsals, I need to move consciously out of the role of the dramaturg to the role of director.

Dramaturgy is part of a director's skill set but can stand alone as a separate skill. It's about making the play the best possible version of itself and helping a writer to realize the story they want to tell. It's a midwife role, rather than a co-creation role. But there has to be quite a clear cut-off point, where I'm transitioning out of that role of midwifery into directing: into thinking about how I'm going to stage the best possible production of this play. Which is very different to thinking about how I'm going to help create the best possible script. When directing I see myself as the play's first audience member. I'm now advocating for the audience. As a director I work mostly on instinct, so I leave a lot of the decision making until I'm in a room with the actors and with the creative team.

There are some directors I would describe more as 'auteurs', where their role in the process is lead artist. They have a strong vision for the production, which they work to create with their team. I'm the other way around: I'm more like an editor. I create space to experiment in the rehearsal room and wait for my colleagues to offer ideas and exciting possibilities which then I edit, riff off and shape, working from instinct.

If I've been helping to develop a new play, as discussed, the play is in my bones and I'm not having to do an intense level of discovery work during rehearsal. When directing a play I haven't developed, this changes: for example my 2022 production of *Henry V* at the Globe. I was still discovering what that play was about, right up until the final night, after six months of performances. In terms of preparing for rehearsal, I go through the whole play and identify the main events of the story, which I write on Post-it notes. That means that at the point in week three or four in the rehearsals – most rehearsal processes last four weeks – where I can't see the wood for the trees, I can return to these main events, to remind me what the important story beats are. By that point, I find you don't always know what the important beats are, because you're so in it. You start to think that the moment that someone, say, puts a plate away is just as crucial as the moment that somebody hides a knife. So, I come back to my Post-it notes and think, 'What is the actual story? What does the audience need to pay most attention to in order to follow it enthrallingly?' And then I'm able to sharpen those moments and make sure that the production is clearly communicating and prioritizing those moments. It becomes my roadmap. If a musician is playing the wrong notes too loudly, you won't hear the song as it was intended. Of course, sometimes that can be exciting, but often I find the play won't work properly if you don't land the story's beats.

The other preparation that I often do is to break down the script into mini-events, inspired by Stanislavski. To do this, I draw a line after each significant change in the scene, breaking it down into short sections. Each section is a dramatic brick if you like: together they make up the scene. Then I label them in a way that sums up the meat of each brick; an example of this might be 'Nora threatens to leave Torvald'. These are not to be confused with my 'major events' Post-it notes which might include, for example: 'Nora leaves Torvald'. As a director, I'm always putting myself in the position of the audience, thinking about what they need in order to experience the full engine of this story. As I can get lost in the subtext of scenes deep in a rehearsal process, it's really helpful for me to establish and then return to the key plot points, or key moments, to make sure the actor's line-by-line choices are still serving the story.

In terms of the design world, is that something that is created in the space, or do you have any starting points with that element?
My design process happens prior to rehearsals. For me, this is important because I make my best work when there are clear parameters to play within and so the set design becomes a playground.

With new writing, I'm not trying to re-interpret or re-imagine the play. I'm trying to deliver the cleanest, clearest possible version of it. With old plays, you're often creating a design that unlocks an interpretation of that story, one that is going to reach out from hundreds of years ago and connect with a contemporary audience. With *Henry V*, I was really interested in its pre-colonial mindset and how this play was written long before the British empire but contains within it the psychological ideas of white supremacy. So, part of my work, with the designer Moi Tran, was about how we could create a space that gave me room to play, to keep it relatively abstract but include something that provoked thinking in the audience about colonization, patriarchy and white supremacy.

Could you give me a flavour of how those conversations took place, prior to rehearsals?
I'm always interested in how creative conversations and responses to a script translate into a tangible set design. Normally, one of the first stages is when the designer and director prepare together a 'white card' version of the set (literally a 3D version of the design made of white card) that is presented to the team who oversee the realization of the set. At that point, things are costed by the production team, so that's where the designer and director get a sense of whether it's over budget or not. If it is, then you have to go back and work out what the really important elements of your design are and negotiate or find creative ways to deliver your concept differently.

Before that, though, the designer and I will have read the script separately, or even together aloud. With *Henry V*, I also included Cordelia Lynn, the dramaturg who was editing the script, in design discussions. Directors often take on dramaturgy, but on this play, I chose not to. Shakespeare is (of course) dead, so I wanted someone on the creative team who could advocate for the writer but was also not afraid to cut and reshape the script. So together, we asked, 'What does this play reveal about the moment we are living in? How do we design something that brings this to attention?'

After the designer and director discuss a response to the play together, the designer will often then go away and do lots of visual research. For *Henry V*, we were thinking a lot about colonization and Moi created mood-boards of manicured, British gardens that had been planted in colonized countries, which we felt was a rich metaphor for the controlling imposition of English rule; bending nature to the colonizers' will. Then an 'anything goes' generation of ideas happened, where we discussed how we might take this idea of manicured, colonial gardens and tell the story of Henry. A really crucial part of the design process is then going back to the text, scene by scene, looking at scenic elements that we are starting to settle on and asking, 'How does this serve the needs of the scene? For example, how might we use these elements to create the war in *Henry V*?' In Moi's visual references, the control of nature kept cropping up, so we went back and forth with shapes and colours, relating them to the playtext. From there, we started to decide on the different elements of the design that were non-negotiable for our version. For *Henry V*, we knew we also wanted to have the British Navy represented, so an idea of a big sail started to develop; hanging over a floor that looked not unlike one of those colonial gardens. These were the initial ideas presented at the white card meeting. From there we started to distil and abstract until we had the right playground for this play.

Let's talk about your role as an artistic director. How do you define the company and select the plays you work on? And how do you choose directors?

As a theatre company, we are rarely going to be someone's first directing gig. We work with directors who might have done several studio shows, who are ready to scale up or who are already working on mainstages. So, we make work of scale, in terms of story and visuals. We are unlikely to do a beautiful and intimate two-hander, but we will do a ten-hander. This is our offer to the theatre ecology: big stories at scale.

We are very audience-centred, too, as a touring company. What may be very interesting to a group of West Londoners might not be interesting in Liverpool, so I am always trying to programme work that has the muscle to engage in a national conversation. As a theatregoer myself, I am looking for what the big, meaty ideas are, that have a finger on the zeitgeist, that are going to get everybody talking. When I'm programming, I want thrilling theatre with social substance. What that means is that it has to be a good night out *and* it has to be politically engaged. We've just produced *Best of Enemies* by James Graham,[1] which is about political commentary during an

---

[1] James Graham's first professional play was *Albert's Boy*, which premiered at the Finborough Theatre in 2005. Since then, his work has included *This House* (2012) at the National Theatre, *Privacy* (2014) and *The Vote* (2015) at the Donmar Warehouse, as well as the musical *Tammy Faye* (2022), co-written with Elton John, which premiered at the Almeida Theatre. *Best of Enemies*, a fictionalized retelling of televised debates during the 1968 Republican and Democratic party conventions in the US, premiered at the Young Vic in 2021, prior to a West End run.

election. But we also make work that is political but with a small 'p', as it were: plays that are concerned with social issues. Last year, for example, I directed a play about sexual assault and patriarchy. I'm always thinking about the audience: are they getting 'bang for their buck'. If they've put down thirty quid to see this show, am I making it worth their while? I look for story-driven pieces. I didn't programme something last year, though it was exquisitely written, because it was too delicate and didn't have enough action in the story. In short, it needs to be a page-turner.

Moving into the rehearsal room, tell me a little about the spirit and the flavour of your processes as a director?
Typically, on day one, we read the play aloud on our feet. We just do it. I really trust the instincts of actors and quite often when actors aren't having to think too much about it you see some of the most exciting choices made in the process. It also takes some of the edge off performing it later down the line, as we've already performed it on day one. If we had to go onstage, there and then, it would be a hot mess, but also brilliant! We have a version of it, out there in the room, that we can always come back to.

I then do a week of 'tablework', and there's really no secret mystery to it. I like to think of it like a book club, where we read it as slowly or as quickly as we want and when we hit moments that are confusing, or spark ideas or questions, we stop and have a chat. I use that as a time to ask the questions I don't know the answers to. For example, 'What has your character done, between leaving the house in the first scene and returning with a broken bottle in the third?' This is a time to fill in the offstage plot of the play, or the backstory.

That gets everyone who is working on the play – mainly the actors, but sometimes also the designers and dramaturgs – to build a shared imagination of the offstage and pre-play events. I also get us to write out the major events of the play (that I have on my Post-it notes) on big pieces of paper, with the actors filling in the imaginative gaps. This acts as our timeline, and we start to add the pre-play and offstage events that we've been discussing around the table. I'd encourage us not to include when a character was born, for example, as that's generally not useful, but a divorce between two characters that happened before the play's action starts might be. If I don't think the events impact on the main story, they don't go on the wall. There must be genuine impact. So, we build a shared sense of the world of the play, and the timeline of it. It's about getting everyone on the same page and into the same world, with a shared sense of backstory and history of characters. That's the first week of rehearsal spent.

In week two, we rehearse the first half (up until the interval, if there is one); in week three, we rehearse the second; in week four we re-rehearse the first and second half, running the play as many times as possible. You judge the fragility of the room in terms of how confident people are feeling. If it's not going to knock confidence, I'll run the first half at the end of week two and the second half at the end of week three but sometimes actors aren't ready to do that and we only run it in the final week.

I try to do a minimum of three runs before we get to the technical period where lights, sound and other elements are added. Trust actors, as they often make discoveries and solve problems by running the play. So, I try to run it as much as possible. I'm also not scared of saying when I don't have the answer, or if we need to leave something because I don't know something yet. When I don't know something, I might also say, 'Make me an offer!' That will give me an idea to respond to. When I'm rehearsing scene by scene, I don't move on until the actors have had at least two goes at running the scene through, without me interrupting. I want to ensure actors key into their instincts without being told what to do by me. I can then key into my instincts when I'm watching, to ask, 'What is this scene making me feel? Is what it's making me feel the intended story for this moment?' And if not, then I have to work out what notes to give in order to unlock how to tell that moment of the story differently, so as to communicate it to an audience. I always try to make my notes to actors playable. If my notes aren't clear, I say, 'I don't have a good note; this is *roughly* the note. Can you translate that into something playable?' If the actors are confused, I'm not communicating clearly. If I can't communicate clearly, that's OK. I might say, 'I'm going to give you a vague note, so please help me to work out a note within it that's juicy for you to play!'

So, overall there's an honesty to my process, I don't pretend to know all the answers or to be right, which frees me to be creative. It also serves as an invitation to an actor or to my creative team to work something out together, rather than putting pressure on me as a director to have the answers and for everyone else to deliver a singular vision.

So, you're allowing the actors agency and ownership of their own process, so that they embody your notes in their own way?
Yes, we work things out together. For years I've said that it's more often not about working out what *is* working, but about the discovery of what's *not* working. It's important to create a vibe in the room where it's OK not to have the answers and you create that by being honest when you yourself don't

know. Then there's a space where everyone can give something a go, which means a more relaxed and collaborative rehearsal process. Ten imaginations bring more interesting possibilities than one imagination.

That said, your role in the room is sometimes to provide solutions, even if they're not perfect, so at some point, I have to make executive decisions. I am clear about that by saying, for example, 'For the next hour, I need us to workshop as many ideas as possible as to how to create this battle scene, then I'll choose one that tells the story the best and we'll rehearse it.'

Do you have any key practitioners or methodologies that are the bedrock of what you do, or any 'go-to' exercises that you often use?
I do use actioning, and I use Marina Caldarone's *Actions: The Actor's Thesaurus*.[2] I think it's genius. I like to give actors instructions that are doable. I find actions so useful in this regard. Actions are essentially verbs. For example: to seduce, to anger, to impress. A series of actions create an event, and series of events create a story. All those smaller actions – 'to intimidate', for example – are key. If something's not working, I go back to the Post-it notes to look at the event and ask what the series of actions is that ensures that the event is inevitable. It forces me to be specific and roots out when I'm chatting nonsense. I use that tool a lot in the rehearsal room. The event must be inevitable.

Do you use that as a tool when something *isn't* working, rather than tablework?
Yes, exactly. Instinct is key and I trust sometimes that the actions will be implicitly right. I often ask actors to *try* things, rather than talk about things. I can tell what it might be if it's in front of me, whereas sometimes if we talk about what we might do, I'm lost. If the scene isn't working, I'll also change our environment. In *Henry V*, a scene didn't work, so we went to play it by a water cooler in a cramped office corridor at the Globe. It immediately felt more like an episode of *Succession*, which was really useful to us, and we borrowed from this exercise in our final execution of the scene. By changing location, we can look at the scene afresh.

Audience is also everything. It's not until I get an audience that I can see which elements are unclear, or boring. So, the earlier you can get an

---

[2] *Actions: The Actor's Thesaurus*, by actor trainer Maria Caldarone, provides lists of transitive verbs as a stimulus for actioning exercises.

audience in the rehearsal room the better. That might be the producer, or the whole costume department: you need audiences in the room. I often have kids in the rehearsal room, as lots of my colleagues are parents. Someone bringing their 15-year-old child in can really focus you: if it's boring, their body language will tell you! Then I can work out how to make it engaging.

Audience awareness and thinking seem to be key themes in this conversation.
Yes, I see the preview period as an extension of the rehearsal, and I'll always ask for more preview time in favour of rehearsal time. In the daytime before each evening preview, I'll change a lot. With *Henry V*, I couldn't initially land the tone of the opening. I try not to hide anything from the actors, but I must also manage their fears. I tell them that the show is in a great place, but that I need us to try something different each preview in order to find the right tone for the top of the show, for example. My mantra in previews is 'suck it and see'. With *Henry V*, we tried four or five different beginnings before it clicked.

How do you judge that moment where things click? Through the audience's energies?
Yes; I might also simply talk to people in the interval to see what's landing or not. I ask to be in a seat in the auditorium where I can see the maximum number of audience members. Have I lost the over-sixties? Are the teenagers engaged? It's through reading the body language and energies of the audience that I am able to finesse and embed the production. And you can often tell from the buzz (or lack of it) in the interval, in the bar or the loos. In certain previews on *Henry V*, we landed the first half of the show, but not the second. It can take a week until you can land both. You have to hold your nerve.

Just watching something over a few nights is also key. Actors solve so many problems themselves as they tune into audiences and get used to the journey of the piece. If someone's asleep during a soliloquy, they adapt what they're doing. It's important to use the audience as a focal point to know where you are with a show. It's not about pandering to the audience but using them as a barometer to tell you what needs cooking and what's overcooked! It's key to use the preview period slowly, I find, observing how different nights tell you different things and slow-cook the show, rather than panicking after the first night and making sudden drastic changes before seeing it again.

Rather than just thinking about the 'what' of rehearsals, directors are now keen to consider the 'how' of rehearsals, which I think is about being the 'tone setter': ensuring that genuine creative work can be achieved in an inclusive manner, so that everyone can take ownership of the work.

I often ask actors in auditions what their process is and what they need in order to do their best work. Sometimes I do a check-in at the beginning and end of each week, seeing where everyone is at. But that's always about the work, as it's a workplace. I want to create an environment where everyone can do their best work. I don't create a therapeutic environment, as that's not my skill set. So instead, I ask people what they need from a process and also tell them what I might need.

16

Josie Rourke

JOSIE ROURKE *is a theatre and film director. From 2012 to 2018, she was Artistic Director of the Donmar Warehouse, and from 2007 to 2011, Artistic Director of the Bush Theatre. She has also worked as a freelance director for Chicago Shakespeare Theatre, the National Theatre and the Royal Court, among others. In 2020, she directed 'Her Big Chance', part of the BBC reboot of Alan Bennett's* Talking Heads *monologues. She made her feature film debut with* Mary Queen of Scots *in 2018, which featured Saoirse Ronan and Margot Robbie.*

Talk me through your pre-production processes and thinking.
It really depends on what the text is that I'm directing. I'm largely a text-based director. I have worked occasionally in other ways: so, I worked with James Graham at the Donmar Warehouse on *Privacy* and *The Vote*, and those plays began with very intensive research processes, where I was much more involved in the creation of the text but that's quite unusual for me. Generally, if the playwright is alive, we might go through a process of examining and thinking and discussing. Perhaps some redrafting will go on. When it's about new plays, some writers will change a new play a lot over the course of your preparation with them and some will hardly change it at all. The volume of discussion you have about it can be roughly the same amount, but that doesn't always lead to change. It's very much dependent on the individual. So, a play that I rehearsed with James Graham[1] would be unrecognizable from the first day to its opening night, it would change so radically. A play that I would direct of Nick Payne's[2] would be pretty much

---

[1] See footnote 1 in Chapter 15, above, for details of Graham's work.
[2] Nick Payne made his Broadway debut in 2015 with *Constellations* (2012), which had earlier played at the Royal Court Theatre. His other work for the stage has included *Sixty Six Books* (2011) for the Bush Theatre and *Elegy* (2016) for the Donmar Warehouse. He created and wrote the BBC TV series *Wanderlust* (2018).

the same: a scene might get swapped around and some dialogue might have been tweaked, but it would be largely and essentially the same play when we got to opening. So, for me, there isn't one particular set practice because playwrights are so different.

Part of the 'job' of theatre directing is a pre-production process, involving practical elements: that of designing the play, working in collaboration with your designer to figure out what the play requires. And, in a way, that's very useful for your process in the rehearsal room, because you'll have asked questions about the most basic unit of action, which are: 'Where do they come on from and go off to?' '*Do* they come on and go off?' 'How far do you want them to go?' and 'Where do they appear from?' Some of the geography of the play will have been set through that design process, so that will just inform how the play shapes within the room. And lots of directors do that very differently. The more experienced I become as a director, the more I look – with certain plays – to engineer a degree of flexibility into them. So, what I try to do through that design process is work out the essential things I need to do, in order to establish what I would call the 'visual grammar' of a play. I sometimes call it the 'physical dramaturgy' of a play, because often if the playwright's around – or even if they're long dead – that's a good way to talk to a designer; to say, 'This play has certain requirements, and it needs you to be able to do certain things.' Which could be anything, like: 'Caius Martius needs to sack the city of Corioles single-handedly, in order that he can become Coriolanus.' When I did *Coriolanus* with twelve chairs and a ladder, we had the ladder because he had to go up *something*, in order to go over the walls of Corioles and sack the city. That's part of the physical dramaturgy of the play. You don't see it, but he needs to *go* somewhere, and return from the *same* place a *different* person. So, working things out like that is important.

I used to run the Bush Theatre, which is a new writing theatre, and one of the things we'd do was connect playwrights with designers as early as possible, just so that when they were writing the play that question of 'What do you see?' was less abstract and more defined. The more mature I get, the more I dare myself to see if I can – with certain plays – prepare less, so that I can respond to performances. I recently set myself the challenge of doing *As You Like It*, just with a piano. It's in the round, and there are four entrances. I began that rehearsal process not knowing where anyone was going to go off or come on from, because there was just a piano onstage and it didn't matter, until we decided *where* and *how* it mattered. You know, you might say, 'We need to locate where the Duke is, so the Duke's going to come on from over there.' And we need to know where the sheepcote is. But you can decide that in the room, with certain elements of design. So, in terms of preparation, when I began as a director I was very, very prepared, in terms of how I thought the play was going to work physically on the stage. I did that in order that I could answer the actors' questions and efficiently stage the play. The more experienced I get as a director, what I try to do is to give myself as much flexibility as possible.

Has that evolved naturally, rather than being a conscious change?
I think so. The thing I'm most interested in *now*, as a director – and I've been directing for nearly twenty years – is trying to follow the instincts of the actor with the text. And trying to let the actor be the investigating force for the character, within the scene. A lot of what I try to do is about removing impediments, in order that I can gain that information, and understand the play through the actor. I think that's probably because – again, as I've gotten more experienced – I've realized something that we all know, which is that a character is going to be very different in the hands of a different actor, but no less valid. And so, that conversation becomes part of the investigation into the play and becomes part of the production for me. It's the thing I'm most fascinated by.

What I *do* do is a lot of really breaking down text. And reading, and re-reading the text a lot. If it's a Shakespeare play, or a classical play, I'll prepare my own edition. I'm nerdy enough to go back to the First Folio.[3] So, with *As You Like It*, I went back to the First Folio. I dumped a file of the First Folio into Word and went through everything. Modernized all the punctuation, tried to work it out. I'll often do that alongside looking at how a couple of editors have worked on published versions of the play, and then – once I've done that exercise, which is incredibly painstaking – I feel like I'm ready to cut and shape. I tend to do that hand in hand with the design process. But I do tend to worry about every word before I start. That's with a classical play.

---

[3]The 'First Folio' is the shorthand title for the collection of thirty-six plays by William Shakespeare first published in 1623, around seven years after the death of Shakespeare himself. The word 'folio' refers to the size of paper, as opposed to the smaller 'quarto' format. Prepared by Shakespeare's actor colleagues John Heminges and Henry Condell, the First Folio is (arguably) the only reliable text for twenty or so of Shakespeare's plays: though some had previously appeared in (often corrupted) quarto form, some – including *The Tempest*, *Macbeth*, *Julius Caesar* and *Twelfth Night* – had not appeared previously. The text was taken from various sources, including prompt books and even Shakespeare's 'foul papers' (working notes). While punctuation is included, the spelling of the Folio is not modernized, and it does not include the interpolations and directions of later editors. All of this means that the Folio is (again, arguably) the most 'authentic' version of Shakespeare's plays available to us today.

All playwrights are different, really. I'm just about to direct *Dancing at Lughnasa* at the National Theatre and I think the author, Brian Friel, had a mistrust of directors, to an extent. That's perfectly understandable. In *Dancing at Lughnasa*, he's baked into that play where things should go and how they should happen. There's a set of instructions towards a production. And some plays do that. So, a lot of preparation is about just analysing the play and asking, 'Is the playwright telling me how they want this to be done? And do I agree with them?' Which I generally do. And how do you arrive at that? And what does that reveal?

Going back to how you prepare, particularly in relation to classical texts, it's interesting that you keep coming back to dramaturgy – either visual, or a dramaturgical exercise with the text.
I have a near-synaesthesia for the shape of stories. So, in an odd way, I do tend to try to get to a point in my brain where I can – kind of – see a play three-dimensionally and understand it as an object. One of the things in rehearsal that's incredibly pleasurable for me, actually, is to go, 'Oh! Right! That's the scene! I see. That's what the intention of the scene is.' It might be different with these actors, but something goes 'click!' in my brain when it clicks in the room, or when it clicks into shape with part of the design process. And so, I think, rather than trying to *create* something, I'm trying to *conceive* something.

You often storyboard, with a 3D quality in relation to your work.
Yes; this is my screensaver. [*Holds mobile phone up; the screensaver is an image of two people sitting on a round carpet, with concentric circles of differently coloured papers surrounding them.*] The actors are Aidan Turner and Jenna Coleman. Sitting on the oval carpet that we rehearsed on for *Lemons Lemons Lemons Lemons Lemons*.[4] Each scene had two numbers: one for its chronological order and one for where it sat within the order of scenes in the play. Then it all had colour-coding for sections that we decided were the sections of the relationship depicted in the play. It was a mnemonic exercise for the actors. And also an acting exercise. Jenna particularly found it useful; she'd go, 'Oh! OK! This section here, this cream section: we're in

---

[4] *Lemons Lemons Lemons Lemons Lemons* by Sam Steiner was first performed at Warwick Arts Centre in 2015. The play is composed of non-chronological scenes that follow the relationship between the two characters, Bernadette and Oliver. As a romance develops between them, they are obliged to negotiate a society where a 'quietude bill' has been passed, permitting each individual to use only 140 words a day. The play questions the importance of language for communication, as well as exploring personal and individual freedoms and relationships.

"coping cream", when this word limit first comes in.' And so, everything got given a title. I wouldn't always do that. I think it depends, from play to play.

I'd say that I'm systematic without a system: what I try to do is to work out what system every play needs. And every play is different, to an extent. A really good question is: 'What's the best way to break this down?' And that could be anything. That could be frequency of language in a poetic text: with *Dancing at Lughnasa*, you can ask, 'How many times is "water" mentioned?' or 'How many times are "birds" mentioned?'

How do you work with your designer?
I think it varies a little, from designer to designer. The other thing I really love is research, so I will try to go to the place. Obviously, I can't go to the Forest of Arden for *As You Like It*, because it doesn't really exist, but I once directed a play that began in the Art Institute in Chicago. I went on a road trip to Iowa, as it was mostly set in Iowa, then drove back to Chicago and so I did that journey. The thing that balances the systematic for me is a kind of lateralism, too. So, when I'm in preparation for a play, I'll go and see a couple of exhibitions. They might be completely irrelevant, but something might click. I was in New York this week and there was a big Edward Hopper[5] exhibition at the Whitney Museum of American Art. I'm about to direct a movie set in Westminster, around Parliament Square, but there were a few things in that Hopper exhibition, in terms of the frames of buildings, where I thought that the way that he was looking at New York in the 1930s could inform the way that I could potentially look at Parliament Square now, using that as a frame. You need something that actually gets you out of the flow of the play and into something else, as that can be really helpful in the visual process. Probably the biggest influence on *Mary Queen of Scots* is Louise Bourgeois.[6] And if you watch the film with that in your head, you can suddenly see it in the work. Directors often say in masterclasses to go to as many galleries as you can and see a lot of stuff, but equally, you might just sit and watch a movie that tells you something. You might just see the

---

[5] American realist painter Edward Hopper was known for taking commonplace subjects from everyday Americana and imbuing them with a subdued drama. Perhaps his most famous (and most widely reproduced) painting is *Nighthawks* (1942), which depicts four people in a downtown diner late at night, seen through the large front window. The light spilling from the diner contrasts the shadowy and deserted city streets outside.
[6] French-American artist Louise Bourgeois was mostly known for large-scale installations. Sharing some similarities with abstract and surrealist schools, one of her most famous works is *Maman* (1999), a huge steel-and-marble sculpture of a 9-metre-high spider, from which six bronzes were made, first appearing at Tate Modern's Turbine Hall in 2000.

shape of a scene, or a frame. Anything can inspire, in that sense. It's not always logical.

Are there ways in which you'll approach rehearsals differently, due to scale or genre? Or, are there things that you will always do, regardless of the play, cast size, genre or scale of house?

I *always* do something different, depending on the play. So, part of my process is working out how to begin. What I tend to do is think quite hard about the group and it's often about working out what, in that first week, is going to create a good group dynamic. Years ago, I stopped doing a lot of tablework with classical plays and did this thing, which I find really useful – especially with a Shakespeare play – where we will read and break down scenes, but we'll do it standing up, at music stands. People can have a chair, if they like, but I generally encourage people, if they're able to, to do it on their feet. Because I think, often, what you have in any acting company of scale, is that people have very different educational backgrounds. And you will have people who are Cambridge-educated Shakespeare nerds, like me, and you will have people – excitingly – who have never done a Shakespeare play before.

I think the thing that it's most important to do, particularly in that first week of rehearsals, is to protect people from what they're trying to collect subconsciously. Within that first week, actors are approaching each other and the play, working out the dynamic of the room. They tend, however experienced they are, to have a degree of nerves in operation: 'Will I be any good?', 'Will this room like me?', 'Did this director *really* want me in this part?', 'Am I right for this character?', 'Can I do this thing?' And so, I often think that one of the things that can occur in that first week, if you're not insanely careful, is that somebody can say something that they feel doesn't land, or fail to understand a moment that's occurring within the group, or just feel like, in some small way, that they've messed up. And it can be tiny. But it can really interrupt the process.

So, the thing I'm actually most interested in is a warmth, a kindness, an openness, a friendliness and creating the idea of a company. Why I do what I do with Shakespeare plays is to ensure that there aren't one or two members of the company who are highly academic, sitting there, talking about the First Folio in great detail. One of the reasons I start with the First Folio and do my own punctuation – all of those things – is very specifically so that there isn't another authority in the room, where people come in with two editions of the play and say, 'Well, it's this and it's this', which holds up the process and – more importantly – can make other people feel thick. As theatre has matured and become more inclusive, that's become less of an issue. I would say that, in my experience, when I began to direct, as a very young director directing big classical plays, it was mainly – and to an extent, understandably – men who were thirty years older than me, arguing about the position of a semicolon! I think that what I do now also allows me to give actors flexibility if they find that something isn't flowing. So, I can say, 'Listen. I didn't put a comma there, because there wasn't one when it was originally published; however, you *could* have a comma, if you wanted to and it would get you through that line slightly better. Or imagine one.' It de-sanctifies it, in a way.

I do think it's my responsibility to understand a little bit about how the conservatoires operate, and how they have operated, at different points in their history. And to know whether I'm talking to an actor who trained at Drama Centre, or an actor who trained at LAMDA, or an actor who trained at RADA, or an actor who trained at university. Or an actor who is a screen actor. One of the really interesting things, for example, about doing *Lemons*, with two actors who've mainly worked on-screen, proportionately to theatre, is that, unlike theatre actors, they don't cut themselves: they keep going because nobody has shouted, 'Cut!' With Jenna and Aidan on *Lemons* we had this little joke, where I started to call them 'flow-monsters', because they would just keep going. And I'd be like, 'Woah! OK, flow-monsters! Just stop …!' It's finding these invented terms and this invented language, in the rehearsal room. I think it's probably fair to say that I tend, as a human being, to be quite aphoristic. I come from a family with a great love of language: my mum's always making up words and I've inherited a bit of that. And I find that incredibly useful; that rather than have a language that's outside of the room, you might say, 'Right, here's a language that's inside of the room..' And I do that all the time.

I believe that becomes inclusive for that room, rather than saying, 'I'm going to impose the language of Stanislavski'. If everyone is from different backgrounds and has different training, then you can create your own language, that makes its own sense and has its own logic for the people in that room.

Yes, it's a word or a term or an idea that was coined in that room, with those people: nobody else has possession of it. Everybody is responsible for using it and for it evolving. It's a great way of unifying people. Nobody is any more educated in it than any other person, which is really important. Which is not to say that it's not also my responsibility to know that, for example, Leah Harvey[7] is very governed by Meisner,[8] so I need to know what that means. There will be other methodologies at play and it's about creating a space that can include that. I don't – almost quite deliberately – action.[9] I would only unit[10] if there was a bit of the script we needed to break down, to understand in the space of the rehearsal room. We might do that as a shared exercise, but we'd agree on the principles of the uniting. Those methods, which are systems of acting, are not everybody's systems. So, it can sometimes leave someone out, or put someone ahead.

I might say, for example, 'If it were an action, I think it would be this' and an actor might reply, 'What's actioning?' Then I might spend ten minutes explaining what actioning is. I'm very aware that if you direct Michelle Terry,[11] for example, she'll come in with her script pre-actioned. If you direct Anne-Marie Duff,[12] she'll have undertaken the action system on that text before she starts work with you. While Leah Harvey is in that space working out how to apply Meisner. So, all that stuff is going on and it's exciting to me. Alfred Enoch,[13] in *As You Like It*, recently, had the entire relationship click for him because a good friend of mine, an academic, came in to chat to the

---

[7] Leah Harvey's stage roles include Hortense in *Small Island* at the National Theatre in 2019 and Lisa in *The Wonderful World of Dissocia* at the Theatre Royal Stratford East in 2022. Their screen credits include the BBC's *Les Misérables* (2019) and the Apple TV+ series *Foundation* (2021).

[8] Drawing on early work by Stanislavski, Meisner technique is an approach to acting developed by American practitioner Sanford Meisner at New York's Neighbourhood Playhouse, where he served as Director of Acting until the 1990s. The Meisner approach encourages the actor to concentrate on the other actors in the immediate environment, rather than focusing on themselves. Some of the exercises the technique uses emphasize repetition, with words becoming of less importance than the underlying emotions. Also see footnote 2 in Chapter 17.

[9] As a rehearsal technique, actioning involves assigning a transitive verb to each of an actor's lines to explain its underlying meaning or subtext; for instance, the character may 'prod', 'encourage', 'harangue' or 'seduce'.

[10] Uniting involves dividing the text into sections (or 'bits'): though definitions differ, a unit/bit tends to mark a moment of action in the text (in contrast to an event, where something changes for every character present in a scene).

[11] Michelle Terry is known predominantly for her work at Shakespeare's Globe, where she assumed the role of artistic director in 2018. Having previously appeared there as Rosalind in *As You Like It* (2015), during her tenure as artistic director, she has appeared as the title role in *Hamlet* (2018), Lady Macbeth in *Macbeth* (2018), and as Viola in *Twelfth Night* (2021).

[12] Anne-Marie Duff has appeared in Channel 4's *Shameless* (2004), *Sex Education* (2020) and films such as *On Chesil Beach* (2017). Her theatre work has spanned from playing the title role in *Saint Joan* (2007) at the Olivier Theatre, to the title role in *Sweet Charity* at the Donmar Warehouse in 2019 and Lady Macbeth in *Macbeth* (2013) at New York's Lincoln Center.

[13] Alfred Enoch appeared in the *Harry Potter* film franchise and his later stage work includes Edgar in *King Lear* (2016) for the Royal Exchange, Ken in *Red* (2018) at Wyndham's Theatre, and Romeo in *Romeo and Juliet* for the Globe Theatre in 2021.

company and said something to him about the ideal of platonic love and he got it, but Alfie's very intellectual in that way. It's really about understanding all of those different things and how they operate alongside each other.

Do you set expectations around when you would like people to be off-book, or highly familiar with the text, or expectations of when you're going to do a stumble-through, or a stagger? Is that in your overall planning?

I don't ask people to be off-book. For example, with *As You Like It*, recently, they had to learn a huge amount of British Sign Language and it's a massive challenge to integrate that. Also, Leah uses Meisner so interestingly that, although they knew it, they needed to be in flow, before they could really speak it without the text. People were really cool with it; it was a very relaxed room.

In complete contrast, Jenna and Aidan turned up and ran lines for *Lemons* for half an hour, every day, before we started rehearsal. But that's a very different play. Also, that's two actors who implicitly know that if one of them goes down, they both go down, because nobody else is there. They were pretty much off-book before they turned up and I completely endorsed it. But, no, I generally feel that you just need to learn your lines in the same way that I need to show up to rehearsals. So I try not to make too big a deal of it.

There are some directors who have a very concrete methodology. What practitioners or methodologies do you draw on, perhaps implicitly or explicitly, even if you don't use that terminology in a room?

I had this extraordinary training, which was compressed really into a two-year period. I spent one year at the Donmar, in which I assisted various directors: Sam Mendes, Michael Grandage (twice), Phyllida Lloyd, Nick Hytner.[14] And then I went from assisting those people to assisting Peter Gill.[15] I'd done all this assisting at the Donmar, and at the end of that year, in

---

[14] Sam Mendes was Artistic Director of the Donmar Warehouse from 1990 to 2002, overseeing its initial opening with Stephen Sondheim's *Assassins* in 1992. Michael Grandage subsequently assumed the role from 2002 to 2012, and was also Artistic Director of Sheffield Theatres from 2000 to 2005. Phyllida Lloyd, perhaps best known for her directing work on the films *Mamma Mia!* (2008) and *The Iron Lady* (2011), was the director of David Mamet's *Boston Marriage* (2001) and Friedrich Schiller's *Mary Stuart* at the Donmar, the latter of which transferred to Broadway in 2009. Nick Hytner was previously Artistic Director of the National Theatre, where his major successes included *The History Boys* (2004) and *One Man, Two Guvnors* (2011); he has also directed films such as *The Madness of King George* (1994) and *The Lady in the Van* (2015).
[15] After helming the Royal Court and the Riverside Studios, Welsh playwright and director Peter Gill founded the National Theatre Studio in 1984 and ran that venue until 1990. His work elsewhere includes a revival of his own play, *The York Realist*, at the Donmar Warehouse in 2018 and *Something in the Air* (2022) at the Jermyn Street Theatre.

a slightly unusual way, Sam Mendes offered me a show at the Donmar and Michael Grandage offered me a show at Sheffield. I then went to the Royal Court for two weeks and that became two years. And then, in the second two years of what I think of as my 'training period', I got this intense understanding of new work. Now, I was insanely lucky, because to move from the Donmar, to the Royal Court, via Peter Gill, is pretty much the most wonderful training you could have, in terms of those contrasts in values, as much as anything else. I also got to observe a number of very successful writers at work.

So, really, if I have a practice, it's from that very close and intensive observation, that ran roughly as long as a slightly extended university process. And I think, probably, as a director, Peter is the most distinct influence on my work. I wouldn't do what Peter does; he is notorious for line-reading. Though, that said, it's not really line-reading: Peter's coming underneath and through the actor into the line. So, if the line is the music, the actor is the instrument, as it were. It will be different from actor to actor, so he's trying to tune you; it's a bit like an orchestra tuning up. It's also the energy of someone who did *all* the jobs in theatre, who came from Wales to be a stage manager at the Royal Court. I'd say that Sam, Michael and Nick don't have distinct methodologies. Sam has an intense idea of team and a way of working, steadily and quietly, with actors. Michael does have a 'know-it-before-you-turn-up-and-block-it-from-day-one' rigour, which is imparted by an actor's irritation at directors not serving clarity; I often think that when I consider his work. Nick is insanely technical; it's not just about technical theatre, it's about how theatre operates: a play as an object in a physical space. But those are not methodologies; those are practices. I think that what I got from Peter Gill was about a director understanding exactly what an actor's practice was. His desire is really to understand the actors, to speak to the part of the actor. It's a kind of purist belief in the encounter between the actor and the text that I'm probably most influenced by. Everything Peter does is about flow and how to get people into, and then keep people in, flow.

It's very refreshing to hear you talk about values and practices.
I think, in a political way, it's the responsibility of the director to work out what the endeavour is. And I think that can sometimes be located in a space that is too sociological. Actually, I was at the National Theatre yesterday and they were holding 'The Why Meeting', where the director is asked to come into a meeting with the artistic director and the management and other people, to say *why* they're doing the play.

It was Peter Gill – more than anyone else, because of his time at the Royal Court – that turned me on to the fact that the endeavour *doesn't* have to be sharply political; it can be collective. It can be about beauty; it can be about poetry. It can be about things that are ineffable, that are rendered effable by a group of people coming together. You can do a play because it's about love. You can also do a play because you're acutely concerned about the mass collection of data. All of these things exist and are valid.

I think your responsibility as director is to identify that shared endeavour and you might do that through process. And that comes more readily to me, because I'm an artistic director. I remember when I was at the Royal Court, under Ian Rickson,[16] the then box office manager – who had been box office manager there for a long time – stood up at the staff meeting and said '*My Zinc Bed*, by David Hare, went on sale on Monday, and in all my time as a box office manager at the Royal Court, it has achieved greater ticket sales than any other play that's ever been programmed. Can anybody explain to me *why* we're doing it?'

I interviewed Rufus Norris a number of years ago and he talked about asking the question, 'Why are we doing this play?'
It's very interesting. I think it's partly a response to the building needing to know why things are happening: 'Why are we doing this?' That *is* the endeavour of it. What goes on in the rehearsal room and what goes on in the programming meeting and what occurs in the marketing meeting. And I can't really do a play if I don't know that.

You've mentioned in a previous interview that one of the roles of the director centres around stress absorption in the room.[17] Could you elaborate on that idea of the director as a 'stress absorber'?
It's a quotation from Sam Mendes, who told me that the role of a director was to absorb stress, and not to give it off. Post-pandemic, one of the biggest and best conversations we're having about theatre is welfare. I think it's a very interesting time to be a director, because I think actors in their twenties now will say, 'Actually, I need Thursday morning off, because I have to do my therapy.' Ten years ago, nobody would have ever said that. And I'm really glad that people now say that. And I think that it is possible to run rooms that are

---

[16]Ian Rickson was Artistic Director of the Royal Court Theatre from 1998 to 2006, where major successes included *Mojo* (1995) and *The Weir* (1997). Following work at the Young Vic and the National Theatre, Rickson presented the Covid-lockdown podcast 'What I Love' in 2020, featuring interviews with actors, writers and producers from the deserted stages of British theatres.
[17]Rourke quoted Mendes in an interview given to the *Guardian* newspaper in 2013; the full text can be found online here: https://www.theguardian.com/stage/2013/apr/21/josie-rourke-donmar-artistic-director-interview.

about welfare, and that are about saying, 'I think we've got to where we can get to now, and it might be 5.45, but let's break fifteen minutes early.'

As a director, you're more focused on people's levels of tiredness. What we did at the Donmar towards the end of my time there and what I try to do now in my rehearsal rooms, is to ask stage management, 'Who are the parents? Who are the care givers? And what do they need? What's helpful to them?' And I want them to say, because I think this space should be able to be compatible with those things. I really believe that.

There is a death of authoritarianism in the rehearsal room. Nobody is banging a stick on the floor anymore, or running a metronome. I hope! But it's not only the demise of a kind of authoritarian figure, but a growing sense of the value of contributions from other people. And, as a director is entitled to their preparation and their space, an actor is entitled to some space around the work that they're making with you in the room. I think that there can be value in giving an actor space for rest, reflection and consideration.

I worked with the choreographer Wayne McGregor a few years ago on *Sweet Charity*, and Wayne is very knowledgeable about how people learn choreography and how the body holds it and remembers. There's an absolute in his methodology about dance practice, which is that you can learn physically for a set amount of time. There comes a point where it's completely useless and you have to stop, in order that you can then come away, and know it. That's about a degree of muscle memory, but it's also about a degree of absorbing and reflecting. And I do think that valuing absorption and reflection is a key thing and something that will actually begin to contribute to this process of evening things out that I'm interested in.

So, it's not about taking the stress of others and absorbing it into yourself; what you're actually trying to do is to reduce the risk of that potential stress in the room?
Yes; actually to create a space where people can say, 'Look, if I could pick my child up at four, that would be amazing!' And if you don't make that invitation, often, people don't say. What you need to be for actors is to be stable for them. I think that you need to be a sort of North Star within that space, so that they can navigate by you. For me, it's more like that. It's more about a kind of steadiness.

17

Roy Alexander Weise

ROY ALEXANDER WEISE *is a theatre and film director. Previously the BBC Theatre Fellow at the Bush Theatre and the Lyric Hammersmith, he then became a trainee director at the Royal Court Theatre, before going on to become an associate director at the Donmar Warehouse in 2019. This interview was conducted during Roy's tenure as Co-Artistic Director of the Royal Exchange, a post which he held from 2019 to 2023. While there his plays included* The Mountaintop *(2021), which he had previously directed in 2016 for the Young Vic.*

Talk me though your pre-rehearsal period; let's start with choosing your play.
That's a really interesting place to start, because I think choosing plays can be really hard. Sometimes, they really jump out at you, they just seep into you as you read them, but some of them don't come off the page straightaway. And actually, I have always found reading plays quite challenging. I don't think they're the easiest thing to read. And I've found that the more I've started being really open about that, the more I realize that I'm not alone. You know, I could read several pages, and be like, 'Woah!' There might be several characters and I have no idea who's who, or what their relationships are and I can't continue until I can really understand what I've read. So, I might read the first ten pages three times before really getting into it, or if I get stuck on a bit that doesn't really make sense, I'll keep going over it until I really get what's going on. So, I start by doing a thorough read of the entire play.

I think, for me, the most important thing in choosing a play to direct is that you feel an umbilical connection to that play; you feel in some way bound, as if a part of you might be lost if you don't get to tell this story. I think that's different to being really excited about a play that you've read. You can read a play and be excited and think it's brilliant, but I think it's a different feeling when you know that the play lives inside of you. When you know that, the experience chimes. I feel as if my entire body gets charged with this electricity that I get from reading the play. And I think that I must always really acknowledge the way that the play makes me feel.

One of the things that I don't really do as a director, or that I'm necessarily very often excited about doing, is coming up with a vision. Because I feel that, for me, it's most important as a director to be able to communicate the emotional experience to your teams. And then you collectively create the vision. So, I make these offerings about how the play needs to feel for the audience, or say, 'They need to think about this' or 'They need to feel this' and then we collectively go on a journey to understand what we need to create: what world the play needs to inhabit, in order for the audience to share that experience with us. So, I think when reading the play, it's important to know how it makes you feel.

Ian Rickson once said in a workshop that you should always try, as far as possible, to read a play all the way through in one sitting. And sometimes I can do that and that's great, because in reading the play all the way through, you're able to have a much clearer sense of the emotional arc of the story and to hold on to that. I think that's a really powerful thing.

What you're also saying is that you're always thinking about the experience that you'll hand over to your audience, right from the start.
Absolutely. I always try to make as many notes as I can after I've finished reading a play, with everything that comes to mind: colours, music, etc. Music is a way in for me. I always feel as if I need to try to find the 'soundtrack' of it, even if I don't end up using that music in the production. I always feel as if it helps me to get a better grasp on the world, because I came from a background of music and that really helps me to start feeling a bit anchored. I also start writing down actors that might be interesting, as well as other creatives, such as lighting designers. I write the themes down as well: a few sentences about what the play's about. Usually, one of the really good tasks to do is to write the story from each character's perspective. This is an exercise I often do in workshops and sometimes in rehearsals as well. Let's take Shakespeare's *Much Ado About Nothing*, but imagine that's it called *Beatrice*, for example. What's the tag-line? 'The story of a woman who needs to defend her honour'? Or, 'The honour of women'? That way, you start understanding the roles that each of the characters play within the story. I find that really useful, because sometimes it's very clear who the protagonist is, but sometimes it's not.

I'm directing a production of *Cat on a Hot Tin Roof* for the Royal Exchange and as a play, it's a real ensemble piece, but it's very easy to read that play and think that it's Brick's story. But actually, it's Maggie's story: Maggie is the cat on a hot tin roof, so Maggie is the person who has the biggest arc. She has the most circumstances and is the most active, in that by the end of the play she makes two massive choices to do things to affect her outcome within this world, to secure her position in that family and, inevitably, to stay on that hot tin roof. I went and did that exercise on my own, in order to understand more clearly that it is Maggie's play. Because I guess we learn that sometimes, the character that's onstage the most is the protagonist, but I think that Brick is somewhere between a protagonist and an antagonist, which makes him really, really fascinating.

Research is huge as well. I might start looking into the world of the play and if there are elements of that world that I don't get, or that feel far removed from me, I might start to collate some research, making lists of the things I need to learn and understand. I try to understand that world through different mediums: podcasts, videos on YouTube, watching documentaries, watching other pieces of fictional storytelling about it, or looking at art in galleries. If I hear that there are exhibitions, or things in museums that are connected to the play, then I'll try to go and see them.

My designer, Milla Clarke, and I went to the Serpentine[1] and they had this really beautiful structure, built as one of their pieces that summer and the idea was like a sanctuary. It was in-the-round and our space is in-the-round. And it felt, because of the religious and political undertones in *Cat on a Hot Tin Roof*, that it might be interesting to go and experience this sanctuary that was created, to go and sit in it and experience it. And it really taught us some stuff about how to create a space that feels like a sanctuary, that feels like it's safe, but then becomes a space that's almost like a ballroom, where so much violence happens. But then being able to go back to it feeling like a sanctuary for moments where we feel we really need to. To try to subtly push those ideas and themes of religion to the fore.

---

[1] Since 2000, the Serpentine art gallery in Kensington Gardens has commissioned a temporary summer pavilion to be built by a leading international architect who has not completed a building in England at the time of the invitation. Recent contributors include Japanese architect Junya Ishigami (2019), South African Sumayya Valy (2021), American Theater Gates (2022) and Lebanon-born Lina Ghotmeh (2023). The pavilion is situated on the lawn for three months for the public to explore.

What about choosing a play for the season as an artistic director? Is that the same process?

As an artistic director, it's about having a good sensibility for audiences as well and having a sense of the things that they like; learning about the things they've responded to in the past. Sometimes, it's about understanding that you're deciding to stretch the ideas that audiences experience, actually. You know it's something that won't be everyone's cup of tea, but you try to tap into those groups whose cup of tea you know it will be. I guess, because we've got an interesting history of a range of different kinds of work, we're fortunate enough to know that there are audiences for all of those. But we've also got to reckon with the realities of box office and wondering about whether it's something that is going to be an easy sell. And sometimes that becomes about looking at the themes, looking at the opportunities, in terms of casting: whether there's any way to get artists of profile, to really endorse the work for the audience as well.

I think that when you read a play as an artistic director, it's also about the entire picture and puzzle that you're creating as a team and the range of stories that you want to offer as well. So, we might really love a play, but we've also got to pay attention to where the plays sit in relation to one another in a season, or across a year and try not to replicate the same styles and patterns or themes, so we're giving the broadest experience to our audiences. And that can be quite challenging, because when you're as close to plays as you can be on the inside, it's easy to see all of the nuances and differences between them, but sometimes audiences want stuff that is drastically different, in contrast to work that they've seen before.

I'm very interested in what you say about coming at each character from their perspective. I like the idea, when working with actors, that you're always the guardian of your own character, no matter what their actions. But you're the first person I've spoken to who really does that as a director in a methodological way. It seems that you're trying, as a director, to remove yourself from a judgement perspective on characters' choices. I'm wondering if that says something about how you bridge into telling the story, or working with the actors on the rehearsal room floor?

If you cannot understand the characters within a play – especially the leading characters – then you're probably not the right director. You might be fascinated by them, but if you're unable to find the reason as to why you have an obsession, or why you're repulsed by a character, you need to explore them. There has to be a desire to reach into them, regardless of what judgement you might make, or what experience you might have emotionally when trying to connect to the character.

I think it's always a big no-no to direct a play if you don't respect the characters in the story, especially the leading characters. And I think that becomes a huge task for you as a director, in theatre especially, because our work predominantly – in terms of time – is working with actors to unpack and to understand the characters; to create authentic versions of these characters. If, as a director, you don't know how to appreciate and love the characters, then it's probably going to be very difficult for you to encourage somebody else to do so. I think that's a really big part of the job, which is why I try to do it so early on, because very soon after that – if it gets green-lit and you're going ahead – you've got to be able to give casting breakdowns, you've got be able to speak with your heart about these characters when you're trying to convince actors to come and work with you. You've got to be able to speak in an impassioned way with your creative teams to invite them into the process as well, to help unpack the play for them. If you don't understand the heart of the story, which is the people, then I think you should really be asking yourself why you're doing the play. And it might be that you're fascinated by a world, or an aesthetic, or a style, but if you're not excited by the people and the story that they tell, about the human beings within, then that will show in your work.

You use words there like 'encourage' and 'invite'. Does this give a flavour of how you might define the role of the director and your approach?
You won't hear me using words like 'dictate', or 'force', or 'must'. Well, sometimes I might use 'must'! It depends on the context. But, yes, I guess to call the director a 'facilitator' is a huge part of it. You're sort of a facilitator, but also an audience member: you're an audience member that has the special skills to help the performers get to the next bit. So, I might say, 'OK, you've just shown me this; this is what I hear, this is what I see. What about if you try to …? What about if …? Think about …' Asking questions is a major part of the role.

I think it's important to allow actors to make discoveries that they can own. But it's also my responsibility to be really clear about the direction of travel, too, so I think it's always really important to say when you don't think something is right. Or to keep an openness to the possibilities of what could happen. You must create a space where people can organically discover and learn, but also, very importantly, let people know when they have found those discoveries. Really impressing and endorsing the ideas, or the offers that are made by the actors that really chime with you. So, sometimes I use language like: 'That's really clear. Great!'

Clarity is really important. Because sometimes a piece of work isn't not good because it's not exciting or dynamic; it's not good because it's not clear. And I think storytelling is communication and communication must be about clarity, or it has to include clarity. Or, if clarity is not a part of it, then it has to be a *conscious* ambiguity. It has to be a choice. So, I often find myself going, 'Oh, great, that was really clear. That was super-clear!' Even if I want to say, 'That was amazing!' I'll say instead, 'Oh, that was the clearest possible version that you could have done!'

The director Katie Mitchell talks about this, too, this idea of being clear and making sure that rehearsal room language is useful. I think sometimes there's a misconception: clarity doesn't mean that there's no dynamic, or no emotional rollercoaster.

The dynamism and the emotion are what allow the story to be clear. So, when you've encouraged actors to really look for those peaks and troughs in a scene, and to really look for those sharp corners, look for those moments that really need to be negotiated by all characters. Then suddenly, you start to unlock the possibilities for each character to respond to and everybody becomes alive to something. And if you've really encouraged the actors to do that detailed work, in terms of understanding who their characters are, starting to understand what sort of choices they might make and what sort of trajectory the character is on, then they start to make offers that begin to really pull out the story with real clarity.

I also think that part of the reason it's important to use language such as 'clear', instead of 'good', is because you shouldn't encourage actors to be chasing merit. I don't think you want actors to be chasing praise. Of course they want to know that they're really good in it and you can tell them that, but ultimately while we're working and creating a piece together, what we're doing is understanding the clearest possible version of the story that we could tell collectively, for the purposes that we have decided together in the collective vision that we've created, in order to have the greatest impact on our audience, so it helps to create a really brilliant through-line. After all, what's good is subjective. How do you quantify 'good'? How do you quantify 'brilliant'? It really depends upon who's watching and who's listening. I think that if you can ensure that there's clarity there, then at least it allows the actor to let go of the idea of whether they're being brilliant in that moment or not.

It allows them to just focus. Not every moment in the story needs to be brilliant: it has to be clear, and to be clear it has to tell the story.

Do you always design prior to rehearsals? Is it always a finished world in that way?
Yes, I'm quite traditional in that sense. The bulk of the work has to be done. Often that's because of the processes that the rest of the production must go through. The design has got to be costed and you've got to know that you can afford it before you sign off on it and it gets built. There's a lot of work that has to happen beyond the work that you do, and I think if you leave too much to that making process and that process of creation, it can be really difficult to deliver, which places a considerable amount of stress and strain on teams that isn't very helpful and doesn't allow people to continue to be really creative. So, a lot of that work does happen before, but there are degrees of openness and flexibility, so that the actors can come in and have opportunities to really impress on the world as well. But you can start with, 'Well, this is where we are.'

With casting, it's important for me to find ways to communicate, as clearly as I can, the direction of travel for a production, too, in order that the actors know what they're getting themselves into. I also allow actors to feel like they have agency in the dramaturgy of the entire story and the production because, really, theatre doesn't need a director, or a design. Sometimes, it doesn't even need a writer. But it will always need performers. And so, ensuring that the performers always have agency in the world is really, really important.

Things like costume – what the actors will wear on their bodies – are so important. I think designers go on quite a careful journey with actors to present a world and a style. But they then also allow the room for an actor to flex and manoeuvre. Sometimes it's about their own comfort: 'I don't want to show this part of my body'; 'When I wear something like this, it makes me feel like that.' It's about ease and comfort, as well as practicality, so the actors will say, for example, 'If I wear that dress, with the really long train, I can't do the scene where I climb up the ladder.' And things like props: there's always a world of props that either gets introduced, or stripped away in the process, while working with actors. Sometimes it can be that lots of business and lots of props start to enter the world and it's really useful. And sometimes, it's really not: sometimes, it's a distraction.

Do you have your roots in any particular practices, practitioners or methodologies?

I feel like I've got a comprehensive toolkit and I hope that what I do is bring that toolkit to the practice and discover which tools people need. If you're an engineer, you rock up to the job with all of your toolkit and you figure out what is needed: 'This pipe needs a wrench', for example. I like to think that's how I work. But I do realize that there are some specific things that I do, like I do love a lot of Stanislavski's work. I particularly love a lot of Meisner[2] as well, because I feel like it's important for actors to develop generosity as collaborators with one another. I think Meisner's work really helps actors to get out of themselves, using the principle of understanding that you are better by giving your focus to somebody else. It feels like a really liberating offer for actors. And that is what we actually do: I might speak to you and I watch you to see how you're receiving what I'm saying. If I then realize that something that I'm saying isn't right, I'll change direction or I'll stop talking. But I won't ever be able to arrive at those choices if I'm not focusing on you; if I'm not placing my attention on you. People in the world actually engage with other people.

Also, actions! I'm a really big fan of actions. Again, because it's about affecting one another. I imagine that there's a laser-light that you shoot from one to another with the text, or sometimes, if I really want to emphasize an actor *giving* a line to another, I'll say, 'Throw that dart!' And then I'll say, 'Where does it go? Where does it hit? Where do you want to hit them? In the crotch? In the shoulder? Point-blank in the forehead? Throw that dart! Go

---

[2] One of Meisner's best-known exercises is the repetition exercise. In pairs, one partner spontaneously makes a remark about the other. The remark is then repeated, back and forth, between the two, in the same manner, until it changes on its own. The object is to react truthfully, allowing the change to occur naturally, rather than by deliberate manipulation. A variation of this is to initially repeat the remark – for instance, 'You have blue eyes' – and then have the actors add their own point of view to the remark: 'I have blue eyes'. The actors then repeat the remark again, instinctually, but allowing it to change in meaning, tone and intensity, and adding to it: 'I have blue eyes, and they're beautiful', for example, followed by 'You have blue eyes, but they squint', allowing the lines to evolve spontaneously and naturally. The next step is to add an activity to this for one of the partners – it may be anything from trying to write a report to changing a baby's nappy. One partner must try to carry out this activity while the other begins the repetition exercise; while still performing the independent activity, that partner must try to follow the rules of the repetition exercise. Any delay in their responding may provoke small responses from the other partner, such as holding out their hands, or raising their eyebrows. Meisner provided two directives for these exercises: 'Don't do anything unless something happens to make you do it' and 'What you do doesn't depend on you: it depends on the other person'. Each partner must pay attention to the other and what they are doing, so as to respond accordingly. This encourages connection to the partner and to the actor's own instincts, as well as an awareness and inhabiting of the space and environment.

again, throw that dart back!' It's always about how you affect one another, how you impact one another. We watch stories because we need to know why the hell we do the things that we do to one another. And I think that that really helps us to get into the belly of stories and character and human behaviour.

Do you use those techniques very specifically, saying, for example, 'We're going to explore some Meisner'? Or is it, again, as and when required?
I did a huge amount of Meisner work – very physical Meisner work – on *The Mountaintop*.[3] I've directed that play three times now. It's a two-hander and it's an hour and forty-five minutes, straight through. The characters are just in a motel room and all they've got is each other. For the bulk of it, actually, for about an hour, all they're doing is talking to each other and so they have to be umbilically connected. There's a sort of story of love, underneath the surface, so it felt to me as if they had to have this intense connection, from the moment that he opens the door and they meet. I would really impress upon the company that Meisner is something that we really need to embed in our training and we might do that work every morning for half an hour. And then, just come to the text, in order to build in that sort of emotional intensity, that language of connection between the actors.

What I've found in my experience is that you can create a process, you can have lots of ideas about how you want your room to be run, but ultimately, your job as a director is to look at everything and everyone that you have, and make the best version that you possibly can with all of that. And that means not being overly ambitious with your design if you don't have enough money, or not pushing your actors too far if you don't have enough time. It's also about understanding what an actor's capacity is, or what an actor's great skill, or great charm is and really using that to their advantage. Because, ultimately, I think audiences want to see everything in the production when it's at its best. And so, you've really got to hone the best of everyone and everything as you make the story. I might sometimes realize that there are

---

[3] *The Mountaintop*, by American playwright Katori Hall, is set entirely in Room 306 at the Lorraine Motel, Memphis, in 1968; it tells the story of a meeting between Martin Luther King Jr. and Camae, who initially appears to be a maid at the motel, but whose true identity is revealed at the climax. Premiering at Theatre503 in London, the play reached Broadway in 2011 and starred Samuel L. Jackson and Angela Bassett. Roy Alexander Weise directed the play for the Young Vic in 2016 (with Gbolahan Obisesan and Ronke Adékoluejo), a UK national tour in 2018 (with Obisesan and Rochelle Rose) and the Royal Exchange Theatre in 2021 (with Adetomiwa Edun and Ntombizodwa Ndlovu).

actors that I'm working with that are not very specific about objectives, wants and needs, so I'll really lean into that.

You reminded me of Kate Wasserberg[4] and her notion of drawing the best out of everyone from a place of love. You also reminded me of Stephen Joseph[5] who apparently said a director's role is 'to make the tea, get the heating right, and get out of the way', i.e. the best way to direct is to create environments where the actors can do their best work.

Absolutely. And I've had the pleasure of watching some incredible directors that say very little in a room. As well as working with some directors who really lead with the word: the word as the weapon and the word as the tool. I think I'm someone who really loves to talk and really crack open the play. I think it's important for everyone to really have a good, solid grounding of why we're doing what we're doing; what we want it to do to other people. For people to really understand the richness a story might hold and the scope and the scale a story might hold, so that everybody knows that they have that room to play within it. Then it's my job to be a conduct or mould, or to open the gates, so that the actors really take off and go in that direction.

---

[4]Kate Wasserberg became Artistic Director of Theatr Clwyd after the departure of Tamara Harvey in 2023 and was previously artistic director at both new writing company Stockroom and Cardiff's The Other Room. Her other directing credits include *Boys from the Blackstuff* at Liverpool's Royal Court (2023), *Alice in Wonderland* (2023) for Liverpool Playhouse, and *Rita, Sue and Bob Too* for Stockroom (then called Out of Joint) in 2017. I interviewed Wasserberg for *Inside the Rehearsal Room*, where she described her process as '[…] very practical and the rest of it is love. I give [the company] a parental love, not in a patronising way, but an unconditional love from someone who wants the best for them. I love the play. It doesn't matter what my doubts might have been. I invest in it utterly. I love the characters. I staunchly defend even the worst character […]' (2022: 92).

[5]Director Stephen Joseph was a pioneer of in-the-round theatre in the UK. The Scarborough Theatre, in which he had been heavily involved, is now named the Stephen Joseph Theatre in his honour, after his untimely death in 1967. His legacy was carried on through the work of playwrights he inspired, including Alan Ayckbourn and Harold Pinter.

References

Abbott, J. (2019), *Improvisation in Rehearsal*, London: Nick Hern Books.
Alfreds, M. (2010), *Different Every Night: Freeing the Actor*, London: Nick Hern Books.
Aquilina, S., ed. (2024), *Stanislavsky and Pedagogy*, London: Routledge.
Ashton, K. (2015), *How to Fly a Horse: The Secret History of Creation, Invention, and Discovery*, New York: Random House.
Barclay, N. (2024), personal communication, 21 March.
Beadle, R. and Fletcher, A. J., eds (2008), *The Cambridge Companion to Medieval English Theatre*, Cambridge: Cambridge University Press.
Benedetti, J. (2008), *Stanislavski and the Actor: The Final Acting Lessons 1935–38*, London: Methuen.
Benedict, D. (2023), 'Rebecca Frecknall: "My job is to unlock the play"', *The Stage*, 16 March. Available online: https://www.thestage.co.uk/big-interviews/streetcar-named-desire-cabaret-director-rebecca-frecknall-almeida-phoenix-theatre-london
Benjamin, J. N. (2023), 'Tristan Fynn-Aiduenu: "The UK has a real thing against revivals of contemporary work"', *The Stage*, 5 July. Available online: https://www.thestage.co.uk/features/tristan-fynn-aiduenu-the-uk-has-a-real-thing-against-revivals-of-contemporary-work
Bharucha, R. (2000), *The Politics of Cultural Practice: Thinking Through Theatre in an Age of Globalization*, Middletown, CT: Wesleyan University Press.
Boenisch, P. M. (2015), *Directing Scenes and Senses: The Thinking of Regie*, Manchester: Manchester University Press.
Bogart, A. (2001a), *A Director Prepares*, London: Routledge.
Bogart, A. (2001b), *A Director Prepares: Seven Essays on Art and Theatre*, London: Routledge.
Bowen, D. (2024), personal communication, 21 March.
Braun, E. (1982), *The Director and the Stage: From Naturalism to Grotowski*, London: Methuen.
Brecht, B. (1976), *Poems, 1913-1956*, ed. J. Willett and R. Manheim, trans. E. Anderson et al., London: Eyre Methuen.
Carlson, M. (2006), *The Haunted Stage: The Theatre as a Memory Machine*, Ann Arbor: University of Michigan Press.
Carnicke, S. M. (2009), *Stanislavsky in Focus: An Acting Master for the Twenty-First Century* (2nd edn), Abingdon: Routledge.

References

Carnicke, S. M. (2023), 'Belief through Knowledge: The Relationship of Knebel's Active Analysis to Stanislavsky's System', *Stanislavski Studies* 11(1): 19–31. https://doi.org/10.1080/20567790.2023.2196284

Coetzee, M.-H. and Groves, K. (2023), 'Touch and consent: towards an ethics of care in intimate performance', *Theatre, Dance and Performance Training* 14(2): 103–18. https://doi.org/10.1080/19443927.2023.2184855

Crawford, T. M. (2015), 'Real Human in this Fantastical World: Political, Artistic and Fictive Concerns of Actors in Rehearsal: An Ethnography', PhD thesis, University of Sydney. Available online: https://ses.library.usyd.edu.au/handle/2123/13803

Donnellan, D. (2005), *The Actor and the Target*, London: Nick Hern Books.

Doran, G. (2023), *My Shakespeare: A Director's Journey through the First Folio*, London: Methuen.

Dromgoole, D. (2022), *Astonish Me! First Nights That Changed the World*, London: Profile Books.

Dugdale, T. (2023), *Directing Your Heart Out*, London: Methuen Drama.

Dunderdale, S. (2022), *Directing the Decades: Lessons from Fifty Years of Becoming a Director*, Abingdon: Routledge.

Eagleman, D. and Brandt, A. (2017), *The Runaway Species: How Human Creativity Remakes the World*, New York: Catapult.

Fisher, M. (2024), '"I loved every single word": tributes to the blistering brilliance of Edward Bond', *The Guardian*, 7 March. Available online: https://www.theguardian.com/stage/2024/mar/07/i-loved-every-single-word-tributes-to-the-blistering-brilliance-of-edward-bond

Fliotsos, A. (2009), 'From Script Analysis to Script Interpretation: Valorizing the Intuitive', *Theatre Topics* 19(2): 153–64.

Fortune, S. (2024), personal communication, 22 March.

Gardner, L. (2023), 'Pooja Ghai: "I'm confident about where I sit in theatre"', *The Stage*, 6 July. Available online: https://www.thestage.co.uk/big-interviews/pooja-ghai-tamasha-big-interview-im-confident-about-my-voice-where-i-sit-in-theatre-and-the-work-i-hold

Gardner, L. (2024), 'If You Can Give Audiences a Good Story and Tell It Well, You Earn Their Attention', *The Stage*, 4 April, 10–13.

Giakoumaki, E. (2024), 'What Will the Performance Spaces of the Future Look Like?', *The Stage*, 20 May, 14–15.

Gillett, J. (2024), 'Teaching Stanislavsky's Core Approach of Action, Imagination, and Experiencing', in Aquilina, S. (ed.), *Stanislavsky and Pedagogy*, 14–35, London: Routledge. https://doi.org/10.4324/9781003333609-2

Goodman, J. E. (2020), *Staging Cultural Encounters: Algerian Actors Tour the United States*, Bloomington: Indiana University Press. https://doi.org/10.2307/j.ctv177thwk

Grecian, L. (2024), personal communication, 11 May.

Halba, H. (2024), 'Stanislavsky and the Pedagogy of Play', in Aquilina, S. (ed.), *Stanislavsky and Pedagogy*, 36–55, London: Routledge. https://doi.org/10.4324/9781003333609-3

Harvey, T. (2023), personal communication (interview).

Harwood, R. (1984), *All the World's a Stage*, London: Secker & Warburg.

Henley, D. (2018), *Creativity: Why It Matters*, London: Elliott & Thompson.

Hilton, A. (2022), *Shakespeare on the Factory Floor*, London: Nick Hern Books.

Igweonu, K. and Okagbue, O. (2013), *Performative Inter actions in African Theatre 1: Diaspora Representations and the Interweaving of Cultures*, Newcastle upon Tyne: Cambridge Scholars Publishing.

Innes, C. and Shevtsova, M. (2009), *Directors/Directing: Conversations on Theatre*, Cambridge: Cambridge University Press.

Jarvis, D. (2024), personal communication, 18 January.

Kemp, R. J. (2023), 'The secret of action: a cognitive exploration of eyewitness accounts of Stanislavsky's Active Analysis', *Stanislavski Studies* 11(2): 189–201. https://doi.org/10.1080/20567790.2023.2255603

Kincaid, B. (2018), *Performing Shakespeare Unrehearsed: A Practical Guide to Acting and Producing Spontaneous Shakespeare*, Abingdon: Routledge. https://doi.org/10.4324/9781351136181

Knebel, M., Vassiliev, A. and Brown, I. (2021). *Active analysis*, Abingdon and New York: Routledge.

Knowles, R. P. (2010), *theatre & interculturalism*, London: Methuen.

Leewananthawet, A. (2016), 'Andragogy and Theatre Directing: Teaching Directing Students Not to be Students', *The International Journal of Arts Education* 11(4): 1–7. https://doi.org/10.18848/2326-9944/CGP/v11i04/1-7

Lopez, J. (2008), 'A Partial Theory of Original Practice', *Shakespeare Survey* 61, 302–17. https://doi.org/10.1017/CCOL9780521898881.023

Mackie-Stephenson, A. (2021), 'Virtual Intimacy Directing: Building Best Practices for Safety and Consent', *Theatre Topics* 31(3): 265–8. https://doi.org/10.1353/tt.2021.0049

Malaev-Babel, A. and Margarita, L. (2016), *Nikolai Demidov: Becoming an Actor-Creator*, London: Routledge.

Mamet, D. (1998), *True and False: Heresy and Common Sense for the Actor*, London: Faber & Faber.

Mark, T. G. (2019), 'Approaches to Play Directing in Contemporary Nigerian Theatre: A Study of Segun Adefila and Bolanle Austen-Peters', *Journal of Contemporary Drama in English* 7(2): 314–32. https://doi.org/10.1515/jcde-2019-0022

Marsden R. (2022), *Inside the Rehearsal Room*, London: Methuen.

McAuley, G. (2012), *Not magic but work: An ethnographic account of a rehearsal process*, Manchester: Manchester University Press.

McCabe, T. (2008), *Mis-directing the Play: An Argument against Contemporary Theatre*, Lanham, MD: Rowman & Littlefield.

McConachie, B., Nellhaus, T., Sorgenfrei, C. F. and Underiner, T., eds (2016), *Theatre Histories: An Introduction* (3rd edn), London: Routledge.

McGonigal, G. (2024), personal communication, 28 March.

Meckler, N. (2023), *Notes from the Rehearsal Room: A Director's Process*, London: Methuen.

Meir, D. (2024), personal communication, 28 March.

Merlin, B. (2014), *The Complete Stanislavski Toolkit: Revised Edition*, London: Nick Hern Books.

Merlin, B. (2023), 'Hear, Today, Now: Active Analysis for the working actor: A "special guest workshop" delivered at The S Word, Prague, 12 November 2022, *Stanislavski Studies* 11(1): 81–97. https://doi.org/10.1080/20567790.2023.2196312

Merlin, B. (2024), 'Framing Stanislavsky: Online Pedagogies in the zoom era', in Aquilina, S. (ed.), *Stanislavsky and Pedagogy*, 73–94, London: Routledge. https://doi.org/10.4324/9781003333609-5

Mermikides, A. (2013), 'Brilliant Theatre Making at the National: Devising, Collective Creation and the Director's Brand', *Studies in Theatre and Performance* 33(2): 153–67.

Millar, M. (2018), *Puppetry: How to Do It*, London: Nick Hern Books.

Miller, A. (2015), *The Crucible*, London: Penguin.

Mitchell, K. (2009), *The Director's Craft: A Handbook for the Theatre*, Abingdon: Routledge.

Mitchell, K. (2015), personal communication (interview), 3 November.

Mitter, S. (1992), *Systems of Rehearsal: Stanislavsky, Brecht, Grotowski and Brook*, London: Routledge.

Moor, A. L. (2023), 'Consent-based actor training as the only way forward', *Theatre, Dance and Performance Training* 14(2): 86–102. https://doi.org/10.1080/19443927.2023.2191986

National Advisory Committee on Creative and Cultural Education (1999), *All Our Futures: Creativity, Culture and Education*, London: Department for Education and Employment.

Norrthon, S. and Schmidt, A. (2023), 'Knowledge Accumulation in Theatre Rehearsals: The Emergence of a Gesture as a Solution for Embodying a Certain Aesthetic Concept', *Human Studies* 46(2): 337–69. https://doi.org/10.1007/s10746-022-09654-2

O'Callaghan, S. (2024), personal communication, 21 March.

Olusanya, E. (2024), personal communication, 21 March.

Patterson, C. (2024), personal communication, 21 March.

Perkins, C. (2024), personal communication, 23 March.

Poore, B. (2016), *theatre & empire*, London: Red Globe Press.

Radosavljević, D., ed. (2013), *The Contemporary Ensemble: Interviews with Theatre Makers*, Abingdon: Routledge.

Rikard, L. and Villarreal, A. R. (2023), 'Focus on Impact, Not Intention: Moving from "Safe" Spaces to Spaces of Acceptable Risk', *Journal of Consent-Based Performance* 2(1): 1–16. https://doi.org/10.46787/jcbp.v2i1.3646

Roberts, N. (2024), personal communication, 22 April.

Roberts, S. (2022), 'Sounding the polyphonic cacophony of *Macbeth* with a young Jozi ensemble', *Shakespeare in Southern Africa* 35(1): 4–18. https://doi.org/10.4314/sisa.v35i1.2

Roughan, H. R. (2023), personal communication (interview).

Rourke, J. (2023), personal communication (interview).

Rushe, S. (2019), *Michael Chekhov's Acting Technique: A Practitioner's Guide*, London: Methuen.

Schmidt, A. and Deppermann, A. (2023), 'On the Emergence of Routines: An Interactional Micro-history of Rehearsing a Scene', *Human Studies* 46(2): 273–302. https://doi.org/10.1007/s10746-022-09655-1

Shepherd, S., ed. (2018), *The Great European Stage Directors* (1st edn), London: Methuen.

Shevtsova, M. (2023), '"Music, singing, word, action": the Opera-Dramatic Studio 1935-1938', *Stanislavski Studies* 11(1): 3–17. https://doi.org/10.1080/20567790.2023.2196294

Shipley, M. (2023), 'Active Analysis in the beginning acting classroom', *Stanislavski Studies* 11(2): 203–17. https://doi.org/10.1080/20567790.2023.2258146

Sicart, M. (2017), *Play Matters*, Cambridge, MA: MIT Press.

Svendsen, Z. (2023), *Climate Conversations: Making Theatre in the Context of Climate Crisis*. London: Donmar Warehouse. https://www.donmarwarehouse.com/wp-content/uploads/2023/07/Climate-Conversations-Making-Theatre-in-the-Context-of-Climate-Crisis-Report.pdf

Symeou, N. (2024), personal communication, 23 March.

Tannahill, J. (2016), 'Why Live? A Question for 21st Century Theatre', *World Literature Today*, January edition: 36–9. Available online: https://www.worldliteraturetoday.org/2016/january/why-live-question-21st-century-theatre-jordan-tannahill

Thomas, J. (2016), *A Director's Guide to Stanislavsky's Active Analysis: Including the Formative Essay on Active Analysis by Maria Knebel*, London: Methuen.

Tohver, T. (2024), personal communication, 30 March.

Weise, R. A. (2023), personal communication (interview).

Wickham, G. (1992), *The Medieval Theatre* (3rd edn), Cambridge: Cambridge University Press.

Yorke, J. (2013), *Into the Woods: How Stories Work and Why We Tell Them*, London: Penguin.

Index

access 50, 60, 75, 85
acting, naturalistic 22
actioning 157, 171, 182, 194–5
Actions: The Actor's Thesaurus
    (Caldarone, Marina) 171
active analysis 109–14
Active Analysis (Knebel, Maria) 109
Actor and the Target, The (Donnellan,
    Declan) 89
actor-musician shows 51
Actor Prepares, An (Stanislavski,
    Konstantin) 109
actors 52–3, 133, 159, 172, 177 *see also*
    casting
    agency 193
    ancient Greek 19
    connections 73
    creativity 48
    embodiment 59, 72, 73
    empowering 74
    focus 156–7
    introductions 75–7
    learning lines 160–1
    moment-to-moment playing 119
    nerves 180
    original practices 29
    praise 192
    production worlds 86
    taking ownership 15
    training 181
Actor's Work: Konstantin Stanislavski, An
    (Benedetti, Jean) 109
adaptation 122
Africa 16
Alfreds, Mike 14, 53
All My Sons (Miller, Arthur) 15

All That Jazz (Fosse, Bob) 16
ancient Greece 19
Angels in America (Kushner, Tony) 105
Antoine, André 22
aphantasia 101
Archers, The radio series 17
artistic directors 135, 150, 190
As You Like It (Shakespeare, William)
    176–7, 179, 182–3
Ashton, Kevin 33
    How to Fly a Horse: The Secret
    History of Creation, Invention, and
    Discovery 32–3
ASM (assistant stage manager) 63
assistant stage manager (ASM) 63
audiences 141, 162, 168–9, 171–2, 190
audiovisuals 139–40
auditions 60–1, 158
authenticity 49
authoritarianism 186
Ayckbourn, Alan 31

backstage 145
band calls 139
Barclay, Nick 130, 131
Barong dance 19
Bazaar and Rummage (Townsend, Sue)
    47
Beauty and the Beast (Villeneuve,
    Gabrielle-Suzanne Barbot de) 145
Beginner's Guide to Devising Theatre, A
    (Thorpe, Jess and Gore, Tashi) 4
bending 32
Benedetti, Jean
    Actor's Work: Konstantin Stanislavski,
    An 109

Index

Best of Enemies (Graham, James) 168–9
Bharucha, Rustom 3
Blackpool Opera House 66–7
blending 32
blocking 114–16
Boden, Stephen 71
Boenisch, Peter M. 11, 25
Bogart, Anne
   Director Prepares, A 54
Bond, Edward
   Saved 119
Bourgeois, Louise 179
Braun, Edward
   Director and the Stage, The 18
breaking 32
breakthroughs 31–2, 33, 74, 115–16, 145
Brecht, Bertolt
   'Curtains, The' 33
British Sign Language (BSL) 69–70
Brooks, Peter 33, 46
BSL (British Sign Language) 69–70
Building a Character (Stanislavski, Konstantin) 109

Caldarone, Marina
   Actions: The Actor's Thesaurus 171
Carlson, Marvin
   Speaking in Tongues: Languages at Play in the Theatre 53
Carnicke, Sharon 112
Carroll, Tim 155
casting 49, 57, 193
   appropriateness 58
   auditions 60–1, 158
   balance 59–61
   colour-blind/colour-conscious 59–60
   inclusive and diverse 57–8, 60, 69–70
Cat on a Hot Tin Roof (Williams, Tennessee) 189
characters 120, 190–1
   backstories 160
   choice doors 120
   costume/props 100
   creating 72

development 88–96
emotion 159–60
given and imagined circumstances 90–1, 105
hotseating 91, 160
'in' the scene 108–9
inner monologue work 107–8
keeping the character's journey alive 103
lists and opposites 93–4, 105–6
moment of orientation 92–3
offstage worlds 102–3
perspectives 188–9, 190
pressing issues 100–2
qualities of 58
timelines and pressures 104
waking up 106–7
check-ins 82, 83–4
Chekhov, Anton 22, 59
   Uncle Vanya 59, 161
Chekhov, Michael 93
choice doors 120
choosing a piece 41, 42–4, 46–7,
   Roughan, Holly Race 168–9
   Weise, Roy Alexander 187–8, 190
choregos 19
choreographers 62
choreography 83, 186
Chronegk, Ludwig 21, 22
Cinderella pantomime 142
clarity 192–3
Clarke, Milla 189
classic theatre 51, 161–2, 177, 180–1
Climate Conversations: Making Theatre in the Context of Climate Crisis (Svendsen, Zoë) 64–5
CM (company manager) 63, 145
Coetzee, Marie-Heleen and Groves, Kaitlin 83
   Touch and Consent: Towards an ethics of care in intimate performance 62
Coleman, Jenna 178–9, 181, 183
collaboration 13, 48
   creative teams 61–4

Index

colonialism 167–8
comedy 51
commitment 48
communication 145, 192
company manager (CM) 63, 145
company stage manager (CSM) 63, 143–4, 145
composers 62
configurations 65–8
conflict 131–2
consent 75, 82–5
consistency 50
Coriolanus (Shakespeare, William; dir. Rourke, Josie) 176
costume 80, 100
costume designers 61
Country Wife, The (Wycherley, William) 32
Cracknell, Carrie 54, 100
Craig, Tinuke 70
Crawford, T. M. 74
creative teams 61–4, 74, 79, 133, 137, 145
  plot sessions 140, 141
creativity 31–3, 48–9
Crucible, The (Miller, Arthur) 15, 67–8
CSM (company stage manager) 63, 143–4, 145
cue lines 26–7
cultural appropriation 46
'Curtains, The' (Brecht, Bertolt) 33

Dancing at Lughnasa (Friel, Brian) 178, 179
Davenant, William 20–1
de la Tour, Frances 33
Demidov, Nikolai 80, 100
demonstration 118
deputy stage manager (DSM) 63, 143
design teams 61–2
design worlds 121–2, 167–8, 176–7, 179, 193
directing
  definitions 11
  director-less theatre 25–9

Directing Your Heart Out: Essays for Authenticity, Engagement, and Care in Theatre (Dugdale, Tom) 73
Director and the Stage, The (Braun, Edward) 18
director-less theatre 25–9
Director Prepares, A (Bogart, Anne) 54
directors
  approach changes 99
  as auteurs 166
  cultural representations of 16–17
  demonstration 118
  ethics 17
  as facilitators 191–2
  gestures 99, 118
  intimacy 17
  necessity of 11
  notes 118, 131, 147, 150
  rehearsal positions 98–9
  rise of 19–23
  role of 4, 11, 13–18, 21, 23, 65, 146
  Roughan, Holly Race 165–6
Director's Craft, The (Mitchell, Katie) 8, 29, 55
Director's Guide to Stanislavsky's Active Analysis, A (Thomas, James) 8, 56, 109
Dodin, Lev 59
Donnellan, Declan
  Actor and the Target, The 89
Doran, Greg 44, 74
  My Shakespeare: A Director's Journey through the First Folio 47, 78
drafts 52
Drama Online 35–6
dramaturgs/dramaturgy 63, 165
  physical 176
dress rehearsals 145, 146–8
Dromgoole, Dominic 13, 14
dropping in 113–14
DSM (deputy stage manager) 63, 143
Duff, Anne-Marie 182

Dugdale, Tom
  Directing Your Heart Out: Essays for Authenticity, Engagement, and Care in Theatre 73
Dunderdale, Sue 60, 78, 131
Dunn, Nina 64
dynamic listening 28

embodiment 59, 72, 73
emotion 159–60
endgaming 119
England 20–1
Enoch, Alfred 182–3
ensembles 11, 59
'Enter Two Gardeners' (Langton, Simon) 17
ethics 17
etudes 110–11, 112
Evans, Daniel 155, 162 n. 7
events, locating the 55–7, 166
events read-throughs 79
exercises
  actions, wants, needs, objectives, tasks and supertasks 88–90
  active analysis 110–12
  atmospheres 128–30
  Bogart's 'The Question' and Meckler's 'The Statement' 54
  character-building/development 88–96
  character lists and opposites 105–6
  characters 'in' the scene 108–9
  characters' offstage worlds 102–3
  choosing a piece 43–5
  consent 84–5
  consent negotiation 84–5
  ghosting 54–5
  given and imagined circumstances 90–2
  groundplans 67–8
  inner monologue work 107–8
  inner motive forces/psychological drives 94–6
  keeping the character's journey alive 103
  locating the events 55–7
  mixed-up rehearsal 127–8
  moment of orientation 92–3
  off-text 123–6
  on-text 123, 126–30
  opposites and polarities 93–4
  pressing issues 100–2
  production analysis 35–8
  production worlds 87
  psychological safety 42 n. 2
  raising the stakes 124–6
  repetition 194 n. 3
  shared improvisations 102–3
  talking and walking your way in 123–4
  theatre games 76–7
  thinking forwards: the 'what for?' 126–7
  timelines and pressures 104, 151–2
  vocal 81, 123–4, 144
  waking up 106–7
  words are the world 87
'Exhibit B' (Bailey, Brett) 46

failure 42
farce 51
fight directors 62
First Folio (Shakespeare, William) 177, 180–1
first nights 149–50
Fischer-Lichte, Erika 46
Fliotsos, Anne
  Teaching Theatre Today 53
Fortune, Steve 131
Fouquet, Jean
  Livre d'Heures pour Maître Étienne Chevalier 20
frames 41–2
France 20, 22, 23
Frecknall, Rebecca 11, 14
Free Your Mind (Boyle, Danny) 61
Friel, Brian
  Dancing at Lughnasa 178, 179

Fritz, James
　Parliament Square 55
furniture 100
Fynn-Aiduenu, Tristan 44, 61

García Lorca, Federico
　House of Bernarda Alba, The 101
　Yerma 121
gender 16–17
genres 50–3
Georg II (Duke of Saxe-Meiningen) 21
Germany 23
ghosting 53–4, 58
Gill, Peter 183, 184–5
Gillett, John 73, 78
gimmicks 33
givens 36
Glass Menagerie, The (Williams, Tennessee) 127
Goodbye Girl, The (Ross, Herbert) 17
Gow, Michael
　Toy Symphony 29
Graham, James 168
　Best of Enemies 168–9
　Privacy 175
　Vote, The 175
Grandage, Michael 183, 184
grasp 77–80
Great European Stage Directors, The (Shepherd, Simon) 11
Grecian, Laura-Ann 82
groundplans 37, 67–8

Halba, Hilary 83–4, 86, 113, 122
Hamlet (Shakespeare, William) 58, 155
harmonization 13, 14
Harvey, Leah 182, 183
Harvey, Tamara 8, 155–63
Headlong Theatre 168
Henry V (Shakespeare, William) 58, 166, 167–8, 171, 172
'Her Big Chance' (Bennett, Alan) 175

Hilton, Andrew 54, 120
Holmes, Sean 119
Home, I'm Darling (Wade, Laura) 161
Hopper, Edward 179
hotseating 91, 160
Hound of the Baskervilles, The (Doyle, Arthur Conan) 145
House of Bernarda Alba, The (García Lorca, Federico) 101
How to Fly a Horse: The Secret History of Creation, Invention, and Discovery (Ashton, Kevin), 32–3
Hughes, Gwenda 98
Hytner, Nick 183, 184

Icke, Robert 141
ideas 78
Igweonu, Kene and Okagbue, Osita 16
improvisation 83, 102–3
inclusion 46–7, 49–50, 75, 82–3 *see also* access
　casting 57–8, 60, 69–70
　Harvey, Tamara 159
　pressing issues 101
　Rourke, Josie 180–1
Inside the Rehearsal Room (Marsden, Robert) 5, 18
　breakthroughs 31
　frames 41–2
　genres 50
　textual interpretation 53
intentions 157
intercultural theatre practices 45–7
interwoven theatre 46
intimacy 82–5
intimacy directors 17, 62, 64
introductions 75–7, 79, 142–3
Irigaray, Luce 17
　This Sex Which is Not One 17

Jarvis, Daniel 81
Jersey Boys musical 4
Joseph, Stephen 196

Kemp, Richard J. 86
kinospheres 129
Knebel, Maria
   Active Analysis 109
knowledge sharing 71–2, 98, 99
Knowles, Rik 45–6
Kushner, Tony
   Angels in America 105

language 85, 181–2
Lemons Lemons Lemons Lemons Lemons (Steiner, Sam) 178–9, 181, 183
lighting 139–41
lighting (LX) designers 61
line-reading 184
listening and responding 3
Livre d'Heures pour Maître Étienne Chevalier (Fouquet, Jean) 20
Lloyd, Phyllida 183
logic texts 29
Lopez, Jeremy 28–9
LX (lighting) designers 61

McAuley, Gay 29
Macbeth (Shakespeare, William) 15, 26, 88–90, 121, 161
McCabe, Terry 15
McGonigal, Gracie 135, 136
McGregor, Wayne 186
magic 33
Mahabharata, The (Vyāsa; dir. Brooks, Peter) 46
maître du jeu 20
Maly Theatre 59, 156
Mamet, David
   True and False 54
Mark, Tekena Gasper 13, 14, 16
Marowitz, Charles 59, 74
Mary Queen of Scots (Rourke, Josie) 175, 179
meaning read-throughs 78–9
Measure for Measure (Shakespeare, William) 44

Meckler, Nancy 55
   Notes from the Rehearsal Room: A Director's Progress 54
media, choice of 44–5
Meiningen Ensemble 21, 22
Meir, Dominic 133
Meisner, Sanford 182 n. 8, 194–5
   Meisner technique 182, 194–5
Mendes, Sam 183, 184, 185
Merchant of Venice, The (Shakespeare, William) 26–7
Merlin, Bella 28, 73, 85, 90
   active analysis 109
   Complete Stanislavsky Toolkit, The 56
   pressing issues 101
methodology 7–8
#MeToo social movement 17, 44
Midsummer Night's Dream, A (Shakespeare, William) 33, 94, 124, 129
Millar, Mervyn 132–3
Miller, Arthur
   All My Sons 15
   Crucible, The 15, 67–8
Misérables, Les (Boublil, Alain and Schönberg, Claude-Michel) 4
Mitchell, Katie 31, 48, 59, 91, 98, 158, 192
   Director's Craft, The 8, 29, 55
Mitter, Shomit 74
model boxes 80
Molière (Jean-Baptiste Poquelin) 20
Moor, Andrea L. 17, 82–3, 100
Mountaintop, The (Hall, Katori) 187, 195
movement directors 62
Much Ado About Nothing (Shakespeare, William) 188
music 138–9, 188
musical arrangers 62
musical directors 62, 139
musicals 51, 81, 144

My Shakespeare: A Director's Journey through the First Folio (Doran, Greg) 47, 78
My Zinc Bed (Hare, David) 185
mystery plays 20

National Theatre At Home 36
naturalism 22, 23
Naturalism in the Theatre (Zola, Émile) 22
new writing 51
Norris, Rufus 185
Norrthon, Stefan and Schmidt, Axel 99
notes 118, 131, 135–6, 147, 150, 188
    auditions 158
    clear 170
    play events 166
Notes from the Rehearsal Room: A Director's Progress (Meckler, Nancy) 54

off-book 160–1, 183
offstage worlds 102–3
Olusanya, Emmanuel 131
'On the Emergence of Routines: An International Micro-history of Rehearsing a Scene' (Schmidt, Axel and Deppermann, Arnulf) 72
openness 3, 180, 191
Othello (Shakespeare, William) 47, 105
othering 45–6
ownership 71

pageants 20
    pageant masters 20
pantomime 51, 158
Parliament Square (Fritz, James) 55
Patterson, Christian 131, 132
Perkins, Chrissie 133
Peter Pan (Barrie, J. M.) 66–7
physical shaping *see* blocking
piecing together 121 n. 1

play/s *see also* texts
    choosing 41, 42–4, 46–7, 168–9, 187–8, 190
    classic 51, 161–2, 177, 180–1
    climaxes 120
    events 55–7, 119, 166
    given and imagined circumstances 90–1
    reading 187–8
    surprises 120
    tension 120
    worlds 73, 86–7, 189
playfulness 122–3
playwrights 15, 91, 175, 176, 178
    ancient Greek 19
    as directors 19, 20–1
    writing styles 23
plot sessions 139–42
PM (production manager) 63, 145
PMF (Production Managers' Forum) 49
points of concentration 111–12, 157
Poore, Benjamin
    Theatre and Empire 46
power 4
pre-production processes 175–7
press nights 150
pressing issues 100–2
previews 148–9, 162, 172
Prince and the Pauper, The (Twain, Mark) 69
Princess and the Pauper, The (Simpson, Dave) 69
Privacy (Graham, James) 175
Producers, The (Brooks, Mel) 16
production/s
    analysis 35–8
    compelling 118–19
    encountering 77–80
    locked in 135
    worlds 73, 86–7, 99–109
production manager (PM) 63, 145
Production Managers' Forum (PMF) 49

production teams 63, 147–8
projecting 114
property-players 20
props 100
prose 26
psycho-physicality 73
psychological safety 42
Pullman, Philip 105–6

R&D (research and development) periods 68–70
read-throughs 78
realism 22, 23
rehearsals
  access 85
  active analysis 109–14
  analysis 35–8
  blocking 114–16
  breakthroughs 31–2, 33, 74, 115–16, 145
  casting 58–61
  character appropriateness 59
  character-building exercises 88–96
  choosing a piece 41, 42–4
  configurations and spaces 65–8
  conflict 131–2
  creative teams 61–4
  creativity 31–3
  debriefs 85–6
  definition 14
  drafts 52
  dress 145, 146–8
  dropping in 113–14
  early rehearsal stage 43
  embodiment 72, 73
  final stages 117–33
  first encounters 74–6
  form emerging 97–9
  form establishing 122
  genres 50–3
  grasp 77–80
  ground rules 75
  Harvey, Tamara 159, 160–1, 162–3

improvisation 83, 102–3
knowledge sharing 71–2, 98, 99
learning lines 160–1
locating the events 55–7
Marowitz, Charles 74
mixed-up 127–8
off-book 160–1, 183
playfulness 122–3
plot sessions 139–42
production worlds 73, 86–7, 99–109
projecting 114
R&D periods 68–70
rehearsal room practices 4
risk 72, 132
Roughan, Holly Race 165, 166, 169–70, 173
Rourke, Josie 180–2
routines 72, 98
run-throughs 120–1, 130–1
safety 82–5
schedules 47, 52, 53
script preparation 53–7
shadowing 113–14
side-coaching 113
strategy 47–50
sub-rehearsals 52
sustainability 64–5
technical 135, 136–46
textual interpretation 53–7
theatre games 76–7
timelines and pressures 104
warm-ups/tune-ups 80–2
reliability 50
research 179, 189
research and development (R&D) periods 68–70
'Reset Better' charter 49, 137–8, 147
reviews 150
rhythm 120–1
Rickson, Ian 185, 188
risk 72, 132
Roberts, Neil 131

Index

Roberts, Sarah 25–6
Robin Hood (Harvey, Tamara) 157, 158
Romeo and Juliet (Shakespeare, William) 15, 55, 78
Rosemary and Thyme TV series 17
Roughan, Holly Race 8, 33, 42, 56, 165–73
Rourke, Josie 8, 14, 52–3, 175–86
    Mary Queen of Scots 179
routines 72, 98
Rubasingham, Indhu 44
run-throughs 120–1, 130–1
Rushe, Sinéad 94
Russia 22, 23

safe spaces 72, 79–80, 132–3
safety 17, 82–5
    psychological 42, 74
Saved (Bond, Edward) 119
Schmidt, Axel and Deppermann, Arnulf 98, 118
    'On the Emergence of Routines: An International Micro-history of Rehearsing a Scene' 72
sensitivity readers 50
Serpentine art gallery 189
set designers 61
SFX (sound) designers 62
shadowing 113–14
Shakespeare, William 161, 162
    As You Like It 176–7, 179, 182–3
    Coriolanus 176
    cue lines 26–7
    First Folio 177, 180–1
    Hamlet 58, 155
    Henry V 58, 166, 167–8, 171, 172
    Macbeth 15, 26, 88–90, 121, 161
    Measure for Measure 44
    Merchant of Venice, The 26–7
    Midsummer Night's Dream, A 33, 94, 124, 129
    Much Ado About Nothing 188
    original practices 25–9
    Othello 47, 105
    Romeo and Juliet 15, 55, 78
    shared lines 27–9
    Titus Andronicus 78
    verse and prose 26
    Winter's Tale, The 27–8
shared lines 27–9
Shepherd, Simon
    Great European Stage Directors, The 11
show reports 150
Sicart, Miguel 122
side-coaching 113
Simpsons, The TV series 17
Singin' in the Rain (Kelly, Gene and Donen, Stanley) 16, 142
sitzprobes 138–9
SM (stage manager) 63
Snow Queen, The (Andersen, Hans Christian) 69
Sorgenfrei, Carol Fischer et al.
    Theatre Histories 18
sound 139–40, 141
sound (SFX) designers 62
soundchecks 138–9
spaces 65–8, 129
Speaking in Tongues: Languages at Play in the Theatre (Carlson, Marvin) 53
stage management team 63
stage manager (SM) 63
stagger-throughs 120
Stanislavski, Konstantin 8, 22
    active analysis 109
    Actor Prepares, An 109
    Building a Character 109
stichomythia 121
storyboards 178–9
'Streetcar Named Marge, A' (Moore, Rich) 17
stress 185–6
stumble-throughs 78, 121 n. 1

sub-rehearsals 52
Succession (Armstrong, Jesse) 171
sustainability 48, 64–5
Svendsen, Zoë
  Climate Conversations: Making Theatre in the Context of Climate Crisis 64–5
Sweet Charity (Simon, Field) 186
symbolism 23
Symeou, Naomi 130–1

Tannahill, Jordan 16
Teaching Theatre Today (Fliotsos, Anne) 53
technical rehearsals 135, 136–46
  band calls 139
  sitzprobes 138–9
  soundchecks 138–9
technical teams 137, 140, 145
technology 21
Terry, Michelle 14, 58, 182
text-based dramaturgy 28–9
texts *see also* play/s
  breaking down 166, 179, 182
  encountering 77–80
  opposites and polarities 93–4
  original practices 29
theatre 44–5
  analysing 35–8
  director-less 25–9
  end-on setting 66
  in-the-round 66
  promenade 66
  roots of, 19
  as shared experience 15–16
  technology 21
  thrust setting 66
  traverse setting 66
  warehouses 66
Theatre and Empire (Poore, Benjamin) 46
'Theatre Casting Toolkit' 58
theatre games 76–7

Theatre Green Book, The (Renew Culture and Buro Happold) 64–5
Theatre Histories (Sorgenfrei, Carol Fischer et al.) 18
themes 78
This Sex Which is Not One (Irigaray, Luce) 17
Thomas, James
  Director's Guide to Stanislavsky's Active Analysis, A 8, 56, 109
Thorpe, Jess and Gore, Tashi
  Beginner's Guide to Devising Theatre, A 4
timecoding 140
timelines and pressures 104, 151–2, 159
Titus Andronicus (Shakespeare, William) 78
Tohver, Tamur 99, 117–18, 135
Touch and Consent: Towards an ethics of care in intimate performance (Coetzee, Marie-Heleen and Groves, Kaitlin) 62
Townsend, Sue
  Bazaar and Rummage 47
Toy Symphony (Gow, Michael) 29
Tran, Moi 167–8
transactional analysis 115
True and False (Mamet, David) 54
tune-ups 80–2
Turner, Aidan 178, 181, 183

Uncle Vanya (Chekhov, Anton) 59, 161
unification 14
uniting 182
useful choices 33

values 48–50, 184
van Hove, Ivo 14–15, 73
verse 26, 161–2
video/AV designers 62
vision 14–15, 35, 38, 86, 188
voice/dialect directors 63

voice exercises 81, 123–4, 144
Vote, The (Graham, James) 175

Wade, Laura
   Home, I'm Darling 161
War Horse (Morpurgo, Michael and Stafford, Nick)
warm-ups 80–2
Wasserberg, Kate 52, 98, 104, 196
Weise, Roy Alexander 8, 187–96
welfare 185–6
well-being coordinators 63
what would it be like (WWIBL) 155
Whelan, Peter 89

Williams, Tennessee
   Cat on a Hot Tin Roof 189
   Glass Menagerie, The 127
Winter's Tale, The (Shakespeare, William) 27–8
women 16–17
WWIBL (what would it be like) 155
Wycherley, William
   Country Wife, The 32

Yerma (García Lorca, Federico) 121

Zola, Émile 22
   Naturalism in the Theatre 22